Praise for *The Cross and the Lynching Tree*

"Once again James Cone demonstrates why he is indispensable as an interpreter of faith, race, and the American experience. Growing up in the shadow of the lynching tree, he reminds us how that darkness falls across our political and cultural landscape today—and how, nonetheless, there is redemption in remembrance."

Bill Moyers
Journalist

"James Cone has rescued the cross from formulaic theologies of salvation by proxy. His brave book lights fires of inquiry on the mysterious bond between suffering and love. After reading it, no aspiring Christian or christian can pretend that the lynching tree is about someone other than ourselves."

Taylor Branch
Author, *Parting the Waters: America in the King Years, 1954-63*

"*The Cross and the Lynching Tree* represents the coming together of the major strands of James Cone's illustrious work in black theology. No one has explored the spiritual world of African Americans with the depth or breadth of Cone. Here he turns his attention to two symbols that dominated not only the spiritual world but also the daily life of African Americans in the twentieth century. In their inextricable tie, he finds both the terror and the hope that governed life under violent racism as well as potent symbols of the African American past and present in the United States."

Henry Louis Gates, Jr.
Alphonse Fletcher University Professor, Harvard University

"James Cone is a world-historical figure in twentieth-century Christian theology. *The Cross and the Lynching Tree* is a powerful and painful song of hope in our dance with mortality—a song Cone courageously has led for over forty years!"

Cornel West
Princeton University

"As James Cone shows, the thousands of black men and women who died on lynching trees were the body of Christ crucified all over again. The lynching tree is our American cross. Yet a resistance to racism that bears the cross, as in Martin Luther King's vision, can overcome the lynching tree—and its successors in our slums, prisons, and execution chambers. Cone's work is devastating and redemptive."

Jim Douglass
Author, *JFK and the Unspeakable*

"This is a book that doctors of democracy, justice, and compassion have prescribed to help us deal with our country's malaise of anger, violence, and amnesia. It forces us to acknowledge the horrors of the past and to see more clearly the mutant forms of racism in the present. Then, it shows us how Grace upstages disgrace through the power of the Cross. It points a way toward forgiveness, reconciliation, and the restoration of the beloved community."

Rev. Dr. James A. Forbes, Jr.
Senior Minister Emeritus, Riverside Church, New York City

"*The Cross and the Lynching Tree* is essential reading, both for its impeccable scholarship and its refusal-to-look-away-theology. James Cone, one of the world's most respected liberation theologians, informs religious scholars as well as lay audiences about the cruel violence African Americans experienced on a colossal scale and on a continual basis. When the cross and the lynching tree are placed side by side, there is no way to deny the agony."

Katie G. Cannon
Annie Scales Rogers Professor of Christian Ethics, Union Presbyterian Seminary

"James Cone teaches us still. In this powerful and personal theological work, Cone exposes not only the deep anxiety that continues to throb beneath our national amnesia about lynching and race, but also the failure of the Christian imagination—the failure of Christian theology. At the heart of Cone's critique lies a passionate quest and challenge for the beloved community. James Cone teaches us still. Will we finally learn?"

M. Shawn Copeland
Associate Professor of Systematic Theology, Boston College

"This book will upset your equilibrium in all the best ways, inviting you to think, challenging you to act. James Cone mines the deep insight of poetry and proclamation, song and sermon to compel us to revisit the cross and the lynching tree as poignant symbols of suffering and struggle. His book is an important reminder that the quest for a post-racial society must pass through parts of American history we do not want to claim as our own."

Robert Michael Franklin
President, Morehouse College

"James Cone challenges us all to join him in the necessary, relentless wrestling with the blind and fallen angels of the white American Christian churches that has marked his life for decades. Moving deep into the broken heart of our long, often brutally racialized national journey Cone focuses on the often-denied terrorism of lynching and on the need for all of us—especially those who claim to be followers of Jesus—to confront the "Lynching Tree" both as a reality of American life and history, and as a paradoxical, possible source of redemptive transformation for a wounded nation."

Vincent Harding
Chairperson, The Veterans of Hope Project

"*The Cross and the Lynching Tree* is a disturbing and yet hopeful meditation upon some of the ugliest and most barbaric practices in our country's tortured racial history. James Cone compels us to confront the horror of lynching with unflinching honesty and profound faith. This seminal work is a worthy addition to his lifelong project of relentless truth-telling with matchless courage."

Bryan N. Massingale
Marquette University

The Cross
and
the Lynching Tree

THE CROSS
and
THE LYNCHING TREE

James H. Cone

ORBIS BOOKS

Maryknoll, New York 10545

Second Printing, February 2012

Founded in 1970, Orbis Books endeavors to publish works that enlighten the mind, nourish the spirit, and challenge the conscience. The publishing arm of the Maryknoll Fathers and Brothers, Orbis seeks to explore the global dimensions of the Christian faith and mission, to invite dialogue with diverse cultures and religious traditions, and to serve the cause of reconciliation and peace. The books published reflect the views of their authors and do not represent the official position of the Maryknoll Society. To learn more about Maryknoll and Orbis Books, please visit our website at www. maryknollsociety.org.

Manufactured in the United States of America

Library of Congress Cataloging in Publication Data

Cone, James H.
    The cross and the lynching tree / James H. Cone.
        p. cm.
    Includes bibliographical references and index.
    ISBN 978-1-57075-937-6 (cloth); e-ISBN 978-1-60833-001-0
    1. African Americans—Religion. 2. Jesus Christ—Crucifixion—History of doctrines. 3. Lynching—United States—History. I. Title.
    BR563.N4C648 2011
    277.3'0808996073—dc22
                                                2011010630

To the memory of Black People
whose lives were lost on the Lynching Tree

They put him to death by hanging him on a tree.

—Acts 10:39

The South is crucifying Christ again
By all the laws of ancient rote and rule . . .
Christ's awful sin is that he's dark of hue,
The sin for which no blamelessness atones; . . .
And while he burns, good men, and, women too,
Shout, battling for his black and brittle bones.

— "Christ Recrucified," Countee Cullen, 1922

Southern trees bear strange fruit,
Blood on the leaves and blood at the root,
Black body swinging in the Southern breeze,
Strange fruit hanging from the poplar trees.

—"Strange Fruit," Abel Meeropol
(a.k.a. Lewis Allen)

Perhaps nothing about the history of mob violence
in the United States is more surprising than how
quickly an understanding of the full horror of lynching has receded from the nation's collective historical
memory.

—W. Fitzhugh Brundage,
Lynching in the New South

Contents

ACKNOWLEDGMENTS

This book has been a long time coming, and I have had a lot of help along the way. Although I cannot mention everyone, I must name many whose assistance and encouragement were essential to bring this work to completion.

No one has been more important to my vocation than the students at Union Theological Seminary, who have inspired and challenged me to be the best scholar and writer I could be. They light the fire and make me feel as I did when I first sat down to write, trying to find the words to express the gospel truth for today.

I also want to thank the faculty, administration, staff, and board of Union, who have supported me in my work since I first arrived in 1969. The journey has been exciting and often difficult, but I have no doubt that Union has been the best place for me to teach black liberation theology.

I would never have become the person and theologian I am today without the nurturing support of the African Methodist Episcopal Church. It was at Macedonia A.M.E. Church in Bearden, Arkansas, and later at churches throughout the state that I first received the opportunity to stand before an audience and speak. While I was still a teenager, trying to find my place in a world that was defined by white supremacy, they told me, "Boy, if you live the Christian faith and study hard, you could become much more than what the segregated South intends and more than you ever thought you could be."

I want to thank many people at colleges, seminaries, universities, churches, and community groups who have invited me to speak, especially Professor David Woodward at Denison

University. I appreciate the support of the entire Denison community, including the president, faculty, students, and staff.

During the several years of researching and writing this book, many people read all or parts of it and offered helpful comments. They include Thomas Ogletree, Tom Driver, Donald Shriver, Gary Dorrien, Ronald Stone, Peter Paris, Larry Rasmussen, Roger Shinn, Chris Hedges, Hilton Als, Kathryn Tanner, Deb Chasman, Jeanne Carter Helpern, Robin Lovin, Farah Jasmine Griffin, Edward Blum, Suzanne Frazier, Michael Lenza, Angelo Corlett, Jon Nilson, C. K. Williams, Joe Hough, and the students in my Niebuhr class.

No one has been more important for my theological journey than the remarkable theologian Gayraud S. Wilmore. From the time I wrote my first book, *Black Theology and Black Power*, Gayraud has supported my work and challenged me to be my best. Together we have written essays and books, and traveled the world—debating and interpreting black liberation theology. His text *Black Religion and Black Radicalism* is necessary for anyone who wants to understand the origins and development of black theology and the black church.

I must thank Elaine Pagels, whom I have known for more than thirty years. She read my book several times and made many helpful editorial suggestions.

No one has been more important in the completion of this book than Robert Ellsberg, editor-in-chief and publisher of Orbis Books. He is not only a friend but an extraordinary editor.

I want to thank my research assistants, Jennifer Heckart and Dwayne Meadows. Jennifer worked with me for several years, finding obscure newspaper and journal articles and rare books, as well as making many helpful suggestions. Dwayne contributed to my research as this project was being completed.

My assistant Victoria Furio has been an invaluable office manager, creating time for me to research and write. I am most appreciative for her commitment and her expert attention to detail.

I also want to thank Bill and Judith Moyers and their remarkable staff. After I had presented my first lecture on "the cross and the lynching tree" at Harvard Divinity School, they invited me to appear on the "Bill Moyers' Journal." Because I was still at the beginning of this work, I hesitated, wondering how I could find the words to talk about the cross and the lynching tree to an American television audience. Talking seriously about religion and race is never easy, especially when focusing on their most controversial symbols. Bill and Judith assured me that I could do it, and I am grateful for their encouragement and support.

Finally, I want to say a word in memory of my mother and father, Lucy and Charlie Cone, who protected my brothers and me from the worst of white supremacy in Arkansas. With an amazing love and wonderful humor, they created a happy home that kept us from hating anybody and instilled in us a belief that we could, with determination, overcome any obstacle placed in our way.

Permissions

"Christ in Alabama," "Harlem (2)," "The Bitter River," and "Goodbye Christ" from *The Collected Poems of Langston Hughes* by Langston Hughes, edited by Arnold Rampersad with David Roessel, Associate Editor, copyright © 1994 by the Estate of Langston Hughes. Used by permission of Alfred A. Knopf, a division of Random House, Inc., and Harold Ober Associates, Inc.

"Night, Death, Mississippi," from *Angle of Ascent: New and Selected Poems* by Robert Hayden. Copyright © 1975, 1972, 1970, 1966 by Robert Hayden. Used by permission of Liveright Publishing Corporation.

"If we must die" and "The Lynching" by Claude McKay courtesy of the Literary Representative for the Works of Claude McKay, Schomburg Center for Research in Black Culture, The New York Public Library, Astor, Lenox and Tilden Foundations.

Poetry by Countee Cullen copyright © by The Amistad Research Center, New Orleans, LA. Administrated by Thompson and Thompson, Brooklyn, NY. Used by permission of The Amistad Research Center.

INTRODUCTION

What was it that made me conscious of possibilities?
From where in the Southern darkness had I caught a
sense of freedom? Why was it that I was able to act
upon vaguely felt emotions? . . . It had been through
books . . . that I had managed to keep myself alive . . .
[and that] had evoked in me vague glimpses of life's
possibilities.

—Richard Wright[1]

Theme for Negro writers will emerge when they have
begun to feel the meaning of the history of the race
as though they in one lifetime had lived it themselves
throughout all of the long centuries.

—Richard Wright[2]

The cross and the lynching tree are separated by nearly 2,000 years. One is the universal symbol of Christian faith; the other is the quintessential symbol of black oppression in America. Though both are symbols of death, one represents a message of hope and salvation, while the other signifies the negation of that message by white supremacy. Despite the obvious similarities between Jesus' death on a cross and the death of thousands of black men and women strung up to die on a lamppost or tree, relatively few people, apart from black poets, novelists, and other reality-seeing artists, have explored the symbolic connections. Yet, I believe this is a challenge we must face. What is at stake is the credibility and promise of the Christian gospel and the hope that we may heal the wounds of racial violence that continue to divide our churches and our society.

In its heyday, the lynching of black Americans was no secret. It was a public spectacle, often announced in advance in newspapers and over radios, attracting crowds of up to twenty thousand people. An unspeakable crime, it is a memory that most white Americans would prefer to forget. For African Americans the memory of disfigured black bodies "swinging in the southern breeze" is so painful that they, too, try to keep these horrors buried deep down in their consciousness, until, like a dormant volcano, they erupt uncontrollably, causing profound agony and pain. But as with the evils of chattel slavery and Jim Crow segregation, blacks and whites and other Americans who want to understand the true meaning of the American experience need to remember lynching. To forget this atrocity leaves us with a fraudulent perspective of this society and of the meaning of the Christian gospel for this nation.

While the lynching tree is seldom discussed or depicted, the cross is one of the most visible symbols of America's Christian origins. Many Christians embrace the conviction that Jesus died on the cross to redeem humankind from sin. Taking our place, Jesus suffered on the cross and gave "his life a ransom for many" (Mk 10:45). We are "now justified by [God's] grace as a gift, through the redemption that is in Christ Jesus, whom God put forward as a sacrifice of atonement by his blood, effective through faith" (Rom 3:24-25). The cross is the great symbol of the Christian narrative of salvation.

Unfortunately, during the course of 2,000 years of Christian history, this symbol of salvation has been detached from any reference to the ongoing suffering and oppression of human beings—those whom Ignacio Ellacuría, the Salvadoran martyr, called "the crucified peoples of history." The cross has been transformed into a harmless, non-offensive ornament that Christians wear around their necks. Rather than reminding us of the "cost of discipleship," it has become a form of "cheap grace,"[3] an easy way to salvation that doesn't force us to confront the power of Christ's message and mission. Until we can see the cross and the lynching tree together, until we can identify Christ with a "recrucified" black body hanging from a lynching tree, there can be no genuine understanding of Christian identity in America, and no deliverance from the brutal legacy of slavery and white supremacy.

I was born in Arkansas, a lynching state. During my childhood, white supremacy ruled supreme. White people were virtually free to do anything to blacks with impunity. The violent crosses of the Ku Klux Klan were a familiar reality, and white racists preached a dehumanizing segregated gospel in the name of Jesus' cross every Sunday. And yet in rural black churches I heard a different message, as preachers proclaimed the message of the suffering Jesus and the salvation accomplished in his death on the cross. I noticed how the passion and energy of the preacher increased whenever he talked about the cross, and the congregation responded with outbursts of "Amen" and "Hallelujah" that equaled the intensity of the sermon oration. People shouted, clapped their hands, and stomped their feet, as if a powerful, living reality of God's Spirit had transformed them from nobodies in white society to somebodies in the black church. This black religious experience, with all its tragedy and hope, was the reality in which I was born and raised. Its paradoxes and incongruities have shaped everything I have said and done. If I have anything to say to the Christian community in America and around the world, it is rooted in the tragic and hopeful reality that sustains and empowers black people to resist the forces that seem designed to destroy every ounce of dignity in their souls and bodies.

This work is a continuation and culmination of all my previous books, each of them, in different ways, motivated by a central question: how to reconcile the gospel message of liberation with the reality of black oppression. But in many ways this book is particularly personal. Its subject brings me back to my first memories of hearing the gospel, as well as back to primal memories of terror and violence that were part of the reality of growing up in the Jim Crow South. As a child, I watched my mother and father deal with segregation and the threats of lynching and was deeply affected by their examples, and by the sacrifices they made to keep their children safe.

Through the black religious experience I caught a vision of my possibility, entered the Christian ministry in the African Methodist Episcopal Church, made my way to college and seminary, and received a Ph.D. in theology at Garrett Biblical Institute (now Garrett-Evangelical Theological Seminary) and Northwestern University in 1965. My journey was long and hard, but I was determined to be more than what America had intended for me. Just as books kept Richard Wright alive and gave him "vague glimpses of life's possibilities," the black church and theological texts kept me wrestling with life and faith, trying to find meaning in a society and an intellectual discourse that did not even acknowledge that I existed. How could I find meaning in a world that ignored black people? I decided that I had to say something about that contradiction.

My first theological cry burst forth with the publication of *Black Theology and Black Power* in 1969. I found my voice in the social, political, religious, and cultural context of the civil rights and black power movements in the 1960s. The Newark and Detroit riots in July 1967 and the assassination of Martin Luther King Jr. in April 1968 were the events that shook me out of my theological complacency, forcing me to realize the bankruptcy of any theology in America that did not engage the religious meaning of the African American struggle for justice. What I studied in graduate school ignored white supremacy and black resistance against it, as if they had nothing to do with the Christian gospel and the discipline of theology. Silence on both white supremacy and the black struggle against racial segregation made me angry with a fiery rage that had to find expression. How could any theologian explain the meaning of Christian identity in America and fail to engage white supremacy, its primary negation? I concluded that it was my responsibility to address the great contradiction white supremacy poses for Christianity in America. Published three months before I arrived at Union Theological Seminary in New York, *Black Theology and Black Power* was followed by *A Black Theology of Liberation* (1970), *The Spirituals and the Blues* (1972), and *God of the Oppressed* (1975). In my next work, *Martin & Malcolm & America: A Dream or a Nightmare* (1991), I returned explicitly to the two figures whose influence had combined implicitly to shape the theme and style of black liberation theology. Most people rejected one and embraced the other—seeing Martin and Malcolm as rivals, nemeses, representing oppositional categories of Christian and black, integration and separation, nonviolence and violence, love and hate. I embraced them both because I saw them advocating different methods that corrected and complemented each other, as they worked for the same goal—the *liberation* of black people from white supremacy. Just as I could not separate Martin from Malcolm, neither could I separate my Christian identity from my blackness. I was *black* before I was Christian. My initial challenge was to develop a liberation theology that could be both *black* and *Christian*—at the same time and in one voice. That was not easy because even in the black community the public meaning of Christianity was *white*. Martin King and Malcolm X gave me intellectual resources and the spiritual courage to attack white supremacy.

In earlier reflections on the Christian faith and white supremacy, I had focused on the social evils of slavery and segregation. How could whites confess and live the Christian faith and also impose three-and-a-half centuries of slavery and segregation upon black people? Self-interest and power corrupted their understanding of the Christian gospel. How could powerless blacks endure and resist the brutality of white supremacy in nearly every aspect of their lives and still keep their sanity? I concluded that an immanent presence of a transcendent revelation, confirming for blacks that they were more than what whites said about them, gave them an inner spiritual strength to cope with anything that came their way. I wrote because words were my weapons to resist, to affirm black humanity, and to defend it.

And yet through all this time I avoided dealing directly with the reality of lynching. As a southern black, the subject brought back such painful feelings. But finally I had no choice. The subject chose me. This symbol of white supremacy was like a wild beast that had seized me by the neck, trying to kill me, and I had to fight it before I could fully live. Reading and writing about the lynching nightmare, looking at many images of tortured black bodies, has been my deepest challenge and the most *painful* experience I have had as a theologian. At times it was almost too heavy for me to bear. The more I read about and looked at what whites did to powerless blacks, the angrier I became. Paradoxically, anger soon gave way to a profound feeling of liberation. Being able to write about lynching liberated me from being confined by it. The cross helped me to deal with the brutal legacy of the lynching tree, and the lynching tree helped me to understand the tragic meaning of the cross.

In writing this book, my primary concern is to give voice to black victims, to let them and their families and communities speak to us, exploring the question: how did ordinary blacks, like my mother and father, survive the lynching atrocity and still keep together their families, their communities, and not lose their sanity? How could they live meaningful lives, knowing that they could be lynched for any small violation of what Richard Wright called "the ethics of living Jim Crow"?[4] I wrestle with questions about black dignity in a world of white supremacy because I believe that the cultural and religious resources in the black experience could help all Americans cope with the legacy of white supremacy and also deal more effectively with what is called "the war on terror." If white Americans could look at the terror they inflicted on their own black population—slavery, segregation, and lynching—then they might be able to understand what is coming at them from others. Black people know something about terror because we have been dealing with legal and extralegal white terror for several centuries. Nothing was more terrifying than the lynching tree.

I do not write this book as the last word about the cross and the lynching tree. I write it in order to start a conversation so we can explore the many ways to heal the deep wounds lynching has inflicted upon us. The cross can heal and hurt; it can be empowering and liberating but also enslaving and oppressive. There is no one way in which the cross can be interpreted. I offer my reflections because I believe that the cross placed alongside the lynching tree can help us to see Jesus in America in a new light, and thereby empower people who claim to follow him to take a stand against white supremacy and every kind of injustice.

1

"Nobody Knows de Trouble I See"

The Cross and the Lynching Tree in the Black Experience

They put him to death by hanging him on a tree.
—Acts 10:39

Hundreds of kodaks clicked all morning at the scene of the lynching. People in automobiles and carriages came from miles around to view the corpse dangling from the end of a rope. . . . Picture cards photographers installed a portable printing plant at the bridge and reaped a harvest in selling the postcard showing a photograph of the lynched Negro. Women and children were there by the score. At a number of country schools the day's routine was delayed until boy and girl pupils could get back from viewing the lynched man.
—*The Crisis* 10, no. 2, June 1915, on the lynching of Thomas Brooks in Fayette County, Tennessee

The paradox of a crucified savior lies at the heart of the Christian story. That paradox was particularly evident in the first century when crucifixion was recognized as the particular form of execution reserved by the Roman Empire for insurrectionists and rebels. It was a public spectacle accompanied by torture and shame—one of the most humiliating and painful deaths ever devised by human beings. That Jesus died this way required special explanation. It made no rational or even spiritual sense to say that hope came out of "a place called Golgotha . . . a place of the skull." For the Jews of Jesus' time the punishment of crucifixion held special opprobrium, given their belief that "anyone hung on a tree is under God's curse" (Deut 21:23). Thus, St. Paul said that the "word of the cross is foolishness" to the intellect and a stumbling block to established religion. The cross is a paradoxical religious symbol because it *inverts* the world's value system with the news that hope comes by way of defeat, that suffering and death do not have the last word, that the last shall be first and the first last.

That God could "make a way out of no way" in Jesus' cross was truly absurd to the intellect, yet profoundly real in the souls of black folk. Enslaved blacks who first heard the gospel message seized on the power of the cross. Christ crucified manifested God's loving and liberating presence *in* the contradictions of black life—that transcendent presence in the lives of black Christians that empowered them to believe that *ultimately*, in God's eschatological future, they would not be defeated by the "troubles of this world," no matter how great and painful their suffering. Believing this paradox, this absurd claim of faith, was only possible through God's "amazing grace" and the gift of faith, grounded in humility and repentance. There was no place for the proud and the mighty, for people who think that God called them to rule over others. The cross was God's critique of power—white power—with powerless love, snatching victory out of defeat.

The sufferings of black people during slavery are too deep for words. That suffering did not end with emancipation. The violence and oppression of white supremacy took different forms and employed different means to achieve the same end: the subjugation of black people. And Christian theology, for African Americans, maintained the same great challenge: to explain from the perspective of history and faith how life could be made meaningful in the face of death, how hope could remain alive in the world of Jim Crow segregation. These were the challenges that shaped black religious life in the United States.

At no time was the struggle to keep such hope alive more difficult than during the lynching era (1880-1940). The lynching tree is the most potent symbol of the trouble nobody knows that blacks have seen but do not talk about because the pain of remembering—visions of black bodies dangling from southern trees, surrounded by jeering white mobs—is almost too excruciating to recall.

In that era, the lynching tree joined the cross as the most emotionally charged symbols in the African American community—symbols that represented both death and the promise of redemption, judgment and the offer of mercy, suffering and the power of hope. Both the cross and the lynching tree represented the worst in human beings and at the same time "an unquenchable ontological thirst"[1] for life that refuses to let the worst determine our final meaning.

Lynching has a complicated and dynamic meaning in American history. Since the publication of Jacquelyn Dowd Hall's *Revolt against Chivalry* (1979), many historians have been investigating lynching, and have even discovered most of the names of the nearly five thousand African American victims.[2] Initially, lynching was not directed primarily against blacks nor did it always mean death to the victim. Mexicans, Indians, Chinese, and whites were lynched—a term that could apply to whipping, shooting, stabbing, as well as hanging. Lynching was an extralegal punishment sanctioned by the community. Many scholars date its origin in Virginia during the Revolutionary War when Charles Lynch or William Lynch (both were called the original "Judge Lynch"), with the support of the community, punished Tory sympathizers. As communities moved westward out of reach of the courts, Judge Lynch was invoked to punish rustlers, robbers, wife abusers, and others who committed what a community perceived as outrageous deeds. Lynching was not regarded as an evil thing but a necessity—the only way a community could protect itself from bad people out of reach of the law.[3] Many western movies show a romanticized view of lynching as hanging rustlers or bank robbers and murderers.

During nearly two-and-half centuries of slavery, blacks were considered valuable property. Their owners usually protected their investment as they would their cows, horses, and other articles of value. Slaveholders whipped and raped slaves, violating them in any way they thought necessary, but they did not lynch them, except in the case of those who threatened the slave system itself, such as Gabriel Prosser, Denmark Vesey, Nat Turner, and other insurrectionists.

The lynching of black America marked an important turning point in the history and meaning of lynching, as the racial component of lynching changed its meaning for both whites and blacks. Lynching as primarily mob violence and torture directed against blacks began to increase after the Civil War and the end of slavery, when the 1867 Congress passed the Reconstruction Act granting black men the franchise and citizenship rights of participation in the affairs of government. Most southern whites were furious at the very idea of granting ex-slaves social, political, and economic freedom. The Ku Klux Klan, initially organized as a social club in Pulaski, Tennessee (1866), soon transformed itself into a vigilante group whose primary purpose was to redeem the South and thereby ensure that America remained a white man's country. Many felt that it was one thing to lose the war to the North but quite another to allow ignorant, uncivilized "niggers" to rule over whites or even participate with them in the political process. White supremacists felt insulted by the suggestion that whites and blacks might work together as equals. Whether in the churches, colleges, and universities, or in the political and social life of the nation, southern whites, who were not going to allow their ex-slaves to associate with them as equals, felt that if lynching were the only way to keep ex-slaves subservient, then it was necessary.

During the Reconstruction era, the South was divided into military districts, which provided blacks some protection from mob violence, so that the Klan had to do its violent work against blacks and their white northern sympathizers in secret, at night, wearing hoods to hide its members' identity. When KKK members were tried in courts, they could usually count on their neighbors and friends to find them "not guilty," since all-white male juries almost never found white men guilty of lynching a black man.

The white South's perspective on the Reconstruction was told in Thomas Dixon's enormously popular novel *The Leopard's Spots* (1902), which sold over one million copies. It was followed by *The Clansman* (1905). Both novels portrayed the Klan as redeemers of the South. D. W. Griffith transformed Dixon's novels into that cinematic masterpiece of racist propaganda *The Birth of a Nation* (1915), first seen at the White House and praised enthusiastically by President Woodrow Wilson. Whites, especially in the South, loved *Birth* and regarded seeing it as a "religious experience." It "rendered lynching an efficient and honorable act of justice" and served to help reunite the North and South as a white Christian nation, at the expense of African Americans. After seeing *Birth*, one white man in Kentucky left the theater so excited that he shot and killed a fifteen-year-old African American high school student. By 1930, according to one report, 90 percent of white southerners had seen *Birth*.[4]

Following Reconstruction and the removal of federal troops from the South (1877), the black dream of freedom turned into a nightmare "worse than slavery,"[5] initiating what black historian Rayford Logan called the "nadir"[6] in black history and what journalist Douglas A. Blackmon appropriately called "slavery by another name."[7] Assured of no federal interference, southern whites were now free to take back the South, to redeem it from what they called "Negro domination," through mob violence—excluding blacks from politics, arresting them for vagrancy, forcing them to work as sharecroppers who never got out of debt, and creating a rigid segregated society in which being black was a badge of shame with no meaningful future. A black person could be lynched for any perceived insult to whites. A white from Florida told a northern critic, "The people of the South don't think any more of killing the black fellows than you would think of killing a flea. . . ." A black Mississippian recalled lynching with these words: "Back in them days, to kill a Negro wasn't nothing. It was like killing a chicken or killing a snake. The whites would say, 'Niggers jest supposed to die, ain't no damn good anyway—so jest go an' kill 'em.'"[8] A firm advocate of white supremacy and even lynching in cases of rape, Bishop Atticus G. Haygood of the Methodist Church complained in 1893 that "Now-a-days, it seems the killing of Negroes is not so extraordinary an occurrence as to need explanation; it has become so common that it no longer surprises. We read such things as we read of fires that burn a cabin or a town."[9] "Their blackness alone," writes historian Joel Williamson in his influential text *The Crucible of Race*, "was license enough to line them up against walls, to menace them with guns, to search them roughly, beat them, and rob them of every vestige of dignity."[10]

Although white southerners lost the Civil War, they did not lose the cultural war—the struggle to define America as a white nation and blacks as a subordinate race unfit for governing and therefore incapable of political and social equality. In the white imagination, the image of black men was transformed from docile slaves and harmless "Sambos," to menacing "black beast rapists," the most serious threat to the virtue of white women and the sanctity of the white home. The image of black women was changed from nurturing "Negro mammies" to salacious Jezebels, nearly as corrupting to white civilization as black men.

The claim that whites had the right to control the black population through lynching and other extralegal forms of mob violence was grounded in the religious belief that America is a white nation called by God to bear witness to the superiority of "white over black."[11] Even prominent religious scholars in the North, like the highly regarded Swiss-born church historian Philip Schaff of Union Theological Seminary in New York (1870-1893), believed that "The Anglo-Saxon and Anglo-American, of all modern races, possess the strongest national character and the one best fitted for universal dominion."[12] Such beliefs made lynching defensible and even necessary for many whites. Cole Blease, the two-time governor and U.S. senator from South Carolina, proclaimed that lynching is a "divine right of the Caucasian race to dispose of the offending blackamoor without the benefit of jury."[13] Lynching was the white community's way of forcibly reminding blacks of their inferiority and powerlessness. To be black meant that whites could do anything to you and your people, and that neither you nor anyone else could do anything about it. The Supreme Court Chief Justice Roger B. Taney had said clearly in the Dred Scott Decision (1857): "[blacks] had no rights which the white man was bound to respect."[14] For many whites, whether in the North or the South, that conviction was unaffected by the end of slavery.

But now, without slavery to control blacks, new means had to be devised, and even a new rationale for control. This was supplied by black men's imagined insatiable lust for white women. Because of their threat to white womanhood, black men must be carefully watched and violently kept in their place, segregated and subordinated. Sexual intercourse between black men and white women was regarded as the worst crime blacks could commit against Anglo-Saxon civilization. Even when sexual relations were consensual, "race-mixing," mockingly called "mongrelization," was always translated to mean rape, and it was used as the primary justification of lynching. It was the moral and

Christian responsibility of white men to protect the purity of their race by any means necessary. During the late nineteenth and early twentieth centuries, it would have been difficult to find white persons who would *openly* object to the right of white men to protect white women from sexual union with black men by means of lynching. William Van Amberg Sullivan, a former U.S. senator from Mississippi, boasted, "I led the mob which lynched Nelse Patton, and I am proud of it. I directed every movement of the mob and I did everything I could to see that he was lynched." Even presidents refused to oppose lynching publicly, and some even supported it. As Theodore Roosevelt said, "the greatest existing cause of lynching is the perpetration, especially by black men, of the hideous crime of rape—the most abominable in all the category of crimes, even worse than murder." On the other hand, black men's assertion of their right to protect their daughters, sisters, wives, mothers, and other women from unwelcome advances from white men could bring down the full weight of Judge Lynch.[15]

Threats of lynching were often more effective than the act itself. In his autobiography, *Born to Rebel*, Benjamin E. Mays, the great president of Morehouse College in Atlanta and teacher of Martin Luther King Jr., recalled the occasion when a white mob confronted him and his father when he was just a child.

> A crowd of white men . . . rode up on horseback with rifles on their shoulders. I was with my father when they rode up, and I remember starting to cry. They cursed my father, drew their guns and made him salute, made him take off his hat and bow down to them several times. Then they rode away. I was five years old, but I've never forgotten them.[16]

While white mob violence against African Americans was an obsession in the South, it was not limited to that region. White supremacy was and is an American reality. Whites lynched blacks in nearly every state, including New York, Minnesota, and California. Wherever blacks were present in significant numbers, the threat of being lynched was always real. Blacks had to "watch their step," no matter where they were in America. A black man could be walking down the road, minding his business, and his life could suddenly change by meeting a white man or a group of white men or boys who on a whim decided to have some fun with a Negro; and this could happen in Mississippi or New York, Arkansas, or Illinois.

By the 1890s, lynching fever gripped the South, spreading like cholera, as white communities made blacks their primary target, and torture their focus. Burning the black victim slowly for hours was the chief method of torture. Lynching became a white media spectacle, in which prominent newspapers, like the *Atlanta Constitution*, announced to the public the place, date, and time of the expected hanging and burning of black victims. Often as many as ten to twenty thousand men, women, and children attended the event. It was a family affair, a ritual celebration of white supremacy, where women and children were often given the first opportunity to torture black victims—burning black flesh and cutting off genitals, fingers, toes, and ears as souvenirs. Postcards were made from the photographs taken of black victims with white lynchers and onlookers smiling as they struck a pose for the camera. They were sold for ten to twenty-five cents to members of the crowd, who then mailed them to relatives and friends, often with a note saying something like this: "This is the barbeque we had last night."[17]

Spectacle lynchings attracted people from nearby cities and towns. They could not have happened without widespread knowledge and the explicit sanction of local and state authorities and with tacit approval from the federal government, members of the white media, churches, and universities. Lynching became so prevalent that the Boston branch of the Colored National League sent a letter to President William McKinley demanding action.

> We have suffered, sir . . . since your accession to office . . .
> from the hate and violence of people claiming to be civi-
> lized, but who are not civilized, and you have seen our suf-
> ferings. . . . Yet you have at no time and on no occasion
> opened your lips on our behalf. . . . Is there no help in the
> federal arm for us, or even one word of audible pity, pro-
> test, and remonstrance? Black indeed we are, sir, but we are
> also men and citizens.[18]

Like others in his office, McKinley refused to condemn lynching publicly, even after the infamous Wilmington, North Carolina, race riot of 1898, during which eleven blacks were killed and
thousands were driven from the city in order to prevent them
from participating in politics.[19]

When the anti-lynching Dyer Bill was passed in the House
of Representatives, January 26, 1922, many blacks hoped that
President Warren G. Harding, a Republican, the party of Lincoln, would urge the Senate to do the same. Ara Lee Settle of
Armstrong Technical High School, Washington, DC, wrote to
him (June 18, 1922), calling his attention to the importance of an
anti-lynching law for the black community. "Mr. President," she
wrote,

> imagine yourself about to be lynched for something of
> which you know nothing about. Men seize you from some
> place of refuge, carry you to the heart of town, place a rope
> around you and burn you, while men, women and children
> are jeering you amidst all your pain and agony. It is enough
> to make one ashamed not to use his full influence against
> this horrible crime.[20]

Yet Harding, like most whites, was unmoved by black suffering. No one in America could claim that they did not know that
whites were lynching blacks, nor could legal authorities claim
ignorance, since lynchers made no effort to hide their identity
or their deeds. Bishop Henry M. Turner of the A.M.E. Church

mocked the euphemism, "At the hands of persons unknown," the typical designation for lynchers that often appeared in newspaper accounts after the fact:

> Strange . . . that the men who constitute these [mobs] can never be identified by . . . governors or the law officers, but the newspapers know all about them—can advance what they are going to do, how and when it was done, how the rope broke, how many balls entered the Negro's body, how loud he prayed, how piteously he begged, what he said, how long he was left hanging, how many composed the mob, the number that were masked, whether they were prominent citizens or not, how the fire was built that burnt the raper, how the Negro was tied, how he was thrown into the fire, and the whole transaction; but still the fiendish work was done by a set of "unknown men."[21]

Unlike Bishop Turner, however, few blacks in the South could fight back with pen or gun and survive. "You couldn't do nothing about those things," Mississippi bluesman Willie Dixon said, as he reflected back on the lynching era in his autobiography. "The black man had to be a complete coward."[22] Yet cowardice is not the right word to describe the black response to lynching and white mob violence; even Willie Dixon had the courage to leave Mississippi for Chicago, where he joined other bluesmen and women, like Muddy Waters, Howlin Wolf, and Etta James, together creating a musical response to lynching that told the world about the cultural power of blacks to preserve and protect their humanity.

Blacks knew that violent self-defense was tantamount to suicide; even affirming blackness in a world defined by white power took great courage. Whites acted in a superior manner for so long that it was difficult for them to even recognize their cultural and spiritual arrogance, blatant as it was to African Americans. Their law was not designed to protect blacks from lynching, especially when blacks acted as if they were socially equal to whites. Should a black in the South lift his hand or raise his voice to reprimand a white person, he would incur the full weight of the law and the mob. Even to look at white people in a manner regarded as disrespectful could get a black lynched. Whites often lynched blacks simply to remind the black community of their powerlessness. Unemployed blacks passing through an area with no white man to vouch for them could easily find themselves on a prison chain gang or swinging from a lynching tree. There were many "sundown towns" in the South and the North—some with signs warning, "Nigger, don't let the sun set on your head,"[23] and others with no signs but which could be fatal to blacks who *happened* to be passing through.

How did southern rural blacks survive the terrors of this era? Self-defense and protest were out of the question, but there were other forms of resistance. For most blacks it was the blues and religion that offered the chief weapons of resistance. At the juke joints on Friday and Saturday nights and at churches on Sunday mornings and evening week nights blacks affirmed their humanity and fought back against dehumanization. Both black religion and the blues offered sources of hope that there was more to life than what one encountered daily in the white man's world.

At the Saturday night juke joint, bluesmen like Robert Johnson, often called the most influential bluesman, spoke back in defiance, refusing to be defined by death's brutal reality—the constant threat of the lynching tree.

> I got to keep movinnnn', I got to keep movinnnn',
> Blues fallin' like hail
> And the day keeps on worryin' me,
> There's a hellhound on my trail.[24]

Blues singers lifted African Americans above their troubles by offering them an opportunity to experience "love and loss" as a liberating catharsis.

Blues grabbed me at midnight and didn't turn me
    loose 'til day
Blues grabbed me at midnight, didn't turn me loose
    'til day,
I didn't have no mama to drive these blues away.[25]

Blacks found hope in the music itself—a collective self-transcendent meaning in the singing, dancing, loving, and laughing. They found hope in the stoic determination not to be defeated by the pain and suffering in their lives. James Baldwin called this hope an "ironic tenacity"! "I've got the blues and I'm too damn mean to cry." "The blues," as Ralph Ellison put it, "is an impulse to keep the painful details and episodes of a brutal experience alive in one's aching consciousness, to finger its jagged grain, and to transcend it, not by the consolation of philosophy but by squeezing from it a near-tragic, near-comic lyricism."[26]

Good morning, blues.
Blues how do you do?
Blues say, "I feel all right but I come to worry you."

On the one hand, African Americans spoke of how they "cried and moaned, about "feel[ing] like nothin', somethin' th'owed away." Yet, in the next line they balanced despair with hope: "Then I get my guitar and play the blues all day." As long as African Americans could sing and play the blues, they had some hope that one day their humanity would be acknowledged.

I remember blacks in Arkansas trying to cope with despair—bad crops, terrible winter, and troublesome white folks—yet they still believed they could make it through the "storm of life" and not be defeated in this "mean old world." "Hard times" were real and concrete, an everyday struggle to survive with dignity in a society that did not recognize their humanity. The dialectic of sorrow and joy, despair and hope was central in the black experience.

> My burden's so heavy, I can't hardly see,
> Seems like everybody down on me.

Despair was real; but it was not ultimate, not the last word. In the closing line, the bluesman reached for hope:

> An' that's all right, I don't worry, oh, there will be a
>   better day.
> The sun's gonna shine on my back door some day.

In the black experience, there was what novelist Richard Wright called the "endemic capacity to live."[27]

> Goin' down to de railroad track,
> Lay ma head on de track.
> Goin' down to de railroad track,
> Lay ma head on de track—

Despair seems to close down the future. But the bluesman stubbornly clings to hope.

> But if I see de train a-comin'
> I'm gonna jerk it back!

This dialectic of despair and hope defined black existence.

> Pocket book was empty,
> My heart was full of pain.

Yet African Americans did not let economic distress and mental anguish have the final say on their existence.

> When you lose your money,
> don't lose your mind.

To be able to speak back to the tragedy of lynching in the blues song was partly to overcome its terror. But the singing of the blues was also a way for ordinary working class and poor blacks to assert loudly and exuberantly their somebodiness, twisting and turning their sweaty bodies to the "low down dirty blues."

"You've never heard a mule sing, have you?" intoned a bluesman, asserting his humanity.

Hope in black possibility, in the dream of a new world, had to be carved out of wretched conditions, out of a world where the possibility of violent death was always imminent. African Americans knew what it meant to "make the best of a bad situation"—to live "under a kind of sentence of death," "not know[ing] when [their] time will come, it may never come, but it may also be any time."[28] "They'd lynch you in a minute,"[29] said Skip James. Charlie Patton of Sunflower, Mississippi, agreed and sang about what he saw:

> Everyday seems like murder here,
> Everyday seems like murder here.
> I'm gonna leave tomorrow,
> I know you don't want me here.

In his study of Richard Wright, Abdul JanMohamed speaks about black subjectivity as "the death-bound-subject"—"the subject who is formed, from infancy on, by the imminent and ubiquitous threat of death."[30] African Americans did not have to see black bodies swinging on southern trees or personally experience mob violence to know that they daily risked death. "I had never in my life been abused by whites," wrote Richard Wright in *Black Boy*, as he reflected back on his boyhood in Mississippi, "but I had already become as conditioned to their existence as though I had been the victim of a thousand lynchings."[31]

The lynching tree was the most horrifying symbol of white supremacy in black life. It was a shameful and painful way to die. The fear of lynching was so deep and widespread that most blacks were too scared even to talk publicly about it. When they heard of a person being lynched in their vicinity, they often ran home, pulled down shades, and turned out lights—hoping the terror moment would pass without taking the lives of their relatives and friends.

Despite such terror, however, blacks did not let lynching completely squeeze the joy out of their lives. There was always a lot of excitement and joy at the juke joints, a people swinging with sexual passion on Friday and Saturday nights because then they could express themselves fully, let themselves go with no thought of tomorrow and the white man's dehumanizing disregard of their humanity. They could have fun, get angry, talk dirty and loud to and about each other, and sometimes even get violent—knowing that the limits of proper behavior were what they set among themselves. At the juke, blacks could even talk back to "The Man" (in black idiom a pejorative term—the white man), telling him in his absence what they could not say to his face. Alabama bluesman Cow Cow Davenport sang about the "Jim Crow Blues":

> I'm tired of being Jim Crowed,
> Gonna leave this Jim Crow town.

Blind Lemon Jefferson moaned the "Hangman's Blues," one of a few songs that confronted directly the reality and fear of lynching.

> Mean ole hangman is waitin' to tighten up that noose,
> Lord, I'm so scared I'm trembling in my shoes.[32]

Blacks enjoyed Friday and Saturday nights so much that they nearly forgot, at least for a few hours, whatever humiliations they endured during the week. As a child growing up in Bearden, Arkansas, during the 1940s and 50s, I remember hearing the blues erupt from the juke joints, especially at "Sam's Place." It sounded so good that one had to move to the sound of B. B. King's "Rock Me Baby," accompanied by "Lucille" (his guitar). But I will never forget the voice of Bo Diddley declaring "I'm A Man"—"M-A-N," spelling it out for emphasis, referring overtly to his sexual prowess and covertly speaking back to the denial of his masculinity and humanity in white society. Bluesman Big

Bill Broonzy was bolder and more explicit, asking, "When Will I Get to Be Called a Man?"

> When I was born in this world, this is what happened
>   to me:
> I was never called a man and now I'm fifty-three . . .
> I wonder when I will be called a man.
> Or do I have to wait 'till I get ninety-three?[33]

When an adult black male is treated like a child in a patriarchal society—with whites calling him "boy," "uncle," and "nigger"—proclaiming oneself a "man" is a bold and necessary affirmation of black resistance. (It was analogous to the Memphis garbage workers carrying large signs saying "I'M A MAN" in defiance of white city government during Martin Luther King Jr.'s last march in 1968.) But it was risky for blacks to assert their humanity overtly during those times; it often had to be camouflaged in blues songs about sexuality at the juke joint.

Although my mother never let her sons go to the juke, one did not have to go there to know what a good time black folks had. The drinking was heavy, people were laughing, and the music was so loud that one could hear it miles away. The people jumped at the juke like there was no tomorrow, "letting it all hang out." That was why one Negro joked with a white man that "he would never want to be white if he could just once be a 'nigger' on Saturday night."

To be able to laugh, to say what's on one's mind, expressing feelings of disgust and rage, was liberating for blacks, who usually remained silent, hat in hand and head bowed in the presence of whites. As Albert Murray put it, the blues was nothing but "a disposition to confront the most unpromising circumstances and make the most of what little there is to go on, regardless of the odds."[34] The blues expressed a feeling, an existential affirmation of joy in the midst of extreme suffering, especially the ever-present threat of death by lynching. B. B. King, who saw a lynching as a child in Mississippi, gave a powerful interview on the meaning of the blues:

> If you live under that system for so long, then it don't bother you openly, but mentally, way back in your mind it bugs you. . . . Later on you sometime will think about this and you wonder why, so that's where your blues come in, you really bluesy then, y'see, because you hurt deep down, believe me, I've lived through it, I know. I'm still trying to say what the blues means to me. So I sing about it.[35]

If the blues offered an affirmation of humanity, religion offered a way for black people to find hope. "Our churches are where we dip our tired bodies in cool springs of hope," wrote Richard Wright in *Twelve Million Voices*, "where we retain our wholeness and humanity despite the blows of death. . . ."[36] On Sunday morning at church, black Christians spoke back in song, sermon, and prayer against the "faceless, merciless, apocalyptic vengefulness of the massed white mob,"[37] to show that trouble and sorrow would not determine our final meaning. African Americans embraced the story of Jesus, the crucified Christ, whose death they claimed paradoxically gave them life, just as God resurrected him in the life of the earliest Christian community. While the lynching tree symbolized white power and "black death," the cross symbolized divine power and "black life"—God overcoming the power of sin and death.

"It is only when we are within the walls of our churches that we can wholly be ourselves," Wright correctly said, "that we keep alive a sense of our personalities in relation to the total world in which we live, that we maintain a quiet and constant communion with all that is deepest in us."[38] At church black people sang of having "been in the storm so long," "tossed and driv'n," "'buked an' scorned," and "talked about sho's you born," "sometimes up," "sometimes down," and "sometimes almost level to the groun.'" "Our going to church on Sunday is like placing our ear to another's chest to hear the unquenchable murmur of the human heart."[39] African Americans sang of having traveled a "lonesome journey," through slavery and segregation, often tired, hungry and home-less, "rambling and running," not knowing where to "roam"—not knowing where to "make my getaway" to find a safe place, free of the "noise of the bloodhounds on my trail." Blacks have been "tore down," "broken-hearted," "troubled in de mind," "way down yon-der" where "I couldn't hear nobody pray," in a valley so deep and dark where death is like "a hammer ringin' on a coffin," "a pale horse an' rider," "a chariot swingin' low," and "a train blowin' at the station." Blacks have tasted "sorrow's kitchen"—that "burden of woe" that compelled them to sing a haunting, mournful sound:

> Sometimes I feel like a motherless chile,
> Sometimes I feel like a motherless chile,
> Sometimes I feel like a motherless chile,
> A long ways from home.

Dread and powerlessness in the face of the ever-present threat of death on the lynching tree impelled blacks to cry out from the depth of their spiritual being:

> Oh, Lord, Oh, My Lord!
> Oh, My Good Lord!
> Keep me f'om sinkin' down!

To sink down was to give up on life and embrace hopeless-ness, like the words of an old bluesman: "Been down so long, down don't bother me." It was to go way down into a pit of despair, of nothingness, what Søren Kierkegaard called "sickness unto death," a "sickness in the self"—the loss of hope that life could have meaning in a world full of trouble. The story of Job is the classic expression of utter despair in the face of life's great contradictions:

> Why is light given to the one in misery,
>   and life to the bitter in soul,

> Who long for death, but it does not come,
>   and dig for it more than for hidden treasures;
> Who rejoice exceedingly,
>   and are glad when they find the grave? (Job 3:20-
>   22)

Unlike Kierkegaard and Job, however, blacks often refused to go down into that "loathsome void," that "torment of despair," where one "struggles with death but cannot die."[40] No matter what trouble they encountered, they kept on believing and hoping that "a change is gonna come." They did not transcend "hard living" but faced it head-on, refusing to be silent in the midst of adversity.

> Great gawdamighty, folks feelin' bad,
> Lost everything they ever had.

A classic expression of the dialectic of despair and hope in black life is found in the spiritual "Nobody Knows." The first three lines accent despair:

> Nobody knows de trouble I've seen,
> Nobody knows my sorrow.
> Nobody knows de trouble I've seen,

But the last line accents hope with an exclamation:

> Glory Hallelujah!

"Nobody Knows" reaches the peak of despair in its repetition of the first line in the third.

African Americans did not doubt that their lives were filled with trouble: how could one be black in America during the lynching era and not know about the existential agony that trouble created for black people? Trouble followed them everywhere, like a shadow they could not shake. But the "Glory Hallelujah" in the last line speaks of hope that trouble would not sink them down into permanent despair—what Kierkegaard described as "not willing to be oneself" or even "a self; or lowest of all in despair at willing to be another than himself."[41] When people do not want to be themselves, but somebody else, that is utter despair.

In another version of "Nobody Knows," the dialectic of doubt and faith is expressed with a focus on Jesus' solidarity with the one in trouble.

> Nobody knows the trouble I see,
> Nobody knows but Jesus,
> Nobody knows the trouble I see,
> Glory Hallelujah!

In the first version of "Nobody Knows," hope is carved out of a tenacious spirit, the stubborn refusal to be defeated by tragedy. The source of the hope carved out of "trouble" and "sorrow," expressed in the "Glory Hallelujah," although not clearly identified, is assumed. In the second version of "Nobody Knows," the source of the hope is Jesus, for he is a friend who knows about the trouble of the little ones, and he is the reason for their "Hallelujah." His divine presence is the most important message about black existence.

During my childhood, I heard a lot about the cross at Macedonia A.M.E. Church, where faith in Jesus was defined and celebrated. We sang about "Calvary," and asked, "Were you there?", "down at the cross," "when they crucified my Lord." "Oh! Sometimes it causes me to tremble, tremble, tremble." The spirituals, gospel songs, and hymns focused on how Jesus achieved salvation for the least through his *solidarity* with them even unto death. There were more songs, sermons, prayers, and testimonies about the cross than any other theme. The cross was the foundation on which their faith was built.

In the mystery of God's revelation, black Christians believed that just knowing that Jesus went through an experience of suffering in a manner similar to theirs gave them faith that God was with them, even in suffering on lynching trees, just as God was present with Jesus in suffering on the cross.

Poor little Jesus boy, made him be born in a manger.
World treated him so mean,
Treats me mean too . . .

Dey whipped Him up an' dey whipped Him down,
Dey whipped dat man all ovah town.

Look-a how they done muh Lawd.

I was there when they nailed him to the cross,
Oh! How it makes me sadder, sadder,
When I think how they nailed him to the cross.

I was there when they took him down . . .
Oh! How it makes my spirit tremble,
When I recalls how they took him down.

The more black people struggled against white supremacy, the more they found in the cross the spiritual power to resist the violence they so often suffered. They came to know, as the black historian Lerone Bennett wrote, "at the deepest level . . . what it was like to be crucified. . . . And more: that there were some things in this world that are worth being crucified for."[42] Just as Jesus did not deserve to suffer, they knew they did not deserve it; yet faith was the one thing white people could not control or take away. "In our collective outpourings of song and prayer, the fluid emotions of others make us feel the strength in ourselves. . . ."[43] They shouted, danced, clapped their hands and stomped their feet as they bore witness to the power of Jesus' cross which had given them an identity far more meaningful than the harm that white supremacy could do them. No matter whose songs they sang or what church they belonged to, they infused them with their own experience of suffering and transformed what they received into their own. "Jesus Keep Me near the Cross," "Must Jesus Bear the

Cross Alone?" and other white Protestant evangelical hymns did not sound or feel the same when blacks and whites sang them because their life experiences were so different. When black people were challenged by white supremacy, with the lynching tree staring down at them, where else could they turn for hope that their resistance would ultimately succeed?

Penniless, landless, jobless, and with no political and social power in the society, what could black people do except to fight with cultural and religious power and pray that God would support them in their struggle for freedom? Black people "stretched their hands to God," because they had nowhere else to turn. Because of their experience of arbitrary violence, the cross was and is a redeeming and comforting image for many black Christians. If the God of Jesus' cross is found among the least, the crucified people of the world, then God is also found among those lynched in American history.

To keep hope alive was not easy for African Americans, facing state-endorsed terrorism nearly everywhere in America. Trouble followed them wherever they went—in the morning, at night, and all day long—keeping them awake and stalking them in nightmares, like a wild beast, waiting to attack its prey.

Although church people, like the blues people, could not escape trouble, they sang "trouble don't last always." The final word about black life is not death on a lynching tree but redemption in the cross—a miraculously transformed life found in the God of the gallows. This faith empowered blacks to wrestle with trouble as Jacob wrestled with his divine opponent till daybreak, refusing to let go until he was "blessed" with meaning and purpose. "Thy name shall be called no more Jacob, but Israel: for as a prince has thou power with God and with men, and hath prevailed" (Gen 32:28 KJV). The spirituals "Wrestling Jacob," "We Are Climbing Jacob's Ladder," and "Wake Up, Jacob" are black people expressing their solidarity with Jacob and his struggle for a new identity. Their identification with Jacob stretches back deep into slavery.

In his book *Army Life in a Black Regiment* (1869), Thomas Went-worth Higginson, called "Wrestling Jacob" "one of the wildest and most striking" of the spirituals he heard during the Civil War.

> O wrestlin' Jacob, Jacob, day's a-breakin';
>   I will not let thee go!
> O wrestlin' Jacob, Jacob, day's a-breakin';
>   He will not let me go!
> O, I hold my brudder wid a tremblin' hand;
>   I would not let him go!
> I hold my sister wid a tremblin' hand;
>   I would not let her go!
>
> O, Jacob do hang from a tremblin' limb,
>   He would not let him go!
> O, Jacob do hang from a tremblin' limb;
>   De Lord will bless my soul.
> O, wrestlin' Jacob, Jacob . . . .[44]

The "tremblin' limb" could be the lynching tree since the lynching terror directed specifically at blacks began during the Civil War.

A similar wrestling occurs in "We Are Climbing Jacob's Ladder."

> We are climbing Jacob's Ladder,
> We are climbing Jacob's Ladder,
> We are climbing Jacob's Ladder,
> Soldier of the Cross.
>
> Every round goes higher higher,
> Every round goes higher higher,
> Every round goes higher higher,
> Soldier of the Cross.

Although Jacob was left with a limp, he won his struggle with God.

Wake up, Jacob, day is a-breaking, I'm on my way;
O, wake up Jacob, day is a-breaking, I'm on my way.
I want to go to heaven when I die,
Do love de Lord!
I want to go to heaven when I die,
Do love the Lord![45]

As Jacob, the God-wrestler, received a new name to reflect his new self, black people's struggle with God in white America also left a deep and lasting wound. Yet they too expressed their hope for a new life in God: "Ah tol' Jesus it would be all right, if He changed mah name," another spiritual that connects with Jacob's experience. The change of name initiates a new conflict, a new struggle. "Jesus tol' me the world would be 'gainst me if He changed mah name."

W. E. B. Du Bois called black faith "a pythian madness" and "a demoniac possession"—"sprung from the African forests," "mad with supernatural joy."[46] One has to be a little mad, kind of crazy, to find salvation in the cross, victory in defeat, and life in death. This is why the meaning of the cross is intensely debated today, especially by secular and religious intellectuals who reject the absurd idea that a shameful, despicable death could "reveal" anything.

Yet the German scholar Martin Kahler has said that the Passion story in the Gospels forms the center of the Jesus story, and everything else in his life and teachings is only a prologue to his death on the cross. Black Christians could agree: they sang more songs and preached more sermons about the cross than any other aspect of Jesus' ministry. To be sure, Jesus' life and teachings are important for the black church community to understand his meaning, especially seeing him in complete solidarity with the oppressed. The classic expression of this aspect of Jesus' ministry is found in the Gospel of Luke. "The Spirit of the Lord is upon me," Jesus said at the beginning of his ministry in a Nazareth synagogue, as he read from "the scroll of the prophet Isaiah," "because he has anointed me to bring good news to the poor. He has sent me to proclaim release to the captives, and recovery of sight to the blind, to let the oppressed go free" (4:18). Black people sang and preached about Jesus being with the poor—healing and feeding them. The resurrection of Jesus is God giving people meaning beyond history, when such violence as slavery and lynching seemed to close off any future.

But the cross speaks to oppressed people in ways that Jesus' life, teachings, and even his resurrection do not. As the German New Testament scholar Ernst Käsemann put it, "The resurrection is . . . a chapter in the theology of the cross." Or the cross is "the signature of the one who is risen."[47] The cross places God in the midst of crucified people, in the midst of people who are hung, shot, burned, and tortured. Seeing himself as a man crucified like Jesus, Isaiah Fountain (January 23, 1920) insisted that "he be executed wearing a purple robe and crown, to analogize his innocence to that of Jesus Christ."[48] Before he was lynched in Oxford, Mississippi (1899), Steve Allen testified to his "peace with God," saying that "Jesus died on the Roman cross for me; through his mercy all my sins are forgiven. I am anchored in Christ." With that testimony, "he went to his death without a tremor."[49] Before Charles Johnston, a black minister, was hanged in Swainbora, Georgia, "he 'preached his own funeral sermon,' inducing the crowd to sing, kneel, raise their hands, and pray along with him."[50]

Blacks did not embrace the cross, however, without experiencing the profound contradictions that slavery, segregation, and lynching posed for their faith. That was why most blacks left white churches during slavery to form their own places of worship. Leaving white churches helped blacks to find their own space for free religious and political expression, but it did not remove their need to wrestle with God about the deeply felt

contradictions that slavery created for faith. "Does the Bible condemn slavery without any regard to circumstances, or not?" roars
Reverend J. W. C. Pennington in 1845. "I, for one, desire to know.
My repentance, my faith, my hope, my love, my perseverance all,
all, I conceal it not, I repeat it, all turn upon this point. If I am
deceived here—if the word of God does sanction slavery, I want
another book, another repentance, another faith, and another
hope."[51] Faith achieved its authenticity only by questioning God,
asking, as the Reverend Nathaniel Paul did, "why it was that
thou didst look on with calm indifference of an unconcerned
spectator, when thy holy law was violated, thy divine authority
despised and a portion of thine own creatures reduced to a state
of mere vassalage and misery?"[52]

Bishop Payne of the A.M.E. Church was so troubled that he
questioned God's existence:

> Sometimes it seems as though some wild beast had
> plunged his fangs into my heart, and was squeezing out its
> life-blood. Then I began to question the existence of God,
> and to say: "If he does exist, is he just? If so, why does he
> suffer one race to oppress and enslave another, to rob them
> by unrighteous enactments of rights, which they hold most
> dear and sacred? . . . Is there no God?"[53]

No historical situation was more challenging than the lynching era, when God the liberator seemed nowhere to be found.
"De courts er dis land is not for niggers," a black man from South
Carolina reflected cynically. "It seems to me that when it comes
to trouble, de law an' a nigger is de white man's sport, an' justice is
a stranger in them precincts, an' mercy is unknown. An' de Bible
say we must pray for we enemy. Drop down on you' knee, brothers, an' pray to God for all de crackers, an' judges, an' de courts,
an' solicitors, sheriffs, an' police in de land."[54] Whether one was
lynched on a tree or in court, the results were the same. "Lord,
how come me here," they sang, "I wish I never was born!"

There ain't no freedom here, Lord . . .
They treat me so mean here, Lord . . .
I wish I never was born!

Throughout the twentieth century, African Americans continued to struggle to reconcile their faith in God's justice and love with the persistence of black suffering. Writer James Baldwin spoke for many: "If [God's] love was so great, and if He loved all His children, why were we, the blacks, cast down so far?"[55] No one knows the answer to that question.

Dealing with nearly four hundred years of ongoing suffering in African American history is enough to make any black person lose faith and roam in a blues-like way, trying to find meaning in an absurd world of white supremacy. Unlike the spirituals and the church, the blues and the juke joint did not lead to an organized political resistance against white supremacy. But one could correctly say that the spirituals and the church, with Jesus' cross at the heart of its faith, gave birth to the black freedom movement that reached its peak in the civil rights era during the 1950s and 60s. The spirituals were the soul of the movement, giving people courage to fight, and the church was its anchor, deepening its faith in the coming freedom for all. The blues was an individual's expression of a cultural defiance against white supremacy, a stubborn refusal to be defined by it. The blues prepared people to fight for justice by giving them a cultural identity that made them human and thus ready to struggle. The blues sent people traveling, roaming, looking for a woman or a man to soothe one's aching human heart. But it was Jesus' cross that sent people protesting in the streets, seeking to change the social structures of racial oppression.

Those of us who confront the brutalities in black history must be self-critical regarding the church as well as the juke joint, the spirituals, and the blues. We cannot be too sure of ourselves—whether we sing the blues or spirituals or both. "One can never wrestle enough with God if one does so out of a pure regard for truth," wrote French philosopher, activist, and mystic Simone Weil. "Christ likes for us to prefer truth to him because, before being Christ, he is truth. If one turns aside from him to go toward the truth, one will not go far before falling into his arms."[56] We know from history that African Americans never stopped affirming their humanity and struggling for justice in their churches and the juke joints. But what does the cross in the Christian scriptures and the black experience of the blues have to say about these enduring atrocities? This is the question that both black secular thought and prophetic faith seek to explain for the African American community, for America, and for the world.

Since black thinkers, whether secular or religious, were influenced by white people who enslaved, segregated, and lynched them, what did their own white religious leaders say about Christians who permitted such atrocities? That is the question to which we turn.

2

"THE TERRIBLE BEAUTY OF THE CROSS" AND THE TRAGEDY OF THE LYNCHING TREE:

A Reflection on Reinhold Niebuhr

> They murdered the negro in cold blood in the jail doorway; then they dragged him to the principal business street and hung him to a telegraph-pole, afterwards riddling his lifeless body with revolver shots. . . . And there the negro hung until daylight the next morning—an unspeakably grisly, dangling horror.[1]
> —Ray Stannard Baker

> Our country's national crime is lynching.[2]
> —James Cutler

The lynching tree—so strikingly similar to the cross on Golgotha—should have a prominent place in American images of Jesus' death. But it does not. In fact, the lynching tree has no place in American theological reflections about Jesus' cross or in the proclamation of Christian churches about his Passion. The conspicuous absence of the lynching tree in American theological discourse and preaching is profoundly revealing, especially since the crucifixion was clearly a first-century lynching. In the "lynching era," between 1880 to 1940, white Christians lynched nearly five thousand black men and women in a manner with obvious echoes of the Roman crucifixion of Jesus. Yet these "Christians" did not see the irony or contradiction in their actions.

As Jesus was an innocent victim of mob hysteria and Roman imperial violence, many African Americans were innocent victims of white mobs, thirsting for blood in the name of God and in defense of segregation, white supremacy, and the purity of the Anglo-Saxon race. Both the cross and the lynching tree were symbols of terror, instruments of torture and execution, reserved primarily for slaves, criminals, and insurrectionists—the lowest of the low in society. Both Jesus and blacks were publicly humiliated, subjected to the utmost indignity and cruelty. They were stripped, in order to be deprived of dignity, then paraded, mocked and whipped, pierced, derided and spat upon, tortured for hours in the presence of jeering crowds for popular entertainment. In both cases, the purpose was to strike terror in the subject community. It was to let people know that the same thing would happen to them if they did not stay in their place. What New Testament scholar Paula Frederickson says about crucifixion in Roman society could be substituted easily for lynching in the United States.

> Crucifixion was a Roman form of public service announcement: Do not engage in sedition as this person has, or your fate will be similar. The point of the exercise was not the death of the offender as such, but getting the attention of those watching. Crucifixion first and foremost is addressed to an audience.[3]

The crucifixion of Jesus by the Romans in Jerusalem and the lynching of blacks by whites in the United States are so amazingly similar that one wonders what blocks the American Christian imagination from seeing the connection.[4]

That the analogy between the cross and the lynching tree

should have eluded the Christian agents of white supremacy is perhaps not surprising. But how do we understand the failure of even the most "progressive" of America's white theologians and religious thinkers to make this connection? A case in point is Reinhold Niebuhr, widely regarded as America's most influential theologian in the twentieth century, and possibly in American history. Among his contemporaries he was unusually attuned to social reality and the "irony" and tragedy of American history. Among white theologians he was particularly sensitive to the evils of racism and spoke and wrote on many occasions of the sufferings of African Americans. Few theologians of the twentieth century focused as much attention on the cross, one of the central themes of his work. And yet even he failed to connect the cross and its most vivid reenactment in his time. To reflect on this failure is to address a defect in the conscience of white Christians and to suggest why African Americans have needed to trust and cultivate their own theological imagination.

Born in 1892 in Wright City, Missouri, Niebuhr was the pastor of Bethel Evangelical Church in Detroit (1915-1928) and later professor of Christian Social Ethics and Theology at Union Theological Seminary in New York (1928-1960), where he was the dominant voice in defining the discipline of Christian social ethics, the study of Christian action in society. "His work had the most important impact on social thought and public policy of any Christian thinker of our time,"[5] writes Ronald Stone, an influential Niebuhr scholar, and his classic texts are still widely read in theology, history, social ethics, sociology, and political philosophy. [6]

Among theologians, Niebuhr was unusual for his wide influence in the secular political world. McGeorge Bundy called Niebuhr "probably the most influential single mind in the development of American attitudes which combined moral purpose with a sense of political reality."[7] His "Christian realism" (as opposed to what he regarded as naïve or idealistic optimism) won the admiration of many secular intellectuals and politicians, including Arthur Schlesinger Jr., Hubert Humphrey, and Jimmy Carter. Even in the present time, President Barack Obama has called Niebuhr one of his favorite philosophers, and his name is invoked frequently by both liberals and conservatives, journalists and politicians, theologians and political philosophers.[8]

Best known for his realist approach in Christian social ethics, Niebuhr rejected pacifism (which he had once espoused), idealism, and perfectionism—the idea that individuals and groups could achieve the standard of love he saw revealed in Jesus' life, teachings, and death. Niebuhr taught that love is the absolute, transcendent standard that stands in judgment over what human beings can achieve in history. Because of human finitude and humanity's natural tendency to deny it (sin), we can never fully reach that ethical standard. The best that humans can strive for is justice, which is love approximated, a balance of power among competing groups. Unlike the advocates of the Social Gospel, who often suggested that we could through love build the Kingdom of God on earth, Niebuhr placed justice, rather than love, at the center of Christian social ethics. Since human beings are finite, Niebuhr reasoned that we can never do anything apart from our interests, especially when we act collectively. According to Niebuhr, democracy—"a method of finding proximate solutions to insoluble problems"—was the political system best adapted to the strengths and limitations of human nature. As he put it famously in *The Children of Light and the Children of Darkness*, "Man's capacity for justice makes democracy possible; but man's inclination to injustice makes democracy necessary."[9]

Since Niebuhr saw justice as a balance of power between groups, whether classes, races, or nations, he saw it always in a state of flux, never achieving perfection in history. To him this meant that we must approach what we do *practically*, knowing that

Nothing that is worth doing can be achieved in our life-time; therefore we must be saved by hope. Nothing which is true or beautiful or good makes complete sense in any immediate context of history; therefore we must be saved by faith. Nothing we do, however virtuous, can be accomplished alone; therefore we are saved by love. No virtuous act is quite as virtuous from the standpoint of our friend or foe as it is from our standpoint. Therefore we must be saved by the final form of love which is forgiveness.[10]

Niebuhr takes his starting point for Christian realism as "the facts of experience," the willingness to "take all factors . . . into account, particularly the factors of self-interest and power."[11] This starting point has significant implications for the question of race. When one begins with the facts of experience and not, as in Karl Barth's theology, with God's revelation, the conversation must confront the brutal realities of racial injustice: slavery, segregation, and lynching. While Barth's theology starts with the Trinity, with a focus on the Word of God, Niebuhr's theology and ethics start with an emphasis on self-interest and power. This difference in starting point caused friction between Niebuhr and Barth for three decades, especially in the context of the World Council of Churches and in the pages of the *Christian Century*.

Niebuhr's realist approach to Christian ethics was deeply connected to the cross, which he identified as the heart of the Christian gospel. "If the divine is made relevant to the human," Niebuhr claimed, "it must *transvalue our values* and enter the human at the point where man is lowly rather than proud and where he is weak rather than strong. Therefore I believe that God came in the form of a little child born to humble parents in a manger. . . ." This "life in the manger ended upon the cross . . . [and we] might end there if we really emulated it."[12]

"Transvaluation of values," a term derived from Nietzsche (who derided Christianity's embrace of the weak), is the heart of

Niebuhr's perspective on the cross. He uses the phrase repeatedly in his writings. We find its meaning whenever he speaks about God's mercy and love in relation to Jesus Christ, especially in his sermons and several of his books. For Niebuhr the revelation of God's transcendent love hidden in Jesus' suffering on the cross is not simply the "keystone" of the Christian faith; it is the very key to history itself. [13]

"The crucified Messiah [is] the final revelation of the divine character and divine purpose." He was rejected because people expected a Messiah "perfect in power and perfect in goodness." But "the revelation of divine goodness in history must be powerless." If human power in history—among races, nations, and other collectives as well as individuals—is *self-interested* power, then "the revelation of divine goodness in history" must be weak and not strong. "The Christ is led as the lamb to the slaughter." Thus, God's revelation *transvalues* human values, turning them upside down.

For Niebuhr, "The cross [is] an ultimate point of illumination on the character of man and God."[14] People reject the cross because it contradicts historical values and expectations—just as Peter challenged Jesus for saying, "The Son of Man must suffer": "Far be it from You; this shall not happen to You." But Jesus rebuked Peter: "Get behind me, Satan!" (Mt 16:21; Mk 8:31, 33). "In the course of a few moments," Peter went from being "the mouthpiece of God" to a "tool" of Satan, because he could not connect vicarious suffering with God's revelation. Suffering and death were not supposed to happen to the Messiah. He was expected to triumph over evil and not be defeated by it. How could God's revelation be found connected with the "the worst of deaths," the "vilest death," "a criminal's death on the tree of shame"?[15]

Like the lynching tree in America, the cross in the time of Jesus was the most "barbaric form of execution of the utmost cruelty," the absolute opposite of human value systems. It turned reason upside down. In his sermon-lecture "The Transvaluation of Values" in *Beyond Tragedy*, Niebuhr turns to Paul to express what it meant to see the world from a transcendent, divine point of view.

> For ye see your calling, brethren, how that not many wise men after the flesh, not many mighty, not many noble, are called. But God has chosen the foolish things of the world to confound the wise; and God hath chosen the weak things of the world to confound the things which are mighty. And base things of the world, and things which are despised, hath God chosen, yea, and things which are not, to bring to naught things that are: That no flesh shall glory in his presence. (1 Cor 1:26-29)

The wise, the mighty, and the noble are condemned because their status in society tempts them to think too highly of their knowledge, power, and heritage. Mary's song, the Magnificat, makes a similar point: "He hath put down the mighty from their seats, and exalted them of low degree." Jesus in the Gospels repeatedly makes the same claim: "The last shall be first and the first last." Or as Niebuhr put it, "The Christian faith is centered in one who was born in a manger and who died upon the cross. This is really the source of the Christian transvaluation of all values. The Christian knows that the cross is the truth. In that standard he sees the ultimate success of what the world calls failure and failure of what the world calls success."[16]

"The cross is the truth" because God is hidden there in Jesus' sacrificial, vicarious suffering. Only faith can see that which cannot be derived from the logic of history or reason. "Faith is able to sense and appropriate an ultimate truth too deep for human reason."[17] This faith is defined by humility and repentance.

"People without imagination," Niebuhr said, "really have no right to write about ultimate things."[18] Certainly it takes a special kind of imagination to understand the truth of the cross.

"Ultimate religious truth," Niebuhr wrote, "can be grasped only in symbolic form, and the Christ of the cross is the supreme symbol of divine grace."[19] For that reason, Niebuhr said, "Only poets can do justice to the Christmas and Easter stories and there are not many poets in the pulpit."[20] In an article from 1929, he displayed his own capacity for that kind of poetic language when he speaks of "the 'terrible beauty' of the cross,"[21] an artful phrase that highlights the paradox of the cross—its power and futility. One needs a powerful imagination to see both tragedy and beauty, futility and redemption in the cross. "Christianity is a faith," Niebuhr wrote, "which takes us through tragedy to beyond tragedy, by way of the cross to victory in the cross."[22]

Few could speak with such eloquence about the cross as Reinhold Niebuhr. When I read his sermons and other theological reflections on the cross, I could almost be listening to a black preacher who can take a congregation through the power of imagination to the foot of Jesus' cross.

> I can see Him as He mounted Calvary and hung upon
> de cross for our sins.
> I can see-eee-ee
> De mountains fall to their rocky knees and when He
> cried
> "My God, my God! Why hast Thou forsaken me?"...
> And about that time Jesus groaned on de cross, and
> Dropped His head in the locks of His shoulder and
> said, "It is finished, it is finished."[23]

Niebuhr writes with a similar poetic imagination, using symbols and myths to tell the terrible truth about the salvation offered in the cross to all who accept with a faith defined by humility and repentance.

And yet, in the end, was there not a limit to Niebuhr's imagination? For all his exquisite sensitivity to symbols, analogies, and the moral dimensions of history, was he ultimately blind to the most obvious symbolic re-enactment of the crucifixion in his own time? Niebuhr's focus on realism ("facts of experience") and the cross (tragedy) should have turned his gaze to the lynching tree, but he did not look there, even though lynching trees were widely scattered throughout the American landscape. Why did Niebuhr fail to connect Jesus' cross to the most obvious cross bearers in American society?

Niebuhr has a complex perspective on race—at once honest and ambivalent, radical and moderate. On the one hand, he says that "in the matter of race we are only a little better than the Nazis"; and, on the other, he is urging "sympathy for anxious [white] parents who are opposed to unsegregated schools." In terms almost as severe as those of Malcolm X, Niebuhr speaks about "God's judgment on America." He calls "racial hatred, the most vicious of all human vices," "the dark and terrible abyss of evil in the soul of man," a "form of original sin," "the most persistent of all collective evils," "more stubborn than class prejudices," and "the gravest social evil in our nation." "If," he concluded, "the white man were to expiate his sins committed against the darker races, few white men would have a right to live."[24]

But, unlike Malcolm, Niebuhr also says that the founding fathers, despite being slaveholders, "were virtuous and honorable men, and certainly no villains." "They merely bowed to the need for establishing national unity" based on "a common race and common language." He even says that the 1896 Supreme Court doctrine of "separate but equal," which made Jim Crow segregation legal in the South, "was a very good doctrine for its day," since it allowed "the gifted members" among ex-slaves, a "culturally backward" people, to show, as a few had done in sports and the arts, "irrefutable proof that these deficiencies were not due to 'innate' inferiorities." In my view these latter views amount to a moral justification of slavery and Jim Crow.

Niebuhr praised the 1954 Supreme Court decision ending segregation in public schools, which he claimed "initiated the first step in the Negro revolt." Yet he was also pleased by the Court's added phrase, "with all deliberate speed," which "wisely" gave the white South "time to adjust" (while also opening a loophole to delay integration). "The Negroes," Niebuhr said, "will have to exercise patience and be sustained by a robust faith that history will gradually fulfill the logic of justice."

Niebuhr's call for gradualism, patience, and prudence during the decade when Willie McGee (1951), Emmett Till (1955), M. C. "Mack" Parker (1959), and other blacks were lynched sounds like that of a southern moderate more concerned about not challenging the cultural traditions of the white South than achieving justice for black people. He cited the distinguished novelist William Faulkner and Hodding Carter, a Mississippi journalist "with a long record of fairness on the race issue," in defense of gradualism, patience, and prudence, so as not to push the southern white people "off balance," even though he realized that blacks were understandably smarting under such a long history of injustice: "We can hardly blame Negroes for being impatient with the counsel for patience, in view of their age-long suffering under the white man's arrogance." Yet, Niebuhr continued in the same essay, "The fact that it is not very appealing to the victims of a current injustice does not make it any less the course of wisdom in overcoming historic injustices."[25]

Niebuhr chose to listen to southern moderates like Faulkner and Carter on race, rather than to civil rights leaders like Martin Luther King Jr., who regarded Faulkner's counsel to "go slow, pause for a moment" as a "tranquilizing drug of gradualism." "It is hardly a moral act to encourage others patiently to accept injustice which he himself does not endure," King wrote, in a response influenced by Niebuhr himself. Because Niebuhr identified with white moderates in the South more than with their black victims, he could not really feel their suffering as his own. When King asked him to sign a petition appealing to President Eisenhower to protect black children involved in integrating schools in the South, Niebuhr declined. Such pressure, he told his friend and Supreme Court justice Felix Frankfurter, would do more harm than good. Niebuhr believed that white ministers from the South would be more effective.[26]

What accounts for the contradictions in Niebuhr's perspective on race? In part they are due to his failure to step into black people's shoes and "walk around in them,"[27] to use the words of Atticus Finch in Harper Lee's classic *To Kill a Mockingbird*. It was easy for Niebuhr to walk around in his own shoes, as a white man, and view the world from that vantage point, but it takes a whole lot of empathic effort to step into those of black people and see the world through the eyes of African Americans.

Niebuhr himself analyzed this dilemma, having persuasively pointed out in his classic, *Moral Man and Immoral Society*, that groups are notoriously selfish and have limited capacity to step outside of their interests and see the world from another group's standpoint. The will-to-survive is so strong that it transmutes easily into the will-to-power. Niebuhr expands on this point in the first volume of his theological masterpiece *The Nature and Destiny of Man*. All human beings are finite and free. Our freedom creates anxiety and insecurity, causing us both as individuals and as groups to seek security among our own kind through various forms of power over others in politics, religion, and knowledge. Groups use both religion and reason to advance their own interests and find it nearly impossible to "feel the pain of others as vividly as they do [their own]."[28]

From a rational and intellectual standpoint, however, Niebuhr did attempt to walk in black people's shoes, recognizing how they had been victims of white racist violence throughout American history. He knew about the brutality of slavery, Jim Crow segregation, and lynching. When he was a pastor in Detroit, the Ku Klux Klan was very active politically, nearly capturing the mayor's office in 1925. There was a near-lynching the same year when Ossian Sweet, a black dentist, bought a house in a white neighborhood and nearly caused a riot after he and a few relatives and friends moved into the dwelling. When a crowd of hundreds of whites assembled, throwing rocks and threatening the occupants, Sweet's brother, Henry, panicked and shot and killed a white man. That led to the arrest of all eleven occupants who were subsequently charged with murder.

During the first trial, with Clarence Darrow as the lead defense attorney, the jury could not reach a decision. But, in a second trial that involved only the shooter, Darrow was able to convince the jury to put themselves in Henry Sweet's shoes, and they brought back a "not guilty" verdict, which surprised many blacks and whites. What made Darrow so effective was his capacity to empathize with blacks and to persuade others to do so, arguing that blacks have as much right as whites to defend themselves when their home is under attack. According to Niebuhr, Darrow "made everyone writhe as he pictured the injustices and immoralities of our present industrial system." But, Niebuhr continued, "The tremendous effect of his powerful address was partially offset by the bitterness with which he spoke. . . ." When Niebuhr thought a little more deeply about Darrow's empathy with black suffering, however, he said, "I suppose it is difficult to escape bitterness when you have eyes to see and heart to feel what others are too blind and too callous to notice."[29]

Niebuhr had "eyes to see" black suffering, but I believe he lacked the "heart to feel" it as his own. Although he wrote many essays about race, commenting on a variety of racial issues in America and in Africa and Asia, the problem of race was never one of his central theological or political concerns.

It has always been difficult for white people to empathize fully with the experience of black people. But it has never been impossible. In contrast to Niebuhr and other professors at Union Seminary, the German theologian Dietrich Bonhoeffer, during his year of study at Union (1930-1931), showed an existential interest in blacks, befriending a black student named Franklin Fisher, attending and teaching Bible study and Sunday School, and even preaching at Abyssinian Baptist Church in Harlem. Bonhoeffer also read widely in African American history and literature, including Walter White's *Rope and Faggot* on the history of lynching, read about the burning of Raymond Gunn in Maryville, Missouri (January 12, 1931), in the *Literary Digest*, "the first lynching in 1931," and expressed his outrage over the "infamous Scottsboro trial." He also wrote about the "Negro Church," the "black Christ" and "white Christ" in the writings of the black poet Countee Cullen, read Alain Locke and Langston Hughes, and regarded the "spirituals" as the "most influential contribution made by the negro to American Christianity." Some of Bonhoeffer's white friends wondered whether he was becoming too involved in the Negro community.[30]

Niebuhr, in contrast, showed little or no interest in engaging in dialogue with blacks about racial justice, even though he lived in Detroit during the great migration of blacks from the South and in New York near Harlem, the largest concentration of blacks in America. He attended socialist and leftist meetings when W. E. B. Du Bois and A. Philip Randolph were present and included such writers and artists as James Weldon Johnson, Langston Hughes, and Countee Cullen of the Harlem Renaissance in his course Ethical Viewpoints in Modern Literature (a course that Bonhoeffer attended). But Niebuhr cites no black intellectuals in his writings. He repeatedly writes about "our Negro minority" (not "our brothers," as he referred to Jews), a phrase that suggests white paternalism. Although Niebuhr allowed his name to be used for the support committee of the Legal Defense Fund of the NAACP (1943), he did not join the organization or attend any of its conferences dealing with racial justice. He often used the word "negro" in the lower case, at a time when the NAACP fought hard to establish its capitalization. He seemed only marginally concerned about justice for black people, even though he firmly opposed racial prejudice in any form.

Unlike his "long love affair with the Jewish people," Niebuhr's lack of a strong empathy with black suffering prevented him from speaking out passionately for justice on behalf of black people, as did Clarence Darrow and many others in the NAACP and the Communist Party. He headed Mayor John Smith's Inter-racial Committee to study racial problems in Detroit and acknowledged "a rare experience to meet with . . . white and colored leaders and talk over our racial problems," which was perhaps the only time he would engage racial issues with black and white leaders together. While serving on the "race commission," Niebuhr saw that "the situation which colored people of the city face is really a desperate one, and no one who does not spend real time in gathering facts can have any idea of the misery and pain which exists among these people. . . ." When Niebuhr saw suffering, he described the facts as he saw them: "Thousands in this town are really living in torment while the rest of us eat, drink and make merry. What a civilization!"[31]

After Niebuhr left Detroit to teach theology and social ethics at Union Seminary in New York, a racial controversy arose at Bethel Church when two African Americans tried to join the congregation and were opposed by a significant number of members. Niebuhr's successor, Adelbert Helm, correctly insisted that racial inclusiveness was a test of the Christian identity of the church. However, when advocates on both sides of the controversy attempted to enlist Niebuhr's help, he apparently criticized the new pastor for his "unpedagogical methods," which led to his dismissal. While Niebuhr was no supporter of racism, he stated, "I never envisaged a fully developed interracial church at Bethel. I do not think we are ready for that," he wrote in a letter to the church council at Bethel. He contended that no congregation "at the present time" is ready to face the "ultimate test." "But," Niebuhr continued, "I do not see how any church can be so completely disloyal to the gospel of love as to put up bars against members of another racial group who apply for inclusion in its fellowship."

Niebuhr knew that denying membership to persons merely on the basis of race was also a denial of the church's Christian identity. Yet he also knew that white churches were not prepared to include blacks, a minority they truly despised, and he was not prepared to deny the Christian identity of white churches on that basis. Reading his letter to the church council at Bethel, one can feel Niebuhr's deep spiritual struggle with this issue, as he blames himself and Bethel at the same time. He correctly surmised that the controversy reflected a failure of his ministry, a profound theological failure; for while he spoke many times against racial prejudice, there is no evidence that he endeavored to address race in a practical way by trying to lead Bethel toward racial inclusion. Even in the race commission report to the mayor, which he chaired, Niebuhr, as Ronald Stone said, "gave no hint of the churches' role in combating segregation."[32] "All religions have an element of ethical universalism in them," Niebuhr wrote later in a column for the *Detroit Times*, which in my view exposes the hypocrisy of his inaction at Bethel. "If this element does not operate to mitigate racial antagonisms there is something the matter with the interpretation of religion. If religious idealism does not help us to live together decently with members of other races and groups, it is not producing the kind of social imagination without which religion becomes a sounding brass and a tinkling symbol."

On the one hand, Niebuhr wrote in *Leaves:* "if a gospel is preached without opposition it is simply not the gospel which resulted in the cross." Yet on the other hand, he avoided controversy at Bethel, especially regarding race: "Here I have been preaching for thirteen years, and crying, 'Woe unto you if all men speak well of you,' and yet I leave without a serious controversy in the whole thirteen years."[33] This indicates that he did not engage the race issue—the greatest moral problem in American history—in any practical way. During most of Niebuhr's life, lynching was the most brutal manifestation of white supremacy, and he said and did very little about it. Should we be surprised, then, that other white theologians, ministers, and churches followed suit?

As a professor at Union Seminary, Niebuhr expressed concern for racial justice not by seeking to establish it on the faculty and among the students but by working with the Delta Cooperative Farm, and also supporting the Southern Tenant Farmers' Union, and the Fellowship of Southern Churchmen. The Delta Farm was a collection of poor white and black farmers laboring together "to throw off the tenant farming system." All of these organizations focused on justice with an accent on racial and economic issues, and received support from the Fellowship of Socialist Christians, which Niebuhr founded. In his essay "Meditations from Mississippi," Niebuhr said, "The Delta Cooperative Farm seems to me the most significant experiment in social Christianity now being conducted in America." "The theological outlook which most of us found congenial," said Sam Franklin, the director of the Delta Farm in Rochdale, Mississippi, "was that of the 'Biblical realism' of the president of our board of trustees, Reinhold Niebuhr."

Niebuhr's work with his theological admirers and former students in the Delta ministry was the closest, and, perhaps, the only time he would engage the black struggle for justice. He had a firm grasp of economic issues, writing several persuasive essays and books on the theme and participating in many socialist organizations, even running for the New York State Senate on the Socialist Party ticket in 1930 and for Congress in 1932. But the issue of race was another matter, as indicated in the controversy at Bethel in Detroit and in his reflections on his visits to the South. Niebuhr discovered that talking about race was a divisive issue, even, or, shall we say, especially among white ministers in Mississippi, who were more concerned about the mixing of the races than about justice for whites and blacks. In the name of "justified pedagogical expediency," Niebuhr said, "we told the ministers the farm would not unnecessarily challenge the prejudices of the south. That is a matter of expediency. Economic cooperation is so necessary that it is worth establishing it *even if scruples must be sacrificed to prejudices in the matter of social and educational relationships.*"

Yet while Niebuhr assured southern ministers that the Delta ministry would not challenge white supremacy, he nevertheless noted at the same time "the public gallows in the city of X" (why not name the city?) where "a hanging is a general fete to which men, women and children are invited." As Niebuhr boarded a train to depart Mississippi, he stated, "a newspaper falls in my hands with an account of a public hanging of two Negro boys, sixteen and eighteen years old." Was not that lynching alone enough for Niebuhr to know that white supremacy could not be ignored in searching for economic justice, or explicating the meaning of the Christian gospel in America? Niebuhr himself preserved class solidarity at the expense of racial justice, which many liberal white-led groups were inclined to do when fighting for justice among the poor.[34]

The public gallows Niebuhr saw and read about in the media in Mississippi should have reminded him of the tree on which Jesus hung and "the involuntary cross" he preached about at Bethel in 1915. In that sermon, he spoke about Simon of Cyrene, the African, bearing Jesus' cross. Black ministers, searching for ways to identify racially with the story of salvation in the scriptures, have since slavery times liked to preach about "Black Simon" (as they called him) who carried Jesus' cross. The Reverend James T. Holly, who wrote "The Divine Plan of Human Redemption in Its Ethnological Development" in the *AME Church Review* (1884), said:

> A son of Ham, Simon the Cyrenian, bore the cross of our
> Lord to the place of crucifixion when this dear Savior was

no longer physically able to carry it. . . . When, therefore, our Savior shall be crowned and seated upon His Throne of Glory, He will doubtless remember in a peculiar manner the race whose son carried His cross for Him and choose from that race the crown nobles who shall minister around His Person in His Royal Palace.[35]

Black literary figures like Countee Cullen and James Weldon Johnson wrote about Black Simon:

> That twisted tortured thing hung from a tree,
> Swart victim of a newer Calvary.
>
> Yea, he who helped Christ up Golgotha's track,
> That Simon who did *not* deny, was black.

In a poetic rendition of the Negro sermon on "The Crucifixion," Johnson wrote:

> Up Golgotha's rugged road
> I see my Jesus go.
> I see him sink beneath the load,
> I see my drooping Jesus sink.
> And then they laid hold on Simon,
> Black Simon, yes, black Simon;
> They put the cross on Simon,
> And Simon bore the cross.[36]

Unlike Dietrich Bonhoeffer, who spent time in black communities despite only being in America for about a year, Niebuhr, in his sermon on Simon and the cross, missed an opportunity to move into the river of the black experience.

I remember ministers preaching about Black Simon when I was a teenager in Arkansas. Although blacks like to think that Simon volunteered to carry Jesus' cross, he did not; it was, as Niebuhr said, an involuntary cross. The Gospel of Mark says that "they compelled" Simon "to carry his cross" (15:21), just as some African Americans were compelled to suffer lynching when another could not be found. Niebuhr could have explored this story with theological imagination, seeing blacks as crucified like Jesus and forced like Simon to carry the crosses of slavery, segregation, and lynching. But he did not.

In the end, Christian realism was not only a source of Niebuhr's radicalism but also of his conservatism. This is especially true of the struggles of the oppressed in the black community for racial justice; for even during his most radical period (1930s), when lynching resurged with a vengeance, he was, at most, a moderate on racial justice. Rather than challenging racial prejudice, he believed it must "slowly erode." Although he did not believe that African Americans could achieve proximate justice without the help of liberal whites, he did not choose to be among those to support actively and passionately the black struggle for justice.[37] He put most of his intellectual energies into other issues, especially injustices in the industrial system in his work with Norman Thomas and other socialists. The riots of the 1960s in the cities surprised him because, like most whites and many black middle-class leaders,[38] as he himself later acknowledged, he failed to see that the 1964 Civil Rights Bill did not "seriously affect the status of unemployed Negroes in Northern ghettos." Despair ensued, and "I, for one," Niebuhr acknowledged, "was slow to gauge its import" (though he could have seen it by looking out his window at Union Seminary near Harlem in New York). Struggling with his own failure and that of his group, Niebuhr reflects, "One wonders how we slept that long."[39]

Like most whites, Niebuhr did not realize the depth of black despair because he did not listen to Malcolm X and other Black Nationalists, who were speaking at Temple No. 7 and in the streets of Harlem, only a few blocks away. Had he turned on the radio or television, he could have heard the eloquent and powerful voice of Malcolm talking about the limits of the bourgeois civil rights movement and its leaders. Malcolm was not interested in proximate justice defined by liberal whites. "The price of freedom is death," he told Harlem blacks. Niebuhr probably heard Malcolm (who could be in New York City during the 1950s and 1960s and not know about Malcolm?) and thought he was just another "crazy Negro." Mike Wallace's 1959 television documentary series "The Hate that Hate Produced" was a media event that few people with even a marginal interest in race missed. Since Niebuhr did not heed Martin King on race but preferred Faulkner and Carter, it is very unlikely that he would have listened to the fiery message of Malcolm X. "While Dr. King was having a dream," Malcolm told a reporter shortly after King's 1963 March on Washington address, "the rest of us Negroes are having a nightmare."[40]

Niebuhr could have heard of the nightmare in the black community from many people. While spectacle lynching was on the decline in the 1950s, there were many legal lynchings as state and federal governments used the criminal justice system to intimidate, terrorize, and murder blacks. Whites could kill blacks, knowing that a jury of their peers would free them but would convict and execute any black who dared to challenge the white way of life. White juries, judges, and lawyers kept America "safe" from the threat of the black community. Thus, the nightmare in black life continued to deepen as progressive whites like Niebuhr remained silent about lynching.

Niebuhr often read poetry. "Religion is poetry," he wrote in his diary. "The truth in the poetry is vivified by adequate poetic symbols and is therefore more convincing than the poor prose with which the average preacher must attempt to grasp the ineffable."[41] There were many voices he might have heard during his time in New York. Before Malcolm, the famous anti-lynching poem "If We Must Die" exploded from Jamaican writer Claude McKay during the "Red Summer" of 1919. It was later recited by Winston Churchill, one of Niebuhr's heroes, in a speech against the Nazis, and it was found on the body of an American soldier killed in action in 1944. McKay, however, was speaking to blacks who were being lynched by whites in northern riots.

> If we must die, let it not be like hogs
> Hunted and penned in an inglorious spot,
> While around us bark the mad and hungry dogs,
> Making their mock at our accursed lot.
> If we must die, O let us nobly die,
> So that our precious blood may not be shed
> In vain; then even the monsters we defy
> Shall be constrained to honor us though dead!
> O kinsmen! We must meet the common foe!
> Though far outnumbered let us show us brave,
> And for their thousand blows deal one death-
>   blow!
> What though before us lies the open grave?
> Like men we'll face the murderous, cowardly pack,
> Pressed to the wall, dying, but fighting back![42]

The writer Richard Wright wrote short stories about the nightmare in black life in *Uncle Tom's Children* (1938); told a story about it in his landmark novel *Native Son* (1940), which he hoped "would leave his readers 'without the consolation of tears'"; wrote a "lyrical essay on the story of the Negro in America" in *Twelve Million Black Voices* (1941); and then gave an autobiographical account of the nightmare in *Black Boy* (1945), "which created almost as much of a sensation when it appeared . . . as had *Native Son*."[43]

Langston Hughes, another New Yorker and poet laureate of Black America, also articulated black dreams not realized.

> What happens to a dream deferred?
> Does it dry up
> Like a raisin in the sun?
> Or fester like a sore—
> And then run?

Does it stink like rotten meat?
Or crust and sugar over—
Like a syrupy sweet?
Maybe it just sags
Like a heavy load.

Or does it explode?[44]

Lorraine Hansberry's New York Critics Award–winning Broadway play *A Raisin in the Sun* (1959), whose title was taken from Hughes's poem, was a powerful portrayal of a Chicago black family trying to realize their dream of moving out of the ghetto to a place where few blacks ever lived. Niebuhr saw Marc Connelly's play *Green Pastures* (1930) and even wrote a review, praising its "warmth and beauty of Negro faith," depicting "a sense of awe for the dignity with which simple men meet the ultimate mysteries of life."[45] *Green Pastures* was a dramatic rendition of black faith seen through white eyes, thus hardly a good source for understanding religion in the nightmare of black life.

Finally, Niebuhr wrote four books on American history but did not deal with racial issues in any substantive manner. When he sent a manuscript of *The Irony of American History* to his historian friend Arthur Schlesinger Jr., Schlesinger called Niebuhr's attention to the glaring omission of the Negro:

> One irony deserving comment somewhere perhaps is the relationship between our democratic and equalitarian pretensions and our treatment of the Negro. This remains, John Quincy Adams called it in 1820, "the great and foul stain upon the North American Union"; and I think you might consider mentioning it.[46]

But Niebuhr did not mention it, finding it apparently not a substantial concern. This was a serious failure by an American religious leader often called this nation's greatest theologian. How could anyone be a great theologian and not engage

America's greatest moral issue? Unfortunately, white theologians, then and since, have typically ignored the problem of race, or written and spoken about it without urgency, not regarding it as critical for theology or ethics.

Niebuhr, by contrast, did acknowledge that "we have failed catastrophically only on one point—our relations to the Negro race." But what about the native people in this land? He claimed that North America was a "virgin continent when the Anglo-Saxons came, with a few Indians in a primitive state of culture."[47] He wrote about Arabs of Palestine and people of color in the Third World in a similar manner, offering moral justification for colonialism. Niebuhr even justified U.S. imperialism, referring to America as being elected by God: "Only those who have no sense of the profundities of history would deny that various nations and classes, various social groups and races are at various times placed in such a position that a special measure of the divine mission in history falls upon them. In that sense God has chosen us in this fateful period of world history."[48]

There is a great difference in the way Niebuhr wrote about Jews, on the one hand, and blacks and other people of color, on the other. When he wrote about Jews, he had engaged in a dialogue with them that began in Detroit and continued throughout his life, culminating in his great address, "The Relations of Christians and Jews in Western Civilization," at the Jewish Theological Seminary, where he urged Christians to stop trying to convert Jews to Christianity. Yet his essay "Justice to the American Negro from State, Community and Church," in *Pious and Secular America*, which spoke of the white fear of the Negro's "cultural backwardness," was not written in conversation with blacks.[49] In contrast to his friend Abraham Heschel, a close friend and supporter of Martin Luther King Jr., Niebuhr made no effort to engage in dialogue with black religious leaders and scholars or to develop friendship with black people with whom he could learn about race as he did with Jews.[50]

The only dialogue Niebuhr is known to have had on race with a radical black intellectual was with James Baldwin, following the September 1963 bombing of the Sixteenth Street Baptist Church in Birmingham that killed four little girls. Niebuhr's former student Thomas Kilgore, then pastor at Friendship Baptist Church in Harlem and the New York director of Martin King's Southern Christian Leadership Conference (SCLC), asked Niebuhr to appear on the Protestant Council radio program with Baldwin to discuss "the meaning of the Birmingham tragedy." It was not clear from the audio tape whether Baldwin had read Niebuhr, but Niebuhr let Baldwin know that "I've read almost everything you've written."

As the moderator, Kilgore started the dialogue by asking Baldwin, "Does the missing face of Christ on the stained glass window, which survived the bombing . . . suggest to you a meaning of the Birmingham tragedy?" At first Baldwin responded with irony: "The absence of the face is something of an achievement, since we have been victimized so long by an alabaster Christ." Then he turned serious, and suggested that "it sums up the crisis we're living through. If Christ has no face, then perhaps it is time that we, who in one way or another, invented and are responsible for our deities, give him a new face . . . and make . . . the whole hope of Christian love a reality. And as far as I can tell," he continued, "it's never been a reality in the 2000 years since his assassination."

Niebuhr agreed with Baldwin that the missing face of Christ represented a deep moral crisis, "the failure of the church" to "give the Christian message the real content . . . the real face of Christ." But he was careful to emphasize that, in contrast to Baldwin's accent on love, groups don't love. "The Negro doesn't love the white man collectively or the white man the Negro collectively," Niebuhr said. We, therefore, must see that "love is the motive, but justice is the instrument." Both agreed that "the white church has failed," and that "the Negro church has really realized itself in this crisis." Niebuhr proclaimed that "Martin Luther King is one of the great Americans of our day."

Although the Baldwin–Niebuhr dialogue did not reveal sharp disagreements, it did reveal different levels of passion in their responses, a gulf of emotional orientation to the racial crisis, reflected in the bombing. Baldwin, identifying with a powerless black minority, was seething with rage, ready to say anything to get white Americans to stop such violence, while Niebuhr, identifying with the powerful white majority, was calm and dispassionate in the face of what most blacks regarded as an unspeakable evil. Baldwin was relentless in his critique of white Americans for failing to live up to their own political and religious traditions about love and justice, even saying that Negroes were the only Christians and the only hope for the country.

> The only people in this country at the moment who believe either in Christianity or in the country are the most despised minority in it. . . . It is ironical . . . the people who were slaves here, the most beaten and despised people here . . . should be at this moment . . . the only hope this country has. It doesn't have any other. None of the descendants of Europe seem to be able to do, or have taken it on themselves to do, what Negroes are now trying to do. And this is not a chauvinistic or racial outlook. It probably has something to do with the nature of life itself. It forces you, in any extremity, any extreme, to discover what you really live by, whereas most Americans have been for so long, so safe and so sleepy, that they don't any longer have any real sense of what they live by. I think they really think it may be Coca-Cola.

While Niebuhr agreed, he did not want to throw out "the white man as white man," and asked "whether there is not a leaven in the other classes that would correspond to the light of truth in the despised minority." Baldwin replied that "I don't mean to say the white people are villains or devils or anything like that," but what "I do mean to say is this: that the bulk of the white . . . Christian majority in this country has exhibited a really staggering level of irresponsibility and immoral washing of the hands, you know. . . . I don't suppose that . . . all the white people in Birmingham are monstrous people. But they're mainly silent people, you know. And that is a crime in itself."

Baldwin's condemnation of the silence of the Birmingham white majority in the face of the killing of children was similar to the speech of Rabbi Joachim Prinz (a refugee from Germany) at the March on Washington. "When I was a rabbi of the Jewish community in Berlin under the Hitler regime . . . the most important thing I learned under those tragic circumstances was that bigotry and hatred are not the most urgent problems. The most urgent and most disgraceful, the most shameful, the most tragic problem is silence."[51]

When Baldwin said, "there is something wrong with the economic structure," Niebuhr quickly said, "But that gets us way *beyond* the racial issue, that becomes a very complex economic issue." "Indeed," Baldwin replied. However, Baldwin had no intention of engaging in a theoretical discussion about socialism and communism or Marx and Lenin. "What is called the racial issue never is a racial issue as it turns out anyway . . . [but] simply the fact that I, visibly, am the descendant of slaves, and a source of cheap labor," which "Americans used 'pathological rationalizations' to defend themselves." As an artist and ex-preacher, Baldwin wanted to shake America out of its complacency about race. "I never believed I was happy down on the levee; I never said I was a happy, shiftless, watermelon-eating darky; the country did. And what is worse, the country believed it. And it still does. They thought I was happy in my place. I was never happy in my place."

Niebuhr missed completely much of what Baldwin was saying. Baldwin was dealing with what Niebuhr had written about thirty years earlier in *Moral Man* when he was Baldwin's age, expressing a similar passion against injustice. Baldwin embodied what Niebuhr called "a sublime madness in the soul," when he wrote that "nothing but such madness will do battle with malignant power and 'spiritual wickedness in high places.'" Of course, this madness is dangerous, but yet necessary because without such madness "truth is obscured." Yet in his dialogue with Baldwin thirty years later, Niebuhr was speaking with a "rationality" that "belongs to cool observers," and Baldwin was speaking to what "ought to be true; and may become true if its truth is not doubted."[52]

Despite all Niebuhr's writing and speaking about racism, he expressed no "madness in his soul," no prophetic outrage against lynching. Even when confronted with the tragedy of the Birmingham bombing, he showed no anger. What Niebuhr said about liberalism could be applied to his own perspective on racism: Liberalism, he said, "lacks the spirit of enthusiasm, not to say fanaticism, which is so necessary to move the world out of its beaten tracks. It is too intellectual and too little emotional to be an efficient force in history." When Niebuhr wrote against liberalism, pacifism, communism, and the easy conscience of American churches, he expressed outrage; but when it came to black victims of white supremacy, he expressed none.[53]

"Mr. Baldwin," Niebuhr asked, trying to move the conversation away from too much focus on race and back to class, "aren't you saying that racial prejudice has aggravated the class . . . of American society?" Baldwin did not take the bait. "No, I'm not saying that," Baldwin rejoined. "Racial prejudice . . . is endemic to human life. . . . Everybody hates everybody. . . . It's about power. . . . I don't care whether Senator Eastland [of Mississippi] or Barry Goldwater [of Arizona] likes me. . . . I do care that they have the power to keep me out of a home, out of a job, and to put my child on a needle. . . . I don't care what they think or what they feel; I care about their power." This, of course, is a theme about which Niebuhr wrote persuasively and extensively.

When Niebuhr spoke about the "horrible lack of communication between the white man and the Negro in Birmingham" and spoke with apparent approval of President Kennedy's "two special representatives," which included a former West Point football coach and a former Army Secretary, whose task was to begin a conversation between the races, Baldwin refused to engage the issue rationally, instead repeating, "It's an insult"— a widespread sentiment in the black community. But Niebuhr seemed not to understand the insult of sending a football coach and Army Secretary to heal the deep wounds of racism in Birmingham. This suggests why it is so hard for whites and blacks to talk about white supremacy; even among progressive intellectuals like Niebuhr, there is too little empathy regarding black suffering in the white community. Lacking empathy, he lacks the passion to engage the unspeakable evil of killing black children.[54]

Had Niebuhr initiated more interchange with radical black intellectuals like Baldwin, as he did with Jewish intellectuals, his theological perspective could have achieved a broader and deeper understanding of race in America. How otherwise can one grasp the complexity of race? Following his dialogue with Baldwin, Niebuhr's perspective showed some signs of growth and deepening. In one of his last essays, entitled "The Negro Minority and Its Fate in a Self-Righteous Nation," Niebuhr, reflecting on the 1967 summer riots and the Kerner report of the National Advisory Commission on Civil Disorders, begins to sound surprisingly like Malcolm X: "For our Negro minority the American 'Dream' of justice has become a 'Nightmare.'" He challenged the white church to be the conscience of the nation, reminding it of its responsibilities—"its sins of omission and commission."[55]

If white Protestant churches failed to be a beacon of leadership in America's racial crisis, part of the responsibility for the failure was due to the way its leading religious spokespersons ignored race in their interpretation of the Christian faith. Niebuhr made a sharp contrast between denominational responses to school integration and other racial issues, praising Catholics for being more progressive and forward looking and criticizing Protestants for their often reactionary backward approach, and reserving his highest praise, rightly, to the Jewish community.

Finally, a personal comment. As a graduate student at Garrett Biblical Institute (now Garrett-Evangelical Theological Seminary) in the late fifties and early sixties, I read Niebuhr; but I focused my study primarily on Karl Barth because I was interested in systematic theology, not ethics. Christian ethics at Garrett was taught by one of the most blatantly racist professors there. By contrast, systematic theology was taught by William Hordern, a Barthian from Canada, who treated me as a human being, capable of thinking theologically. Furthermore, I liked Barth's unrelenting focus on Jesus Christ as God's Word, which resonated with the image of Jesus as Friend and Savior, the most dominant motif in the black Christian experience.

I realize now that I should have ignored the separation of theology and ethics in the Garrett curriculum, as well as Niebuhr's modest claim of not being a theologian. It was not until I left seminary and began to deal with the "facts" of the black struggle for justice in society that I returned to Niebuhr, especially his *Moral Man and Immoral Society*. Reading Niebuhr's reflections on power and self-interest among individuals and collectives in the context of the black liberation struggle was an intellectual revelation. "The white race in America will not admit the Negro to equal rights if it is not forced to do so," Niebuhr wrote. "Upon this point one may speak with a dogmatism which all history justifies."[56] What Niebuhr said about love, power, and justice helped me to understand that moral suasion alone would never convince whites to relinquish their supremacy over blacks. Only Black Power could do that, because power, as Frederick Douglass said long before Niebuhr was born, concedes nothing without struggle.

Though I seldom referred to him in the text, I wrote my first book, *Black Theology and Black Power* (1969), with Niebuhr on my mind and (along with Barth) as one of my intellectual guides in theology. Both Barth and Niebuhr were necessary. Barth helped me to understand the complexity of the Western theological tradition while Niebuhr helped me to relate it to the struggle for justice in society.

When I came to Union Seminary in 1969, I was in awe of its liberal theological tradition, largely because Niebuhr's spirit was still there, challenging me to be the best I could be. Although I never met him, since he had retired nine years earlier, I do remember that when I first walked in the halls of Union Seminary to interview for a position, Larry Jones, dean of students and the first black to serve on the staff, turned to me and said, "You should be grateful to have the opportunity to teach at the place where Reinhold Niebuhr and Paul Tillich taught theology." Had he been white, I would not have ignored the negative implications of that comment. When one considers that Union Seminary was founded in 1836 and that no blacks had served on its faculty until the 1960s, that no black student had been accepted into its doctoral program until the 1970s, and that only a small number of black Master of Divinity students were graduates, Union could not have escaped criticism on matters of race. Like most seminary professors, those at Union did not say much, if anything, about episodes of lynching. Instead, they chose to focus on academic theology that could defeat fundamentalism, especially in support of Professor Charles Augustus Briggs (whose chair I occupy), who was tried for heresy for using historical criticism in his interpretation of the Bible. Why, then, didn't Union faculty and board make a similar stand against slavery, segregation, and lynching?

I looked at Dean Jones with a smile on my face and said, "I am very pleased to be walking in the same academic halls that Niebuhr and Tillich walked."

Today I teach a course on Niebuhr because of his profound reflections on human nature, the cross, and creative social theory, focusing on justice, self-interest, and power. My understanding of the cross is deeply influenced by his perspective on the cross. Thus, I have never questioned Niebuhr's greatness as a theologian, but instead admired his intellectual brilliance and social commitment. What I questioned was his limited perspective, as a white man, on the race crisis in America. His theology and ethics needed to be informed from critical reading and dialogue with radical black perspectives.

Niebuhr's close friend and former colleague in theology and social ethics, John Bennett, was the president of Union when I was called to teach there. Bennett sent him a copy of my newly published book, *Black Theology and Black Power*, telling him of my recent appointment as assistant professor of theology and warning him that "you will find this book in many ways difficult to take." But, Bennett continued, "Though one may be very critical of much in this book, I think it is an excellent statement of the mind of a thoughtful young black militant." When Niebuhr sent Bennett his response to my book, Bennett called me in his office and read Niebuhr's letter to me.

At the time, I tended to shield myself from white theological perspectives, since they had shown no appreciation for a theological voice like mine, both black and radical. I listened respectfully as Bennett read his letter. "Thank you for sending Professor Cone's *Black Theology and Black Power*," Niebuhr wrote. "I was tremendously interested in the book, and am not as critical as you anticipated that I would be. After all, the negroes are the most genuine proletarians that we have in our middle class culture, and there is bound to be some resentment in our negro minority which he expresses adequately."

I was surprised that Niebuhr had such a clear and sympathetic understanding of the meaning of black rage, something few whites ever grasp. But Niebuhr had "two points of criticisms." Appropriately, one had to do with the influence of Barth, and the other, more serious point, had to do with my tendency to dismiss the progress of integration, especially my silence on "the negro politician and statesman—Senator [Edward] Brooks of Massachusetts . . . or Thurgood Marshall of the Supreme Court, and the whole slew of negro mayors. . . ." He concluded his letter with a statement that surprised me: "I think he will be an excellent man on your faculty."[57] Niebuhr's affirmation of my presence at Union meant much to me then and still means much to me today.

I wish that my time at Union had coincided with Niebuhr's. I would have enjoyed engaging race and theology with him as I did with John Bennett, Paul Lehmann, Tom Driver, Roger Shinn, Beverly Harrison, and other members of the Union faculty. I would have granted some validity to his criticism of the Barth influence, which is less today. But the critique about integration is another matter. It would have been challenging to engage him on my failure to appreciate the progress in integration. What most whites call "integration" (or in the language of today, diversity) is often merely "tokenism." There is very little justice in any educational institution where black presence is less than 20 percent of the faculty, students, and board members. There is no justice without power; and there is no power with one, two, or three tokens.

Although Niebuhr is often called a "prophet," and he claimed that "all theology really begins with Amos," he was no prophet on race. Prophets take risks and speak out in righteous indignation against society's treatment of the poor, even risking their lives, as we see in the martyrdom of Jesus and Martin King. Niebuhr took no risks for blacks. On the one hand, "Courage is the primary test of prophesy," Niebuhr said. "There is no national community today in which the genuine word of God does not place the prophet in peril." But, on the other hand, Niebuhr acknowledged his prophetic limits in *Leaves*, especially appropriate regarding his views on race: "I am a coward myself . . . and find it tremendously difficult to run counter to general opinion." [58]

Niebuhr was by no means alone in his failure to express prophetic rage against racial injustice and his silence on lynching. In 1935, John Bennett wrote a book on *Social Salvation* and did not even mention the need to be saved from racial injustice, especially lynching, which was resurgent during that decade. Bennett and I talked about his blindness, and he responded with *The Radical Imperative: From Theology to Social Ethics* (1975), addressing social issues he omitted to mention in his earlier text, especially race. [59]

Before Niebuhr and Bennett, Walter Rauschenbusch, the Social Gospel movement's greatest theologian, expressed his frustration: "For years the problem of the two races seemed to me so tragic, so insoluble that I have never yet ventured to discuss it in public." [60] The Social Gospel advocates held conferences on the status of the Negro in Mohonk, New York, in 1890 and 1891 and felt no need to invite any blacks, because, as Lyman Abbott said, "A patient is not invited to the consultation of the doctors on his case." [61]

In contrast to Niebuhr and many Social Gospel theologians, there were a few white preachers who did oppose lynching and who noted the connection between the lynching of African Americans and the crucifixion of Jesus. Among these was Episcopalian Quincy Ewing, who served parishes in Louisiana and Mississippi, participated in the founding of the NAACP, and was widely praised by black leaders. He preached and wrote against the lyncher as "a murderer in the eyes of Almighty God." Andrew Sledd, a professor of Latin at Emory College, ended his silence with an essay, "The Negro: Another View," after seeing the lynching of Sam Hose. Like nearly all whites who opposed lynching, he did not deny whites were a superior race, but that alone did not justify lynching blacks. His dissent cost him his job at Emory, which was later restored. E. T. Wellford wrote a book entitled *The Lynching of Jesus* (1905).

"Lynch law is usually credited as an American product," he wrote. "The most awful application of it, however, belongs to the first century." In a sermon (1903), Atlanta minister John E. White of Second Baptist Church asked a penetrating question but did not develop it: "Will it be considered 'one-sided' if I suggest that Christ was lynched by a legalized mob, and coming out of that stupendous event was a divine force and truth which will cure the lynching evil and settle all problems of evil in the world?"[62]

Niebuhr was a Christian theologian of the cross who knew all about Jesus' solidarity with the poor and the consequences he suffered for that from the Roman Empire. If the American empire has any similarities with that of Rome, can one really understand the theological meaning of Jesus on a Roman cross without seeing him first through the image of blacks on the lynching tree? Can American Christians see the reality of Jesus' cross without seeing it as the lynching tree? How could Niebuhr make the tragedy of the cross the central theme in his theology while ignoring the obvious tragedies of slavery, segregation, and lynching in the United States? Even confronting the death of four children in a Birmingham church and a dialogue with James Baldwin about the event, Niebuhr did not summon the language and passion to speak adequately to that event. What is missing in his language about Calvary was the racial context that defined the actual cross bearers in American society. Unless we look at the "facts of experience," as Niebuhr's own realism demanded, what we say about the cross remains at the level of theological abstraction, like Karl Barth's Word of God, separated from the real crosses in our midst.

One who made the connection real was Billie Holiday, with "Strange Fruit," her signature song about southern lynching. When she sang that song, in the words of Elijah Wood, "You feel as if you're at the foot of the tree." Upon hearing another singer, Josh White, sing "Strange Fruit" in Chicago, Brigitte McCulloch, a German woman who grew up in "war-torn Hamburg, Germany," did with her imagination what Niebuhr did not do, even though he identified with the Jews there: "On those southern trees, along with black men, hung the murdered Jews," she said, "hung all the victims of violence. And one survived to tell the story, to tear our hearts apart, to make us feel and remember."[63] Niebuhr's heart and those of most white religious leaders unfortunately remained unmoved.

Just as Martin Luther King Jr. learned much from Reinhold Niebuhr, Niebuhr could have deepened his understanding of the cross by being a student of King and the black freedom movement he led. King could have opened Niebuhr's eyes to see the lynching tree as Jesus' cross in America. White theologians do not normally turn to the black experience to learn about theology. But if the lynching tree is America's cross and if the cross is the heart of the Christian gospel, perhaps Martin Luther King Jr., who endeavored to "take up his cross, and follow [Jesus]" (Mark 8:34) as did no other theologian in American history, has something to teach America about Jesus' cross.

3

Bearing the Cross and Staring Down the Lynching Tree

Martin Luther King Jr.'s Struggle to Redeem the Soul of America

I will die standing up for the freedom of my people.
—Martin Luther King Jr.

If a man hasn't discovered something that he will die for, he isn't fit to live.
—Martin Luther King Jr.

Only a year after twenty-six-year-old Martin Luther King Jr. began to preach at Dexter Avenue Baptist Church in Montgomery, Alabama, the lynching of fourteen-year-old Emmett Louis "Bo" Till in Mississippi shook the black community in the South and the nation. In a sermon at Dexter, King called the Till lynching "one of the most brutal and inhuman crimes in the twentieth century."[1] Although the U.S. Supreme Court's *Brown v. Board of Education* (1954) decision had outlawed segregation in public schools, the Till lynching was a shocking reminder of the enduring power of white supremacy. Because he had whistled at a white woman and reportedly said "bye baby" as he departed from a store on August 24, 1955, Emmett Till was picked up four days later around 2:00 A.M., beaten beyond recognition, shot in the head, and thrown in the Tallahatchie River, "weighted down with a heavy gin fan."[2]

To a remarkable extent, the Till lynching would provide the spark that lit the fire of resistance in the Negro masses, inspiring them, as King said, to "rock the nation" and to demand their "freedom now."[3] "This was the beginning of the civil rights movement in Mississippi in the twentieth century," said grassroots leader Amzie Moore. "It galvanized the country," recalled John Lewis, the Georgia congressman and veteran civil rights activist. "A lot of us young black students in the South . . . weren't sitting in just for ourselves—we were sitting in for Emmett Till. We went on Freedom Rides for Emmett Till."[4] Cleveland Sellers, another young activist in the civil rights movement, remembered: "The atrocity that struck me the most was Emmett Till's lynching. . . . There was something about the cold-blooded callousness of Emmett Till's lynching that touched everyone in the community."[5] Black people throughout the country were outraged that white racists would stoop so low as to lynch an innocent child. Roy Wilkins, the executive head of the NAACP, spoke for many: "It would appear from this lynching that the State of Mississippi has decided to maintain white supremacy by murdering children."[6]

If anything was remarkable about the Till lynching, it was not so much the callousness of the deed as the militant response it evoked. If lynching was intended to instill silence and passivity, this event had the opposite effect, inspiring blacks to rise in defiance, to cast off centuries of paralyzing fear. The signal of this change was marked by the actions of Mamie Till Bradley, Emmett's mother, who refused to allow this heinous act, like so many similar cases, to remain in the shadows or to fade from public memory. When Emmett's body was brought back to Chicago, she insisted that the sealed casket be opened for a three-day viewing, exposing "his battered and bloated corpse" so that "everybody can see what they did to my boy." She exposed white brutality and black faith to the world and, significantly, expressed a parallel meaning between her son's lynching and the crucifixion of Jesus. "Lord you gave your son to remedy a condition," she cried out, "but who knows, but what the death of my only son might bring an end to lynching."

It was as if she was pleading with God to let her son's death count for something—to help save other black boys from Emmett's fate. "Darling, you have not died in vain," she said to Emmett, as she "looked at that horribly mangled monstrosity"; "your life has been sacrificed for something." Six hundred thousand people viewed his bruised body and attended the funeral, and many millions more saw the *Jet* magazine photos that traveled around the world.[7] "This is not for Emmett," Mrs. Bradley said, "because my boy can't be helped now, but to make it safe for other boys. Unless an example is made of the lynchers of Emmett, it won't be safe for a Negro to walk the streets anywhere in America."[8]

John Lewis, who was fifteen at the time, reacted like many black teenagers: "I was shaken to my core," he recalled in his memoir. "He could have been me. *That* could have been me, beaten, tortured, dead at the bottom of a river."[9] The Till lynching shook me up too. I was seventeen, beginning my second year at Shorter College in North Little Rock, Arkansas, where I was the daily news reporter to the student assembly, focusing on local, state, national, and world events. I read stories to the college community about the atrocity, the trial and acquittal of the accused men. Like Lewis, I remember saying to myself, "Emmet Till could have been *me!*" My older brothers felt the same way, as did most young males we knew.

While African Americans had heard about many previous lynchings, the murder of Emmett Till was an unforgettable event, a horror etched in black memory forever. He was so young; only fourteen—just a child from Chicago, not really aware of the etiquette of Jim Crow culture in Mississippi and what it could mean if he failed to observe the "ways of white folk." Although blacks followed the trial closely, they knew that the two white men directly responsible for the shameful act, J.W. Milan and Roy Bryant, would never see a day in jail, even though they admitted in court to the federal crime of kidnapping. (They were acquitted by an all-white jury after an hour of deliberation.) Crimes against blacks seldom led to conviction; instead, the perpetrators were often rewarded for putting "niggers" in their place. And when white men *were* convicted, which was rare, the punishment was usually just a slap on the wrist. One Mississippi court awarded the family of a lynched victim just one dollar for their loss.

For Mamie Till Bradley, the lynching of her only son was indeed a very heavy cross to bear, as it was for other parents who lost their sons and daughters to Judge Lynch. Black Christians saw in her response to her son's lynching a reflection of the spiritual struggles of Job. On the one hand, Mrs. Bradley's prayers reflected the obedient and patient spirit of the biblical Job: "Lord, take my soul, show me what you want me to do and make me able to do it" (Job 1-2). Yet, on the other hand, there was the rebellious spirit of the angry Job, who, feeling wronged by God, cried out "in the anguish of my spirit" and "the bitterness of my soul." "Why have you made me your target?" (Job 7:11, 20). Mrs. Bradley also railed at God: "Why did You do this[?] Why are You so cruel that You would let this happen? Why do You allow this kind of persecution?"[10]

Such questions are often found on the lips of parents who lose a child to a much-too-early death. But with a loss involving violence or lynching, so unjust and so unnecessary, the agony was even deeper, extending down the corridors of history for blacks who dared not forget what white supremacy meant for their children. Mrs. Bradley, however, was not left alone in her agony. She spoke about a strange experience, a voice that said to her: "Mamie, it was ordained from the beginning of time that Emmett Louis Till would die a violent death. You should be grateful to be the mother of a boy who died blameless like Christ. Bo Till will never be forgotten. There is a job for you to do now."[11]

Suffering always poses the deepest test of faith, radically challenging its authenticity and meaning. No rational explanation can soothe the pain of an aching heart and troubled mind. In the face of the lynching death of an innocent child, black Christians could only reach into the depth of their religious imagination for a transcendent meaning that could take them through despair to a hope "beyond tragedy." For Mrs. Bradley, the voice she heard was the voice of the resurrected Jesus. It spoke of hope that, although white racists could take her son's life, they could not deprive his life and death of an ultimate meaning. As in the resurrection of the Crucified One, God could transmute defeat into triumph, ugliness into beauty, despair into hope, the cross into the resurrection. And so, like Paul, Mrs. Bradley was "afflicted in every way, but not crushed; perplexed but not unto despair; persecuted, but not forsaken; struck down, but not destroyed" (2 Cor 4:8-9).

We do not know what really happened in Mrs. Bradley's revelatory experience; its meaning remains locked in mystery. What we do know is that her spirit of resistance caught fire in black communities throughout the nation, justifying the claim of author Clenora Hudson-Weems that Emmett Till was "the sacrificial lamb of the civil rights movement."[12] Only three months after the Till lynching, Rosa Parks refused to give up her seat on a city bus in Montgomery, and a "New Negro" was born. Rather than ride segregated buses in humiliation, blacks decided to walk the streets with pride until the walls of segregation, like the Jericho walls, "come tumblin' down."

What was it that cast out black people's fear of death and sent them flowing into the streets—defying mob violence? Many reasons certainly, not all of them stemming from Christian faith. Secular activists like Robert Moses, James Forman, and Stokely Carmichael drew inspiration from other sources, like Albert Camus' *The Rebel* and Frantz Fanon's *The Wretched of the Earth*. With Camus, they said, "Better to die on one's feet than to live on one's knees."[13] But for poor southern blacks, who had little formal education in philosophy or political philosophy, it was religion that offered the only resource—and the language—to fight against segregation and lynching.

Martin Luther King Jr. came to embody this faith, courage, and intelligence. His faith was derived from the black church; his courage originated from his faith; and his intelligence came from his intellectual discipline, deepened and expanded at Morehouse College, Crozer Seminary, and Boston University. What he learned in college and graduate school helped him to reflect critically on faith and to develop from it a method of social change that would transform race relations in the United States. When he accepted the invitation to become the leader of the Montgomery bus boycott, King knew he was risking his life. Other blacks knew it too. As he often put it, "Freedom is not free."

It is one thing to teach theology (like Niebuhr, Barth, Tillich, and most theologians) in the safe environs of a classroom and quite another to live one's theology in a situation that entails the risk of one's life. King agreed fully with Dietrich Bonhoeffer, the Christian pastor hanged in 1945 by the Nazis for resisting Hitler: "When Christ calls a man, he bids him come and die."[14]

Like Reinhold Niebuhr, whom he studied in graduate school, King believed that the cross was the defining heart of the Christian faith. Unlike Niebuhr, his understanding of the cross was inflected by his awareness of the lynching tree, and this was a significant difference. While the cross symbolized God's supreme love for human life, the lynching tree was the most terrifying symbol of hate in America. King held these symbols together in a Hegelian dialectic, a contradiction of thesis and antithesis, yielding to a creative synthesis.[15]

In considering the subject of God and the problem of race in America, King reflected that God's love created blacks and whites and other human beings for each other in community (thesis). White supremacy was the sin that separated them in America and in much of the world (antithesis). God reconciled humanity through Jesus' cross, and thereby white supremacy

could never have "the final and ultimate word" on human relationships (synthesis). God's reconciling love in the cross empowered human beings to love one another—bearing witness with
"our whole being in the struggle against evil, whatever the cost."
Thus, blacks and whites together were free to create the American Dream in society and the Beloved Community in our religious life.

Like Reinhold Niebuhr, King believed that love in society is
named justice. King came to see early that "the Christian doctrine of love operating through the Gandhian method of nonviolence was one of the most potent weapons available to the
Negro in his struggle for freedom."[16] Hate and white supremacy
lead to violence and alienation, while love and the cross lead to
nonviolence and reconciliation.

There was, however, an important difference between Reinhold Niebuhr and Martin Luther King Jr. that partly accounts
for why King became a martyr in the civil rights movement
while Niebuhr remained safely confined in his office at Union
Seminary teaching Christian social ethics, never risking his life
in the fight for justice. Unlike King, Niebuhr viewed agape love,
as revealed in Jesus' cross, as an unrealizable goal in history—
a state of perfection which no individual or group in society
could ever fully hope to achieve. For Niebuhr, Jesus' cross was
an absolute transcendent standard that stands in judgment over
any human achievement. The most we can realize is "proximate
justice," which Niebuhr defined as a balance of power between
powerful collectives. But what about groups without power?
Niebuhr did not have much to say to African Americans, a
10-percent minority, except to recommend nonviolence, which
he believed might advance the cause of civil rights, while never
winning full justice.[17] Niebuhr's moderate view was not one to
empower a powerless group to risk their lives for freedom. That
might have been why he did not talk to militant black groups or
black nationalists in Harlem. He had very little to say to them.

If blacks had followed Niebuhr's theology of proximate justice, there would have been no *militant* civil rights movement because, practically speaking, blacks had no prospect of success against the power of white supremacy. Niebuhr believed that laws that violated the mores and customs of the southern white majority would not be obeyed; if such laws were enforced, the result would be anarchy. On that basis, he was practical and cautious in his support of the integration of schools in the South and praised the Supreme Court's *Plessy v. Ferguson* (1896) decision, which made segregation legal, and perhaps that is why he was silent about the Till lynching at a time when his powerful theological voice was desperately needed.

Although Martin Luther King Jr. was strongly influenced by Reinhold Niebuhr, he had a different take on love and justice because he spoke to and for powerless people whose faith, focused on the cross of Jesus, mysteriously empowered them to fight against impossible odds. In contrast to Niebuhr, King never spoke about *proximate* justice or about what was *practically* possible to achieve. That would have killed the revolutionary spirit in the African American community. Instead, King focused on and often achieved what Niebuhr said was impossible. "What do you want?" King would call out before a demonstration. "Freedom!" the demonstrators would shout back, ready to face angry white mobs and policemen. "When do you want it?" King would ask, his voice reaching a crescendo. "Now!" was the resounding response, as the protestors would begin walking and singing together, "Ain't Gonna Let Nobody Turn Me Around."

"Not tomorrow, not next week, but *now!*" was the persistent cry for freedom among people who had never known it. "I am tired of fighting for something that should have been mine at birth," King often said. That kind of language created a revolutionary spirit that sent people into the streets, prepared to shoulder the cross, ready to meet whatever fate at the hands of mobs or the police. There was no talk about proximate justice— that little bit of justice that whites dole out to blacks when they get ready. God's justice called for black people to bear witness to freedom now, even unto death. That was why Fred Shuttlesworth, the movement's most courageous freedom fighter, said, "You have to be prepared to die before you can begin to live." This justice language was defined by a love of freedom derived directly from Jesus' cross, and it led more than forty martyrs to their deaths in the civil rights movement.

Martin King lived the meaning of the cross and thereby gave an even more profound interpretation of it with his life. Reinhold Niebuhr analyzed the cross in his theology, drawing upon the Son of Man in Ezekiel and the Suffering Servant in Isaiah; and he did so more clearly and persuasively than any white American theologian in the twentieth century. But since he did not live the meaning of the cross the way he interpreted it, Niebuhr did not see the real cross bearers in his American context. The crucified people in America were black—the enslaved, segregated, and lynched black victims. That was the truth that King saw and accepted early in his ministry, and why he was prepared to give his life as he bore witness to it in the civil rights movement.

Martin Luther King Jr. initially encountered the meaning of the cross at home and at Ebenezer Baptist Church in Atlanta, where his father was the pastor. At Ebenezer, young Martin heard a lot of singing and preaching about the cross. Black Christians sang, "Surely He Died on Calvary," as if they were actually there. They felt something redemptive about Jesus' cross—transforming a "cruel tree" into a "Wondrous Cross." Blacks pleaded, "Jesus Keep Me near the Cross," because "Calvary," in a mysterious way they could not explain, was their redemption from the terror of the lynching tree.

Though wonderful and beautiful, Jesus' cross was also painful and tragic. Songs and sermons about the "blood" were stark reminders of the agony of Jesus' crucifixion—the symbol of the physical and mental suffering he endured as "dey whupped him up de hill" and "crowned him wid a thorny crown." Blacks told

the story of Jesus' Passion, as if they were at Golgotha suffering with him. "Were you there when dey crucified my Lord?"
"Dey nailed him to de cross"; "dey pierced him in de side"; and
"de blood came twinklin' down."

> Jesus, my darling Jesus,
> Groaning as the blood came spurting from his wound.
> Oh, look how they done my Jesus.

But through it all, "he never said a mumbalin' word"; "he just
hung down his head and cried," and "then he . . . died."

> O see my Jesus hangin' high!
> He look so pale an' bleed so free:
> O don't you think it was a shame,
> He hung three hours in dreadful pain?[18]

Instead of attempting to explain the saving power of the cross
rationally, black Christians recognized it as a mystery, beyond
human understanding or control. In remembrance of Jesus' last
week, leading to his death, blacks at Ebenezer and other black
churches, celebrating the sacrament of "Holy Communion,"
raised their voices to acknowledge "a fountain filled with blood,"
"drawn from Immanuel's veins"; "blood," they believed, "will
never lose its power," because "there is power in the blood," and
"nothing but the blood."[19]

Since most ministers had little or no formal training in
academic theology, they spoke from their hearts, appealing to
their life experience, biblical stories, and the Spirit of God that
empowered them to struggle for dignity and freedom. They proclaimed what they felt in song and sermon and let the truth of
their proclamation bear witness to God's redemptive presence
in their resistance to oppression. Their sense of redemption
through Jesus' cross was not a propositional belief or a doctrine
derived from the study of theology. Redemption was an amazing
experience of salvation, an eschatological promise of freedom

that gave transcendent meaning to black lives that no lynching tree could take from them.

> Ain't you glad, ain't you glad,
> that the blood done sign your name?

When blacks sang about the "blood," they were wrestling not only with the blood of the crucified carpenter from Nazareth but also with the blood of raped and castrated black bodies in America—innocent, often nameless, burning and hanging bodies, images of hurt so deep that only God's "amazing grace" could offer consolation.

As a child, Martin King heard his father and other ministers preach about Jesus' death and his power to save not only from personal sins but also from "the hatred, the violence, the vitriolic and vituperative words of the mobs, . . . aided and abetted by the law and law enforcement officers."[20] Ministers often preached sermons about Jesus' crucifixion, as if they were telling the story of black people's tragedy and triumph in America. The symbol of the cross spoke to the lives of blacks because the likeness between the cross and the lynching tree created an eerie feeling of mystery and the supernatural. Like Jesus, blacks knew torture and abandonment, with no community or government capable or willing to protect them from crazed mobs. "Oh, way down yonder by myself," in Georgia, Mississippi, and Texas, "and I couldn't hear nobody pray. In the valley, on my knees, with my burden," "O my Lord, O my Lord, what shall I do?"

In their spiritual wrestling, black Christians experienced the weakness and power of God's love revealed in the cross—mysteriously saving them from loneliness and abandonment and "the unspeakable violence . . . by blood thirsty mobs."[21] Black ministers preached about Jesus' death more than any other theme because they saw in Jesus' suffering and persecution a parallel to their own encounter with slavery, segregation, and the lynching tree.

The assertion that Jesus' cross is the answer to the lynching tree, as young Martin heard preachers proclaim at Ebenezer and later appropriated for himself, is a stunning claim. How could Jesus' death in Jerusalem save blacks from mob violence nearly two thousand years later in America? What did salvation mean for African Americans who had to "walk through the valley of the shadow of death," or those forced to swing from a lynching tree? As a young Christian thinking about the ministry as a voca-tion, Martin King had to wrestle with the great contradictions that mob violence posed for black life and Christian identity.

Born in 1929 on the eve of the Great Depression, thirty years after the lynching of Sam Hose, and twenty-three years after the infamous Atlanta riot, Martin Luther King Jr. was never far from black suffering. Ministry appealed to him because he "felt the inescapable urge to serve society," to do something about black suffering. It was, he said, in his application to Crozer Seminary, "a sense of responsibility which I could not escape." King's own experiences of segregation and injustice as a child and a teenager disgusted him. Forced to sit behind a curtain on a train, he said, "I felt as though that curtain had dropped on my personhood."[22] In those formative years the Klan was as active as ever, striking fear with their hooded night marches and burning crosses, a powerful reminder that not all crosses were liberating and loving, even when Jesus' name was invoked. White ministers sometimes served as mob leaders, blessing lynchings, or citing the stories of Ham and Cain to justify white supremacy as a divine right.

Martin King first encountered lynching in conversations with his parents. His father, "Daddy King," would later, in his auto-biography, describe his first childhood glimpse of Judge Lynch, an event so terrifying that "I thought I was going to pass out." A group of disgruntled white men, complaining about "niggers" taking their jobs, had decided to take their frustrations out on a black man who worked with them at the mill. Hearing their conversation, as he walked near them from work, the black man knew his life was in grave danger, but it was too late to retreat or to pass unnoticed. He just smiled as he walked briskly, hoping to make it home without incident. But this was not to be.

"What the hell are you laughin' at, nigger?" one man shouted. "I ain' laughin', suh, honest I ain't. . . . Jus' on ma way home is all. . . ." He was in the wrong place at the wrong time. There was no exit. He was a scapegoat like Jesus. "Nigger come struttin' down the road like he thinks he's up North someplace. Pocket full of money. Laughin' at white folks." It was payday and they tried to take his money. "This money fo' my chil'ren now," the black man screamed, fighting back. "I cain' let you have that." They proceeded to kick and beat him severely—"blood pouring out of the man's mouth," as he cried out in painful agony. "They pulled him right past me," Daddy King remembered; "it was as if I hadn't even been there watching." Then "one of them took off his belt and wrapped it around the Negro's neck. They lifted him up and tied the end of the belt to this tree and let him go . . . his feet about five or six inches off the ground."[23] Like Jesus, hanging on a cross, this nameless black victim, hanging on a Georgia tree, was left to die a shameful death—like so many other innocent blacks, completely forgotten in a nation that did not value his life.

Merely a child at the time, Daddy King was shocked into silence, as he helplessly watched a lynching take place only a few feet away. "All I could do was to run on home, keep silent, never mentioning what I'd seen to anyone, until many, many years later, when I understood it better."[24]

Openly to fight white supremacy in the deep South during the 1950s and '60s was unthinkably perilous. Even at a distance of more than fifty years, we can still sense the fear. When King agreed to act as the most visible leader in the civil rights movement, he recognized what was at stake. In taking up the cross of black leadership, he was nearly overwhelmed with fear. This fear reached a climax on a particular night, January 27, 1956, in the early weeks of the Montgomery bus boycott, when he received a midnight telephone call threatening to blow up his house if he did not leave Montgomery in three days. Later he told how that call created a "spiritual midnight," as he thought about what could happen to him, his wife, and newly born baby girl.

Later recalling this incident, King told how fear drove him from bed to the kitchen where he prayed, "out loud," pleading, "Lord, I'm down here trying to do what's right. . . . But Lord, I must confess that I'm weak now, I'm faulting, I'm losing my courage." Yet then, like Mrs. Bradley, King said he heard a voice: "Martin Luther, stand up for righteousness. Stand up for justice. Stand up for truth. And lo I will be with you, even to the end of the world."[25]

Interestingly, that message echoed the words of an elderly, unlettered woman, who was "affectionately called Mother Pollard." At an earlier mass meeting where King was urging the people to continue the boycott of the buses, she had perceived his doubt and fear. He did not speak with the conviction she was accustomed to hearing. When she confronted him, King denied anything was wrong. "You can't fool me," she told him. "I know something is wrong. Is it that we ain't doing things to please you? Or is it that the white folks is bothering you?" Before he could reply, she said, "I don told you we is with you all the way. . . . But even if we ain't with you, *God's gonna take care of you*."[26]

"God's gonna take care of you"—it was an eschatological promise Martin Luther King Jr. never forgot. It was the same promise he would later hear in his kitchen—words also found in a popular hymn, "Never Alone," which he cited often to renew his spirit when threats against his life overcame him.[27]

Three nights after that threatening call, while he was at a boycott meeting, King's house was bombed. Fortunately, his wife and daughter and a family friend escaped harm, having moved to the back of the house when they heard something land on the porch. When told at the meeting that his house had been bombed, King calmly asked about the safety of his family and then went home to comfort them.

"Strangely enough," he said later, "I accepted the word of the bombing calmly. My religious experience a few nights before had given me the strength to face it." When an angry crowd of blacks gathered with guns ready for revenge, King raised his hand and calmed them, saying, "We cannot solve this problem through retaliatory violence. We must meet violence with non-violence. . . . We must love our white brothers no matter what they do to us. We must make them know that we love them."

As King saw it, the most powerful religious authority for black Christians was Jesus Christ, and Jesus' teachings on love and nonviolence became his primary focus: "Jesus still cries out in words that echo across the centuries: 'Love your enemies; bless them that curse you; pray for them that despitefully use you.' This is what we must live by."

Loving whites who hated and killed them was not easy for African Americans. Only God could empower black Christians to love hateful whites, and even God could not guarantee that they would return love for hate, nonviolence for violence. But King believed that God was the only hope for a minority to achieve justice. "Remember, if I am stopped, this movement will not stop, because *God is with the movement*." [28]

A few weeks later, when a reporter asked him whether he was afraid, King replied:

No, I'm not. My attitude is that this is a great cause. This is a great issue we are confronted with and the consequences for my personal life are not particularly important. It is the triumph of the cause that I am concerned about, and I have always felt that ultimately along the way of life an individual must stand up and be counted and be willing to face the consequences, whatever they are. If he is filled with fear, he cannot do it. And my great prayer is always that God will save me from the paralysis of crippling fear, because I think when a person lives with the fear of the consequences for his personal life, he can never do anything in terms of lifting the whole of humanity and solving many of the social problems that we confront.[29]

On the very anniversary of his vision in the kitchen—having learned about the discovery of twelve sticks of unexploded dynamite on his porch the previous night—King recalled the experience in a sermon. Although he and his family were again unhurt (having spent the night at a friend's house), he acknowledged that the attempted murder had disturbed him profoundly. Recalling his kitchen experience, he told the congregation how God had removed his fear. "I realized that there were moments when I wanted to give up and I was afraid but You gave me a vision in the kitchen of my house and I am grateful for it." He told his listeners that "I went to bed many nights scared to death." But then,

> early on a sleepless morning in January, 1956, rationality left me. . . . Almost out of nowhere I heard a voice that morning saying to me, "Preach the gospel, stand up for truth, stand up for righteousness. Since that morning I can stand up without fear.
>
> So I'm not afraid of anybody this morning. Tell Montgomery they can keep shooting and I'm going to stand up to them; tell Montgomery they can keep bombing and I'm going to stand up to them. If I had to die tomorrow morning I will die happy because I've been to the mountain top and I've seen the promised land and it's going to be here in Montgomery.[30]

When Martin King was at his darkest moment and the "midnight of death" was at his door, he turned to the God of the cross. But the threatening call on January 27, 1956, was only the *first* of many "midnights" King would face. As he would later note, we do not know what we truly believe or what our theology is worth until "our highest hopes are turned into shambles of despair" or "we are victims of some tragic injustice and some terrible exploitation." What sustained him was the sense of God's love, which gave him "the interior resources to bear the burdens and tribulations of life," "come what may."[31]

King struggled with the meaning of the cross for his life at various crisis moments in the civil rights movement. Shortly after he resigned as pastor of Dexter in Montgomery and moved to Atlanta to become co-pastor of Ebenezer with his father and full-time leader of a national civil rights movement as president of the Southern Christian Leadership Conference (SCLC), King was arrested for a minor traffic violation and sentenced, like a "hardened criminal," with handcuffs on his wrists and chains on his legs, to four months in the Georgia State Prison in Reidsville (230 miles from Atlanta). With his wife eight months pregnant, King began to realize existentially what bearing the cross of white supremacy would mean as he also voluntarily bore the cross of black leadership. Two crosses—white supremacy and black leadership, one imposed and the other freely assumed—weighed heavy on his young life. "I know the whole experience is very difficult for you to adjust to," he wrote to Coretta, "especially in your condition of pregnancy, but as I said to you yesterday *this is the cross that we must bear for the freedom of our people.* . . . I have the faith to believe that this suffering that is now coming to our family will in some little way serve to make Atlanta a better city, Georgia a better State, and America a better country. Just how I do not yet know, but I have faith to believe it will. . . . Our suffering is not in vain."[32]

Yet King had no "martyr's complex." "I'm tired of the threat of death," he proclaimed in a stressful moment during the later protests in Chicago. "I want to live. I don't want to be a martyr. And there are moments when I doubt if I am going to make it through. . . . But the important thing is not how tired I am; the important thing is to get rid of [injustice]."[33] King just wanted to follow Jesus, even if it led to his own death. He really believed what Jesus said to his disciples: "If any man would come after me, let him deny himself and take up his cross and follow me" (Mt 16:24).

Bearing the cross was a frequent theme in King's sermons. Preaching at Dexter on his return from a visit to Palestine in 1959, Martin King, following the black religious tradition on Simon of Cyrene, recalls that in the story of the crucifixion, "when Jesus fell and stumbled under that cross, it was a black man that picked it up for him and said, 'I will help you,' and took it on up to Calvary." When we realize that blacks "have been dominated politically, exploited economically, trampled over, and humiliated," King told the Dexter congregation, "I think one day God will remember that it was a black man that helped His son in the darkest and most desperate moment of his life. . . . It was a black man who picked up that cross for him and who took that cross on up to Calvary. God will remember this. And in all our struggles for peace and security, freedom and human dignity, one day God will remember that it was a black man who aided his only-begotten son in the darkest hour of his life." Like other black ministers before him, King connected the story of the black struggle for dignity with the biblical story of Calvary. In merging the two stories, he was enabled to face his own coming death.[34]

How did King live with the daily threat of death for more than twelve years? No one was more at risk than he. The cross of Jesus is the key to King's willingness to sacrifice his life, not only for the freedom of black people ("I will die standing up for the freedom of my people") but also for the souls of whites and the redemption of America. "If physical death is the price I must pay to free my white brothers and sisters from the permanent death of the spirit, then nothing could be more redemptive." "To redeem the soul of America" was the motto of SCLC, which meant creating the American Dream and the Beloved Community. The cross protected King from the paralyzing fear of death, giving him the courage to fight for racial justice, no matter the cost. With the cross at the center of his faith, he could even love the people he knew were trying to kill him, following Jesus' example on the cross, "Father, forgive them; for they know not what they do" (Lk 23:34).

Between the kitchen experience in Montgomery and his last sermon in Memphis, King was hounded by death. "He talked about death all the time," Andy Young recalled in later years. In fact, every time SCLC made preparations for a new engagement against segregation, King knew he could be killed. He often discussed this with his associates, warning them about the dangers that lay before them. "I want to make a point that I think everyone here should consider very carefully and decide if he wants to be with this campaign," he said to his staff as they prepared for a confrontation with white supremacy in Birmingham. "There are something like eight people here assessing the type of enemy we're going to face. I have to tell you that in my judgment, some of the people sitting here today will not come back alive from this campaign. And I want you to think about that."[35]

King developed a sense of humor to ease the tension and to enable himself and others to endure in the face of the violence that would engulf their lives. He preached mock funeral sermons for his friends. As Andy Young put it, Martin King "knew, more than anybody else, that every time he made a commitment to something like this [Birmingham] he was committing his life. . . . He thought in everything he did it meant his death. He would never say it that way. He would always say it in terms of us. He would say for instance, 'Now Andy, Bull Connor doesn't play.' He said, with a touch of hyperbole, 'They had fifty bombings in the last year, and you might not come back. You better let me know what kind of eulogy you want.' And even though he was talking about me, he knew he was talking about himself."[36]

The more resistance King received from white supremacy the more he turned to his faith and talked about the cross and the

fered, the more he turned his eyes to Golgotha, the place of the skull, where Rome executed slaves, insurrectionists, and bandits. "Down at the cross" is where King experienced a divine affirmation of his ministry and of God's love and "promise never to leave me alone." "However dismal and catastrophic may be the present circumstances," King proclaimed, "we know we are not alone, for God dwells with us in life's most confining and oppressive cells."[42]

Martin King's perspective on the cross was not derived from reading theological texts in graduate school. His view of the cross was shaped by his reading of the Bible through the black religious experience, and his "personal suffering" in his fight for justice. "My personal trials have . . . taught me the value of unmerited suffering." Suffering could create bitterness and hate or one could "seek to transform the suffering into a creative force." When King thought about Jesus hanging on the shameful cross, he also saw God transform a tragic situation into something redemptive. Referencing Paul, King wrote,

> There are some who still find the cross a stumbling block, and others consider it foolishness, but I am more convinced than ever before that it is the power of God unto social and individual salvation. So like the Apostle Paul I can now humbly and proudly say, "I bear in my body the marks of the Lord Jesus." The suffering and agonizing moments through which I have passed over the last few years have also drawn me closer to God. More than ever before I am convinced of the reality of a personal God.[43]

King saw in Jesus' unmerited suffering on the cross God's answer to black suffering on the lynching tree. Even in the face of the killing of four little girls in the Sixteenth Street Baptist Church in Birmingham (September 15, 1963), King did not lose his faith that love is redemptive, even for the whites who committed the unspeakable crime. In his "Eulogy for the Martyred Children," King said that "they did not die in vain. God still has a way of wringing good out of evil. History has proven over and over again that unmerited suffering is redemptive." He contended that their "innocent blood" could "serve as a redemptive force" to transform "our whole Southland from the low road of man's inhumanity to man to the high road of peace and brotherhood."

> So in spite of the darkness of this hour we must not despair. We must not become bitter; nor must we harbor the desire to retaliate with violence. We must not lose faith in our white brothers. Somehow we must believe that the most misguided of them can learn to respect the dignity and worth of human personality.

Although many in the movement were Christians like King and deeply believed in nonviolence as redemptive, yet it was difficult, as it perhaps was for King, to still maintain that belief in the face of murdered children. The murdered children reminded blacks of the lynching of Emmett Till and the fact that white supremacy would stop at nothing to subjugate African Americans. Some blacks wanted to abandon nonviolence and give the white racists a taste of their own medicine. It was a natural human reaction. But King, unlike others, never wavered in his commitment to the way of love. "Love," he often said, "is the most durable power" in the world. It could conquer evil, even white supremacy.

Then King spoke directly to the "bereaved families," as he had done as a pastor at Dexter in Montgomery and Ebenezer in Atlanta and would also have to do again and again for freedom fighters murdered in the civil rights movement. As he searched for words of faith that would console them in their great loss, King said,

> I hope you find consolation from Christianity's affirmation that death is not the end. Death is not a period that ends

the great sentence of life, but a comma that punctuates it to more lofty significance. Death is not a blind alley that leads the human race into a state of nothingness, but an open door which leads man into life eternal. Let this daring faith, this great invincible surmise, be your sustaining power during these trying days.

It is one thing to talk about suffering philosophically in the calm atmosphere of a graduate seminar and quite another to talk about the death of innocent children who were killed while worshiping Jesus. The death of children is perhaps the deepest test of faith, especially for parents who have to live with the loss the rest of their lives. "At times life is hard, as hard as crucible steel," King told them.

> It has its bleak and painful moments. Like the ever-flowing waters of a river, life has its moments of drought and its moments of flood. Like the ever-changing cycle of the seasons, life has the soothing warmth of the summers and the piercing chills of its winters. *But through it all, God walks with us.* Never forget that God is able to lift you from fatigue of despair to the buoyancy of hope, and transform dark and desolate valleys into sunlit paths of inner peace.[44]

For King, Jesus never promised that his disciples would not suffer. Quite the opposite: suffering is the inevitable fate of those who stand up to the forces of hatred. Jesus freely accepted the consequences that led to Calvary without turning away. He called upon his disciples to do the same. Just as God was with Jesus in his suffering, black Christians believed that God is with us in our suffering too.

Unlike most Christians, however, King accepted Jesus' cross, knowing that following Jesus involved suffering and, as it did for Jesus, the possibility of an unjust death. Even as a child, King's favorite song was "I Want to Be More Like Jesus"; and as a minister and civil rights activist, he put that song into practice by taking up the cross of black leadership until he, like Jesus, was killed trying to set people free. While King never thought he had achieved the messianic standard of love found in Jesus' cross, he did believe that his suffering and that of African Americans and their supporters would in some mysterious way redeem America from the sin of white supremacy, and thereby make this nation a just place for all. Who can doubt that those who suffered in the black freedom movement made America a better place than before? *Their suffering redeemed America from the sin of legalized segregation.* And those blacks among us who lived under Jim Crow know that that was no small achievement.

While for King and many African American Christians the cross may have been God's answer to the lynching tree, it was no easy answer, no matter how deep one's faith. There is no sufficient answer to the challenge of persistent and deep suffering without a deep spiritual wrestling with life and death in the "midnight of human existence, as human beings search for the eternal message of hope . . . that dawn will come."[45]

At no time was Martin King more aware of the threats on his life than when he made the decision to go to Memphis to march with striking sanitation workers. Theologian John Macquarrie is among those who have compared King's decision to go to Memphis with Jesus' decision to go to Jerusalem. His analogy is a telling one. Seeking to explain "the voluntary element in the death of Jesus," Macquarrie wrote,

> There is an example in recent history which appears to me to provide an illuminating parallel. In the spring of 1968, Martin Luther King went to the city of Memphis to help resolve a bitter labour dispute with racial overtones. He did not go to Memphis to die, but in the hope he could help change people's minds there. As we all know, he was assassinated in the course of his visit, and many people look on

his death as martyrdom. Though he had not gone there to die, and though his mind may well have been preoccupied with hopes for the future rather than with the prospect of death, he had known very well for a long time that death was a constant possibility so long as he continued to speak and work for his cause. In the case of Jesus, something similar must have been true.[46]

A similar comparison was made about Jesus and King by Benjamin Mays when he was asked whether King's martyrdom was inevitable.

Inevitable, not that God willed it. Inevitable in that any man who takes the position King did . . . if he persists in that long enough, he'll get killed. Now. Anytime. That was the chief trouble with Jesus: He was a troublemaker. So any time you are a troublemaker and you rebel against the wrongs and injustices of society and organize against that, then what may happen is inevitable.[47]

Just as Jesus knew he could be executed when he went to Jerusalem, King knew that threats against his life could be realized in Memphis. Like Jesus' disciples who rejected the idea that his mission entailed his suffering and death (Mk 8:31-32), nearly everyone in King's organization vigorously opposed his journey to Memphis, not only because of the dangers but because of the need to focus on the coming Poor People's Campaign in Washington. But King, like Jesus, felt he had no choice: he had to go to Memphis and aid the garbage workers in their struggle for dignity, better wages, and a safer work place. He had to go because his faith demanded it.

Martin King, living daily under the threat of death, often repeated similar words about his spiritual "mountain top" and his vision of the "promised land." But on the night before his assassination in Memphis, he etched them into our national memory.

I got into Memphis. And some began to say the threats. . . . What would happen to me from some of our sick white brothers? Well, I don't know what will happen now. We've got some difficult days ahead. But it doesn't matter to me now. Because I've been to the mountaintop. And I don't mind. Like anybody, I would like to live a long life. . . . But I'm not concerned with that now. I just want to do God's will. And he has allowed me to go to the mountain. And I've looked over. And I've seen the Promised Land. I may not get there with you. But I want you to know tonight, that we, as a people, will get to the Promised Land. . . . I'm not worried about anything. I'm not fearing any man. Mine eyes have seen the glory of the coming of the Lord.[48]

No theme was more important in King's thinking about the cross than the hope that emerges out of terrible circumstances. Even when he saw his dream turned into a nightmare—cities burning in America, war raging in Asia, government and the media highly critical of him, and rejected by many black leaders in the civil rights movement as either too militant or too conservative—King refused to lose hope or to relinquish the belief that "all reality hinges on moral foundations." He focused his hope on Jesus' cross and resurrection. "Christ came to show us the way. Men love darkness rather than the light, and they crucified Him, there on Good Friday on the Cross it was still dark, but then Easter came, and Easter is the eternal reminder of the fact that the truth-crushed earth will rise again." No matter what disappointments he faced, King still preached hope with the passion of a prophet: "I still have a dream, because, you know, you can't give up on life. If you lose hope, somehow you lose that vitality that keeps life moving, you lose that courage to be, that quality that helps you to go on in spite of all."[49]

Love and hope, which Martin King found in Jesus' cross and resurrection, did not erase the pain of suffering and its challenge for faith. No black Christian could escape the problem of evil that has haunted Christians throughout history. That is why the cross and redemptive suffering are not popular themes today among many Christians, especially among womanist, feminist, and other progressive theologians, who often criticize Martin King on this score.[50] Theology is always so contextual that it is difficult for young theologians today, as it was also back then, to understand King's profound, existential, and paradoxical truth. I, too, was slow to embrace King's view of redemptive suffering. Have not blacks, women, and poor people throughout the world suffered enough? Giving value to suffering seems to legitimize it.

Whatever we may say about the limits of King's perspective on the cross and redemptive suffering, he did not legitimize suffering. On the contrary, he tried to end it, sacrificing his own life for the cause of others. "Greater love hath no man than this, that a man lay down his life for his friends" (John 15:13). That was precisely what King did. He, along with a host of others, black, white, and other Americans of many walks of life, sacrificed their bodies and lives for our freedom today.

Though we are not fully free and the dream not fully realized, yet, *we are not what we used to be and not what we will be.* The cross and the lynching tree can help us to know from where we have come and where we must go. We continue to seek an ultimate meaning that cannot be expressed in rational and historical language and that cannot be denied by white supremacy. Poetry is often more helpful than prose in expressing our hope. Through poetic imagination we can see the God of Jesus revealed in the cross and the lynching tree. Those who saw this connection more clearly than others were artists, poets, and writers.

4

The Recrucified Christ
in Black Literary Imagination

The South is crucifying Christ again
By all the laws of ancient rote and rule:
The ribald cries of 'Save Yourself' and 'Fool'
Din in his ears, the thorns grope for his brain,
And where they bite, swift springing rivers stain
His gaudy, purple robe of ridicule
With sullen red; and acid wine to cool
His thirst is thrust at him, with lurking pain.
Christ's awful wrong is that he's dark of hue,
The sin for which no blamelessness atones;
But lest the sameness of the cross should tire
They kill him now with famished tongues of fire,
And while he burns, good men, and women, too,
Shout, battling for his black and brittle bones.
　　　—"Christ Recrucified," Countee Cullen, 1922

Like Countee Cullen, many black poets, novelists, painters, dramatists, and other artists saw clearly what white theologians and clergy ignored and what black religious scholars and ministers merely alluded to: that in the United States, the clearest image of the crucified Christ was the figure of an innocent black victim, dangling from a lynching tree. Such victims were not abstract or anonymous symbols. They were particular people; they had names; their passion was recorded (by their very murderers) in souvenir photos like those of Rubin Stacey, hanged on a lynching tree in Fort Lauderdale, or Laura Nelson and her son swinging from a bridge in Oklahoma, or Cleo Wright burned to a crisp in a street in Sikeston, Missouri.[1]

Most black artists were not church-going Christians. Like many artists throughout history, they were concerned human beings who served as society's ritual priests and prophets, seeking out the meaning of the black experience in a world defined by white supremacy. As witnesses to black suffering, they were, in the words of African American literary critic Trudier Harris, "active tradition-bearers of the uglier phases of black history."[2]

In the wake of slavery and the Civil War, there was so much ugliness in black life that one would have had to be blind not to see it. And nothing, absolutely nothing, was uglier than lynching in all of its many forms: hanging, burning, beating, dragging, and shooting—as well as torture, mutilation, and especially castration. And yet so many were blind, deaf, and dumb. What enabled artists to see what Christian theologians and ministers would not? What prevented these theologians and ministers, who should have been the first to see God's revelation in black suffering, from recognizing the obvious gospel truth? Did it require such a leap of imagination to recognize the visual and symbolic overtones between the cross and the lynching tree, both places of execution in the ancient and modern worlds?

"People without imagination really have no right to write about ultimate things,"[3] Reinhold Niebuhr was correct to observe. No one can claim that black preachers' sermonic orations lacked rhetorical imagination. Yet both white theologians such as Niebuhr and black preachers throughout African American history either did not see the parallels between the cross and the lynching tree or else they were too fearful of the dire consequences—loss of social status, work, and possibly life—to make the connection. In short, they lacked imagination of the most crucial and moral kind.

It takes a powerful imagination, grounded in historical experience, to uncover the great mysteries of black life. "We have been in the storm so long," "tossed and driven," singing and praying, weeping and wailing, trying to carve out some meaning in tragic situations. The beauty in black existence is as real as the brutality, and the beauty prevents the brutality from having the final word. Black suffering needs radical and creative voices, prophetic advocates who can tell brutal and beautiful stories of how oppressed black people survived with a measure of dignity when they were not meant to. Who are we? Why are we here? And what must we do to achieve our full humanity in a world that denies it? Those artists who accepted the challenge of answering these questions shouldered a heavy burden. As Countee Cullen wrote,

> I doubt not God is good, well-meaning, kind . . .
> Yet do I marvel at this curious thing:
> To make a poet black, and bid him sing![4]

While black ministers and religious scholars did not ignore the lynching tree—no black person could do that!— still they did not connect it explicitly with the cross, even while preaching about Jesus' suffering in Palestine and its analogies with black suffering in America. Only artists and writers wrestled with the deep religious meaning of the "strange fruit" that littered the American landscape. In the land of "the United States of Lyncherdom"[5] (to use Mark Twain's provocative and apt phrase), a land whose religious discourse was defined by the one who was "put . . . to death by hanging him on a tree" (Acts 10:39), black writers, novelists, visual artists, and poets, like Countee Cullen of the Harlem Renaissance, with their feet grounded in the "tragic beauty" of the black experience, saw the liberating power of the "Black Christ" for suffering black people.

> How Calvary in Palestine,
> Extending down to me and mine,
> Was but the first leaf in a line
> Of trees on which a Man should swing

> World without end, in suffering
> For all men's healing, let me sing.[6]

To say that Christ "was but the first leaf in a line of trees on which a man should swing" suggested that Christ, poetically and religiously, was symbolically the first lynchee—the one who "bought my redemption on a cross" and "shape[d] my profit by His loss." Lynched victims were transformed, by this association, into martyrs. As Cullen wrote, "The South is crucifying Christ again," and this time "he's dark of hue," and

> They kill him now with famished tongues of fire,
> And while he burns, good men, and women, too,
> Shout, battling for his black and brittle bones.[7]

Both lynching and Christianity were so much a part of the daily reality of American society that no black artist could avoid wrestling with their meanings and their symbolic relationship to each other. Christians, both white and black, followed a crucified savior. What could pose a more blatant contradiction to such a religion than lynching? And yet white Christians were silent in the face of this contradiction. Black poets were not silent. They spoke loud and clear. Walter Everette Hawkins, in his narrative poem "A Festival in Christendom" (1920), exposed the religious hypocrisy of whites who participated in the spectacle lynching:

> And so this Christian mob did turn
> From prayer to rob, to lynch and burn.
> A victim helplessly he fell
> To tortures truly kin to hell;

With bitter irony, Hawkins draws out the parallels between Jesus' suffering in Jerusalem and the passion of a lynched black victim in the heart of Christian America.

> They bound him fast and strung him high,
> They cut him down lest he should die

Before their energy was spent
In torturing to their heart's content.
They tore his flesh and broke his bones,
And laughed in triumph at his groans;
They chopped his fingers, clipped his ears
And passed them round as souvenirs.

No one could grow up in the black community without knowing the details of Jesus' sacrificial death at Calvary. Hawkins invoked that memory as he linked the "human sacrifice" at a lynching scene with Jesus' crucifixion.

They bored hot irons in his side
And reveled in their zeal and pride;
They cut his quivering flesh away
And danced and sang as Christians may;
Then from his side they tore his heart
And watched its quivering fibres dart.
And then upon his mangled frame
They piled the wood, the oil and flame. . .
And they raised a Sabbath song,
The echo sounded wild and strong,
A benediction to the skies
That crowned the human sacrifice.[8]

From Henry Smith's lynching in Paris, Texas (1893), to Emmett Till's in Money, Mississippi (1955), and beyond, black artists and writers have made the lynching theme a dominant part of their work, and most have linked black victims with the crucified Christ as a way of finding meaning in the repeated atrocities in African American communities. The site of "the ghastly body swaying in the sun" as "women thronged to look"[9] was a graphic reminder of Jesus hanging on a cross. In this spirit, Gwendolyn Brooks, the first black Pulitzer Prize winner, wrestling with the meaning of the mob violence during the desegregation crisis in Little Rock in 1957, was inspired to conclude her poem "The Chicago Defender Sends a Man to Little Rock" with a powerful christological declaration: "The loveliest lynchee was our Lord."[10]

They say a picture is worth a thousand words. Perhaps that accounts for the powerful impact of James Allen's *Without Sanctuary* (2003), a photographic account of "the lynching industry," a phrase that W. E. B. Du Bois used as the subject of one of his editorials in *The Crisis* magazine, February 1915. I draw a distinction between these pictures of lynched victims and the imaginative work of black visual artists who sought to convey the underlying meaning of these events. These photographs, a type of pornography, were initially part of the apparatus of the lynching spectacle, created by photographers at the scene who sold them for profit as souvenirs for members of the lynching party, who then displayed them in family albums and gave them to friends and relatives who could not be present. First shown at the small Roth Horowitz Gallery in New York City (2000) and then at the larger New York Historical Society, James Allen's collection of lynching photos was also shown at the Martin Luther King Jr. National Historical Site in downtown Atlanta to 176,000 viewers who reacted with tears, anger, resentment, and clenched jaws, and then at the black Jackson State University in Jackson, Mississippi, a state with the largest number of lynched victims, followed by Texas and Georgia. These images brought home in lurid details the black experience in America.

When I saw these pictures in New York and in Atlanta, there was a hushed silence among the black and white viewers, as they marched slowly, contemplating the contorted agony of black bodies dangling from trees, bridges, and lampposts. (I could not help wondering about the relationship between the whites who committed these lynchings and the whites I work with at Union Seminary.[11]) And I wondered how many viewers pondered the theological and relational meanings of the white supremacy that put blacks on trees in America and the religious hatred and political fear that put Jesus on a Roman cross in first-century Palestine? Countee Cullen saw clearly that there had to be a connection between these two horrible events:

> "Lynch him! Lynch him!" O savage cry,
> Why should you echo, "Crucify!"[12]

Where was God in these agonizing deaths? "Likely there ain't no God at all," said Jim in Cullen's *The Black Christ*, for "God, if He was, kept to His skies, and left us to our enemies." What is the meaning of a lynched victim's cry of "Why me, Oh, Lord! What did I do to deserve this?" and Jesus' excruciating cry of abandonment, "My God, My God, why hast thou forsaken me?" (Mk 15:34 KJV). How can we explain in religious terms nearly five thousand lives "so wantonly cut down"? To look at these images is to see what Cullen saw:

> This is a cruel land, this South,
> And bitter words to twist my mouth
> Burning my tongue down to its root[13]

Soon after Allen's *Without Sanctuary* was published, the U.S. Senate issued a historic apology to the "families of more than 5,000 lynching victims across the country for its failure to enact an anti-lynching law first proposed 105 years ago."[14] The House of Representatives passed the NAACP-initiated anti-lynching legislation several times, but it was always defeated in the Senate, whose members, especially in the South, insisted that lynching was a necessary tool to protect the purity of the white race. It is always "better late than never" to correct past injustices. But as the British statesman William Ewart Gladstone once observed, "Justice delayed is justice denied." That truth is confirmed by the legacy that lynching has bequeathed us. An apology, although important and welcomed by many blacks, is not justice.

While the Senate refused to enact a federal law against lynching, black artists relentlessly exposed the political and religious hypocrisy of lynching in America. In competition with each other, both the NAACP and the Communist Party sponsored anti-lynching exhibitions in 1935 featuring drawings, paintings, and sculptures by many participating artists.

Some artists, including whites, Mexicans, Japanese, as well as blacks, displayed their work in both exhibitions. Generally, non-black artists addressed a white audience and focused mostly on the brutality against black bodies and the racism of the lynchers. Black artists usually addressed the black community and thus tended to avoid white brutality and the helplessness of the black victims. They focused more on black subjectivity—the dignity of the black victims and the suffering of the black community, and they were much more likely to allude to the spiritual agency of black people through parallels with the suffering of Christ.

E. Simms Campbell, a native of St. Louis, submitted a charcoal drawing, "I Passed Along This Way" (1935), which shows a Christ figure carrying a cross up a hill alongside a black man being pulled with a rope around his neck.[15] Hale Woodruff, a native of Nashville, Tennessee, submitted two prints—one called "Giddap!" (1935), which portrayed a black man mounted on a wagon with a rope around his neck, his shirt opened with the mark of a cross on his chest, with whites screaming obscenities, as one man with a raised switch in hand prepares to make the horses go and leave the victim swinging. The other was called "By Parties Unknown" (1935), which showed a lynched black man dumped on the doorsteps of a black church with a rope around his neck, flowers growing where the rope touches the ground, suggesting some form of new life and a possible redemption.

When artists used religious symbols, they often pointed not only to the black victim as Christ but also to the hypocrisy of the white churches. In their anti-lynching crusade, the NAACP encouraged visual artists to create images that would counter the lynching photos of lynchers and their supporters, especially in the churches. A few white artists, like Julius Bloch, a Jew from Germany, also used religious symbolism. He produced an oil painting called "The Lynching" (1932), which portrays "a Christ-like figure of a black man, eyes heavenward, tied to a tree with a ladder behind it and surrounded by white men with rope and whip preliminary to the rituals of torture and killing."[16]

When visual artists painted an image of Christ on the cross and painted him *black*, they were also referencing Christ as a lynched victim. Simply turning him from white to black switched the visual signifiers, making him one with the body of lynched black people in America.

No one focused on this theme with more literary passion and creative theological insight than W. E. B. Du Bois of the NAACP. Most scholars call Du Bois an agnostic.[17] Though he certainly had little use for doctrines, dogma, or organized religion, I believe he was a man of deep faith. His faith was expressed in the conviction that evil does not have the last word and that there is a spiritual force for right that cannot be crushed or defeated. He wrote extensively about lynching. In *The Souls of Black Folk* (1903) and especially in his poems and parables in *The Crisis* and *Darkwater* (1920), Du Bois prefigured the theological and christological insights about the Black God and Black Christ in black liberation theology during the late 1960s and early '70s. Although not a great poet or a master storyteller, Du Bois's poems and stories always had great theological and biblical insight. In "The Riddle of the Sphinx," he waits

> Till some dim, darker David, a-hoeing of his corn,
> And married maiden, mother of God,
> Bid the black Christ be born![18]

In his story "Jesus Christ in Texas," a stranger appears as a messianic figure, a "mulatto" with "hair hung in close curls far down the sides of his face and his face was olive, even yellow."

On seeing him the black butler "dropped to his knees," breaking precious china, as he exclaimed: "My Lord and my God!"— the exact words of Thomas to Jesus following his resurrection (John 20:28 KJV). The stranger meets a black convict in the woods and gives him cupped hands of water, "bathe[s] his hot head, and gently [takes] the chains and irons from his feet." "Why, you are a nigger, too," the convict says. Later, the convict is lynched, but "behind him the roped and swaying form below hung quivering and burning a great crimson cross." "There, heaven-tall, earth-wide, hung the stranger on the crimson cross, riven and bloodstained, with thorn-crowned head and pierced hands." Then, "a voice came out of the winds of the night," saying to the convict what Jesus said to one of the thieves in Luke's Gospel, "This day thou shalt be with me in Paradise!" (Lk 23:43 KJV).[19]

While Du Bois was not a conventional Christian, he read the Bible seriously and carefully. He cites the Gospels verbatim to make his theological points about the Black Christ in his parables. All his parables and poems have parallels with the stories about the iconoclastic Jesus in the Gospels, a Jesus whose values disrupted the status quo because he showed solidarity with poor blacks. Whites did not understand the religious meaning of his disruptive appearance. In the story "Second Coming," a black baby is born as the Black Christ in Valdosta, Georgia, giving hope to oppressed blacks. "I never saw niggers act so," the governor says to a visiting white bishop from New York. "They seem to be expecting something."[20]

In *The Souls of Black Folk* and other essays, Du Bois condemned "white religion" as an "utter failure." "A nation's religion is its life, and as such white Christianity is a miserable failure." He could not reconcile white Christianity with the Gospels' portrayal of Jesus. For Du Bois, true Christianity was defined by "the life and teaching of Jesus of Nazareth and the Golden Rule." The white church's treatment of blacks was "sadly at variance with this doctrine." "It . . . assiduously 'preaches Christ crucified' in prayer meeting *patios*, and crucifies 'niggers' in unrelenting daily life."[21] Du Bois then proceeded to outline the "plain facts":

> The church aided and abetted the Negro slave trade; the church was the bulwark of American slavery; and the church to-day is the strongest seat of racial and color prejudice. If one hundred of the best and purest colored folk of the United States should seek to apply for membership in any white church in this land tomorrow, 999 out of every 1,000 ministers would lie to keep them out. They would not only do this, but would openly and brazenly defend their action as worthy of followers of Jesus Christ.

Du Bois elaborated on why the white Christ was not the biblical Christ:

> Yet Jesus Christ was a laborer and black men are laborers; He was poor and we are poor; He was despised of his fellow men and we are despised; He was persecuted and crucified, and we are mobbed and lynched. If Jesus Christ came to America He would associate with Negroes and Italians and working people; He would eat and pray with them, and He would seldom see the interior of the Cathedral of Saint John the Divine.[22]

Du Bois used the NAACP's magazine *The Crisis* to keep the religious meaning of the lynching theme before the American public, especially the black community. The December 1916 issue of *The Crisis* conveyed this message in a powerful painting called "Christmas in Georgia," which depicts a black man, held up with the silhouette image of Christ, while an angry mob of white men hoist the victim with a rope. On the tree on which the black man hangs there is a sign that reads, "Inasmuch as ye did it unto the least of these, My brethren, ye did it unto Me." The contradictions between the gospel message and the reality of lynching—or more precisely, the relation between what white Christians did to blacks and what the Romans did to Jesus--was reflected in a photo that appeared in the December 1919 issue of *The Crisis* with the title "The Crucifixion in Omaha." It was a photo of a burned victim, with a throng of white men observing their handiwork.

The same issue of *The Crisis* contained Du Bois's story "The Gospel of Mary Brown," illustrated with a photo of a black Madonna, holding a black baby in her arms. In Du Bois's story, obviously a retelling of Luke's Gospel account of Jesus' birth, Mary is black, living in a cabin by the creek, when a woman says to her (using the words of the angel Gabriel), "Fear not, Mary: for thou hast found favor with God." Then Mary reads the Magnificat from an "Old Book," citing the exact words of Luke 1:46, 48: "My soul doth magnify the Lord. . . . For He hath regarded the low estate of his handmaiden, for behold, from henceforth generations shall call me blessed. . . ." The child is called Joshua, the Hebrew name for Jesus, and "His skin was black as velvet." "And the child grew and waxed strong in spirit, filled with wisdom, and the grace of God was upon him." When he is twelve, his mother finds him "sitting in the midst of the deacons, both hearing them and asking them questions: Why were colored folk poor? Why were they afraid?" Joshua works on the plantation—plowing, picking and hoeing cotton, and driving mules. He soon learns to be a carpenter.

Whites become exceedingly angry when they hear Joshua preach: "Blessed are the poor; blessed are they that mourn; blessed are the meek; blessed are the merciful; blessed are they which are persecuted. All men are brothers and God is the Father of all." Whites complain bitterly: "He's putting ideas into niggers' heads." "Behold, he stirreth up the people." Then "they seized him and questioned him," saying, "What do you mean by this talk about being brothers—do you mean social equality?" "What do you mean by 'the meek shall inherit the earth'—do you mean the niggers will own our cotton land?""What do you mean by saying God is you-all's father—is God a nigger?" "Joshua flamed in mighty anger," appropriating the words of Jesus and John the Baptist in the Gospels, calling the whites "hypocrites," "serpents,""generation of vipers" who will not"escape the damnation of hell!"

Just as Jesus was taken before Pilate, so too Joshua is taken before a northern Judge, who finds no fault in him, nothing that would warrant a lynching. "Kill the nigger," the mob shouts. "Why," the Judge replies, "what hath he done?" "Let him be crucified," the crowd insists. Like Pilate, "the Judge washed his hands of the whole matter, saying: 'I am innocent of his blood.'" Like Jesus, Joshua "was sentenced for treason and inciting murder and insurrection . . . they stripped him, and spit upon him, and smote him on the head, and mocked, and lynched him." Like Jesus in Luke's Gospel, Joshua says, "Father, forgive them, for they know not what they do." His mother cries out to God, questioning divine justice. While the questioning of God's justice has biblical warrants, especially in the Hebrew Bible, the words Du Bois chose for Mary's lips came directly out of the black experience of suffering.

> God, you ain't fair!—You ain't fair, God! You didn't ought to do it—if you didn't want him black, you didn't have to make him black; if you didn't want him unhappy, why did you let him think? And then you let them mock him, and hurt him, and lynch him! Why, why did you do it God?

These questions, demanding God's explanation for black suffering, sit at the nerve center of black religion in America, from the slave trade to the prison industrial complex of today. Black religion comes out of suffering, and no one has engaged the question of theodicy in the black experience more profoundly than Du Bois. Yet, he did not end Mary's gospel on a note of despair with Joshua's death on a lynching tree. "Mary—Mary—he is not dead: He is risen!" Joshua appears to her and repeats the orthodox Christian claim about being crucified, dead, and buried, descending into Hell, rising from the dead on the third day, ascending to Heaven and sitting at the right hand of the Father, and returning to judge "the Quick and the Dead."[23]

Many students of Du Bois are surprised by this hopeful ending. He was not a conventional Christian. But Du Bois was fundamentally a man of the black experience, and thus a man of deep religious faith. One cannot be defined by this experience and not struggle with religious contradictions. "Why did God make me an outcast and stranger in mine own house?"[24] It is a question that runs throughout African American history. To hold onto the conviction that suffering does not have the last word—as Du Bois did—is to assume an essentially religious stance. That was why Du Bois did not end the "Gospel of Mary Brown" with the lynching. And yet, in most of Du Bois's other stories about the lynched Black Christ, there is no resurrection. The story entitled "Pontius Pilate" ends with the despairing cry of abandonment in Mark's Gospel: "My God, my God! Why hast Thou forsaken me!"[25] In the tale "The Son of God," Joshua is "seized by a mob" that "hanged him at sunset." While his father, Joe, "buried his head in the dirt and sobbed," his mother, Mary, never loses hope and repeatedly proclaims, "He is the Son of God." "Behold, the Sign of Salvation—a noosed rope."[26]

Somewhat like his use of the concept of "double consciousness" to explain the African American search for identity, Du Bois used the paradox of faith and doubt together to explain the meaning of the black religious experience. One cannot correctly understand the black religious experience without an affirmation of deep faith informed by profound doubt. Suffering naturally gives rise to doubt. How can one believe in God in the face of such horrendous suffering as slavery, segregation, and the lynching tree? Under these circumstances, doubt is not a denial but an integral part of faith. It keeps faith from being sure of itself. But doubt does not have the final word. The final word is faith giving rise to hope. And hope is the theme of Du Bois's brief reflection "Easter."

> The winter of despair has long lain upon our souls.... Now all has changed. This is the Resurrection Morning.... This alone is real. These other things that fill and, alas! must fill our pages—murder, meanness, the hurting of little children, the dishonoring of womanhood, the starving of souls—all these are but unsubstantial smoke and shadow that hide the real things. This reality is ever there, howsoever dark the darkness that blackens and hides it.[27]

Nothing challenged Du Bois's faith as much as the Atlanta race riots of 1906, during which a mob of white men, incited by an alleged assault on four white women, took their violent revenge on the black community. Twenty-five African Americans were killed, hundreds injured, and thousands driven from their homes. Du Bois responded with his "Litany at Atlanta," in which he echoes the language of Psalm 44 to wrestle with a God who "saved us from our enemies" and who also "cast off and put us to shame." The psalmist intoned, "Yea, for thy sake we are killed all the day long; we are counted as sheep for the slaughter. Awake, why sleepest thou, O Lord? Arise, cast us not off forever" (Ps 44:9, 22-23). Similarly, in Du Bois's prayer, he struggles to make sense out of divine silence in the face of the indiscriminate slaughter in Atlanta. "O Silent God," Du Bois prays,

> Listen to us, Thy children: our faces dark with doubt are made a mockery in Thy Sanctuary. . . . Bewildered we are and passion-tossed, mad with the madness of a mobbed and mocked and murdered people; straining at the armposts of Thy throne, we raise our shackled hands and charge Thee, God, by the bones of our stolen fathers, by

the tears of our dead mothers, by the very blood of Thy crucified Christ: What meaneth this?

This is the question that suffering black people of faith cannot escape. "Surely Thou, too, art not white, O Lord, a pale, bloodless, heartless thing!"

Such spiritual wrestling did not arise out of abstract reasoning but from enduring and confronting the reality of inexplicable suffering. But no matter how incongruous suffering was for Du Bois and other blacks, it could not destroy their faith. Suffering deepened their faith. So Du Bois followed his questions with a heartfelt affirmation: "Forgive the thought! Forgive these wild, blasphemous words! Thou art still the God of our black fathers."[28]

It is one thing to think about the cross as a theological concept or as a magical talisman of salvation and quite another to connect Calvary with the lynching tree in the American experience. To speak of the Black Christ in a land lighted by the burning crosses of the Ku Klux Klan challenged the imagination of black artists. Du Bois led the way, inspiring other artists and writers to speak movingly about the cross, lynching, and burning black bodies.

Robert Hayden's brilliant poem "Night, Death, Mississippi" (1962) speaks about the lynching theme in the voice of a sadistic white man too old and ill to "be there with Boy [his son] and the rest" but still remembering when "Time was" like "White robes in the moonlight."

> In the sweetgum dark.
> Unbucked that one then
> and him squealing bloody Jesus
> as we cut it off.

In three references to Jesus, Hayden's poem implies a parallel to the crucifixion. The second reference invokes Jesus as a moral voice that follows the son's excitement as he tells about the lynching spree that initiated him into adulthood:

> Then we beat them, he said,
> beat them till our arms was tired
> and the big old chains
> messy and red.

> O Jesus burning on the lily cross.

The final reference comes in the voice of the son, as he relives the excitement:

> Christ, it was better
> than hunting bear
> which don't know why
> you want him dead.[29]

What a complicated, linguistically sophisticated poem! It is significant that the voices of the white man and his son use Christ's name in vain: "Bloody Jesus," "O Jesus," "Christ." They are using the name as a colloquialism. The poet, however, deftly uses the name to connect the crucified Christ and the lynched figure. He at once makes this connection, and at the same time shows the vile ignorance and profanity of the perpetrators.

When black artists and writers looked at the cross and the lynching tree and reflected on their relationship to Jesus and the mob violence of whites against blacks in American history, they saw a Black Christ hanging and burning on a white cross. In "Burnt Offering" (1939), poet James Andrews connects the lynching/burning of a black man to animal sacrifice in the Hebrew Bible:

> A Fatted calf, a priestly fire;
> The sacrificial knife, a dire
> Foreboding of a bloody thing.
> It plunges deep, death takes its prize;

And smoke ascends toward the skies:
Burnt offering.

A lonely tree, a surging crowd
With clubs and stones and voices loud;
A black man as a calf they bring.
Upon a newer Cross he dies,
And smoke ascends toward the skies:
Burnt offering.[30]

In Claude McKay's sonnet "The Lynching" (1922), a reference to the crucifixion is found in the first quatrain:

His Spirit in smoke ascended to high heaven.
His father, by the cruelest way of pain,
Had bidden him to his bosom once again;
The awful sin remained still unforgiven.

The black lynched victim is the son of God who is "bidden" to his father's bosom once more, "by the cruelest way of pain" (lynching) because man's "awful sin remained still unforgiven." Like the "star" in Bethlehem (Mt 2:10),

All night a bright and solitary star
(Perchance the one that ever guided him,
Yet gave him up at last to Fate's wild whim)
Hung pitifully o'er the swinging char.
Day dawned, and soon the mixed crowds came to view
The ghastly body swaying in the sun:
The women thronged to look, but never a one
Showed sorrow in her eyes of steely blue:
And little lads, lynchers that were to be,
Danced round the dreadful thing in fiendish glee.[31]

Lorraine Hansberry, author of *A Raisin in the Sun* (1959), the longest-running Broadway play by a black writer, wrote a poem entitled "Lynchsong," about the "legal lynching" of Willie McGee in Laurel, Mississippi, in 1951.

Laurel:
Name sweet like the breath of peace

Blood and blood
Hatred there
White robes and
Black robes
And a burning
Burning cross

>   cross in Laurel
>   cross in Jackson
>   cross in Chicago

And a
Cross in front of the
City Hall
In:
New York City

Crosses were everywhere in America—"burning crosses" killing black people.

Lord
Burning cross
Lord
Burning man
Lord
Murder cross

Night was a scary time in the African American community in Laurel—"bitter like the rhyme of a lynchsong." Through poetic imagination, one "can hear Rosalee" and "see the eyes of Willie McGee," which meant that could be me.

My mother told me about
Lynchings
My mother told me about

The dark nights
and dirt roads
and torch lights
and lynch robes

  sorrow night
  and a
  sorrow night

The
faces of men
Laughing white
Faces of men
Dead in the night

  sorrow night
  and a
  sorrow night.[32]

However, the lynched Black Christ was not the only Christ that artists saw. They also saw a mean White Christ symbolized in white Christian lynchers, the ones who justified slavery and segregation. Walter White, national secretary of the NAACP and author of several novels and the important book *Rope and Faggot*, indicted Christianity for creating the fanaticism that encouraged lynching. "It is exceedingly doubtful if lynching could possibly exist under any other religion than Christianity," he wrote. "Not only through tacit approval and acquiescence has the Christian Church indirectly given its approval to lynch-law . . . , but the evangelical Christian denominations have done much towards creation of the particular fanaticism which finds its outlet in lynching."[33]

The identification of lynched black victims with recrucified Christ figures did not remove the contradiction that the lynching tree posed for faith. Countee Cullen, the adopted son of a Methodist minister, was both secular and religious, a believer and a doubter—all at the same time in the same poem, "The Black Christ."

> God could not be, if He deemed right,
> The grief that ever met our sight.[34]

Artists recognized that no real reconciliation could occur between blacks and whites without telling the painful and redeeming truths about their life together. Life creates art or, as the black poet Langston Hughes put it, "life makes poems."[35] What Sterling Brown said about Claude McKay could be said of most artists. They "look[ed] searchingly at reality and reveal[ed] its harshness."[36] Unlike preachers and theologians, artists and writers were not bound by the inherited, static religious tradition of white supremacists. Black artists were defined by their creative resistance against an oppressive status quo. They were free to say anything that gave black people liberating visions of their humanity. During the Harlem Renaissance, Du Bois put the matter plainly and bluntly, even though many of the younger artists disagreed with him.

> All art is propaganda and ever must be, despite wailing of purists. I stand in utter shamelessness and say that whatever art I have for writing has been used always for propaganda for gaining the right of black folk to love and enjoy. I do not care a damn for any art that is not used for propaganda. But I do care when propaganda is confined to one side while the other is stripped and silent.[37]

No artists expressed the black transvaluation of values and fused their art with such an affirmation of the ways of black folk and a critique of the ways of white folk as Langston Hughes, often called the poet laureate of black America. Asked by two white student editors of *Contempo* to write a poem about the nine Scottsboro Boys, who were falsely accused but convicted of rape of two white prostitutes on a train, Hughes wrote "Christ in Alabama," which was published on the occasion of his scheduled appearance at the University of North Carolina in Chapel Hill. In this poem he identified Christ with an illegitimate black offspring of a white man and a black woman.

> Christ is a nigger,
> Beaten and black—
> *Oh, bare your back.*
>
> Mary is His mother,
> *Mammy of the South,*
> *Silence your mouth.*
>
> God is His father—
> *White Master above*
> *Grant Him your love.*
>
> Most holy bastard
> Of the bleeding mouth,
> *Nigger Christ*
> *On the cross of the South.*

The poem angered many whites at the university and in the community. "Nothing but a corrupt, distorted brain could produce such sordid literature," said one white man. A politician angrily said: "It's bad enough to call Christ a bastard but to call Him a nigger—that's too much."[38]

The uproar pleased Hughes because it drew attention to lynching and its religious contradictions. He also wrote a poem about "the lynching of two fourteen-year-old boys, Charles Lang and Ernest Green, beneath the Shabuta Bridge over the Chicasawhay in Mississippi." Its title, "The Bitter River," referred to bodies swallowed up by a stream of hate, but it could also be interpreted as a reference to "drink mingled with gall" (Mt 27:34 KJV), the bitter substance given to Jesus on the cross, which he refused.

. . . Oh, tragic and bitter river
Where the lynch boys hung,
The gall of your bitter water
Coats my tongue.
The Blood of your river
For me gives back no stars.
I'm tired of the bitter river!
Tired of the bars![39]

Hughes wrote poems and stories about many lynchings, at the same time exposing the contradictions of white churches and American democracy. "I believe that anything which makes people think of existing evil conditions is worthwhile," he said in response to the controversy about his "Nigger Christ." "Sometimes in order to attract attention somebody must embody the ideas in sensational forms. I meant my poem to be a protest against the domination of all stronger peoples over weaker ones."[40] That is what Jesus' life, teachings, and death were about—God's protest against the exploitation of the weak by the strong.

As in his poem "Christ in Alabama," Hughes was always shaking people up; sometimes he regretted it, even though he spoke the truth. He saw a great difference between the "Nigger Christ" and the White Christ, and he often lambasted the latter so sharply that people began to label him—incorrectly—as an atheist and a communist. Since the Communists defined racial justice as central to their program, Hughes (like other writers, including Richard Wright and Ralph Ellison) became closely associated with them, and even traveled to Russia. During his close association with the Communists, he wrote two poems that he later regretted for the rest of his life. Both appeared about a year after "Nigger Christ"; one was called "Good Morning Revolution" and the other "Goodbye Christ," which caused him the most trouble. He was in Russia when he was inspired to write:

> Good-morning, Revolution:
> You're the very best friend
> I ever had.
> We gonna pal around together from now on. . . .[41]

While poems embracing revolution were well received in Russia, they were not in the United States, especially by evangelical Christians and patriotic citizens. However, it was his poem "Goodbye Christ" that particularly disturbed Christians and their sympathizers.

> Listen, Christ,
> You did alright in your day, I reckon—
> But that day's gone now.
> They ghosted you up a swell story, too,
> Called it Bible—
> But it's dead now.
> The popes and the preachers've
> Made too much money from it.
> They've sold you to many
>
> Kings, generals, robbers, and killers—
> Even to the Tzar and the Cossacks,
> Even to Rockefeller's Church,
> Even to THE SATURDAY EVENING POST.
> You ain't no good no more.
> They've pawned you
> Till you've done wore out.

That kind of talk offended the white Christian community and even African Americans were not happy about it. They regarded it as blasphemy against Jesus and his church. Hughes, however, initially seemed not to care as he replaced biblical heroes with communists.

> Goodbye
> Christ Jesus Lord God Jehova,

Beat it on away from here now.
Make way for a new guy with no religion at all—
The real guy named
Marx   Communist   Lenin   Peasant   Stalin   Worker
    ME—

I said, ME!

Naming persons still living is what got Hughes in trouble.

Go ahead on now,
You're getting in the way of things, Lord.
And please take Saint Gandhi with you when you go.
And Saint Pope Pius,
And Saint Aimee McPherson,
And big black Saint Becton,
Of the Consecrated Dime.
And step on the gas, Christ!
Move!
Don't be so slow about movin'!
The world is mine from now on—
And nobody's gonna sell ME
To a king, or a general,
Or a millionaire.[42]

Hughes was denounced in both black and white churches for this poem, especially by the evangelist Aimee McPherson, who organized demonstrations against him and prevented several of his readings. Hughes paid a heavy price for this one poem both financially and in terms of his reputation. Later, he publicly renounced "Goodbye Christ" and attributed it to the immaturity of his youth.

Artists force us to see things we do not want to look at because they make us uncomfortable with ourselves and the world we have created. That was why Hughes, Du Bois, and other black artists were persecuted. White supremacists defined lynched victims as "black beast rapists," as savages and criminals deserving torture and death. But artists, writers, and other prophetic figures saw African American culture as something sacred and empowering.

It was not easy for blacks to find a language to talk about Christianity publicly because the Jesus they embraced was also, at least in name, embraced by whites who lynched black people. Indeed, it was white slaveholders, segregationists, and lynchers who defined the content of the Christian gospel. They wrote hundreds of books about Christianity, founded seminaries to train scholars and preachers, and thereby controlled nearly two thousand years of Christian tradition. Cut off from their African religious traditions, black slaves were left trying to carve out a religious meaning for their lives with white Christianity as the only resource to work with. They ignored white theology, which did not affirm their humanity, and went straight to stories in the Bible, interpreting them as stories of God siding with little people just like them. They identified God's liberation of the poor as the central message of the Bible, and they communicated this message in their songs and sermons.

This liberating religious tradition is what Hughes and other black poets inherited, and it was the source for their identifying Christ as black and recrucified on the lynching trees of America. It was a kind of "commonsense" theology—a theology of the grassroots, for which one needed no seminary or university degree in religion. It was commonsense theology that led Hughes to compare the federal government's indictment and persecution of W. E. B. Du Bois, the taking of his passport, as analogous to the Roman persecution of Jesus. "Somebody in Washington wants to put Dr. Du Bois in jail," Hughes said, "just as Somebody at Golgotha erected a cross and somebody drove nails into the hands of Christ. Somebody spat on His garments. Nobody remembers their names."[43]

Black artists are prophetic voices whose calling requires them to speak truth to power. Their expressions are not controlled by the institutions of the church. More than anyone, artists demonstrate our understanding of the need to represent the beauty and the terror of our people's experience.

Unlike the black literary tradition, the black church tradition has not been careful in making a distinction between the two Christs, even though such a distinction is implied in their language and life. The White Christ gave blacks slavery, segregation, and lynching and told them to turn the other cheek and to look for their reward in heaven. Be patient, they were told, and your suffering will be rewarded, for it is the source of your spiritual redemption. Rejecting the teaching of black and white churches that Jesus' death on the cross saved us from sin and that we too are called by him to suffer as he did, some black scholars, especially women, reject any celebration of Jesus' cross as a means of salvation. Theirs is a just and powerful critique of bad religion and theology, which must be reckoned with so as not to make suffering a good in itself. To that womanist challenge we turn in the next chapter.

5

"Oh Mary, Don't You Weep"

A colored woman accused of poisoning a white one
was taken from the county jail and stripped naked
and hung up in the county courthouse yard and her
body riddled with bullets and left exposed to view! O
my God! Can such a thing be and no justice for it?[1]
—Ida B. Wells

Southern trees bear strange fruit
Blood on the leaves and blood at the root
Black body swinging in the Southern breeze
Strange fruit hanging from the poplar tree
—"Strange Fruit," Abel Meeropol
(a.k.a. Lewis Allen)

When a mob in Valdosta, Georgia, in 1918 failed to find
Sidney Johnson, accused of murdering his boss, Hampton Smith, they decided to lynch another black man, Haynes
Turner, who was known to dislike Smith. Turner's wife, Mary,
who was eight months pregnant, protested vehemently and
vowed to seek justice for her husband's lynching. The sheriff,
in turn, arrested her and then gave her up to the mob. In the
presence of a crowd that included women and children, Mary
Turner was "stripped, hung upside down by the ankles, soaked
with gasoline, and roasted to death. In the midst of this torment,
a white man opened her swollen belly with a hunting knife and
her infant fell to the ground and was stomped to death."[2]

Most people assume that the "strange fruit . . . swinging in
the Southern breeze" that Billie Holiday sang about at the New

York Café Society in 1939 was a black male body. But the "black body" in her rendition of Abel Meeropol's poem "Strange Fruit" has no sex. The "blood on the leaves and blood at the root" were beaten out of the bodies of black men, women, and children. No black person was exempt from the risk of becoming the scapegoat of white supremacy in America, not even the unborn, whose mothers, like Mary Turner, were lynched while trying to protect their families.

"When I look at those pictures," an Atlanta teacher said, reacting to the photos in James Allen's *Without Sanctuary*, "I don't see a lifeless body. I look at those pictures and I see my son, I see my brother, I see my father. If I look at that lifeless body long enough, I see myself"[3]—or, as she might have added, my daughter, sister, mother. When we look at a lynched black victim transfigured as the recrucified Black Christ, we might as well be looking at "a colored woman . . . stripped naked and hung in the county courthouse yard and her body riddled with bullets and left exposed to view!"[4] That was the point made by woman-ist theologian Jacquelyn Grant when she used the experience of poor black women as the lens for interpreting the meaning of Jesus Christ today. "The significance of Christ is not found in his maleness, but in his humanity," writes Grant. "This Christ, found in the experiences of black women," "the oppressed of the oppressed," "is a black woman."[5] Unfortunately, the powerful image of "Christ as a Black Woman" has been left out of our spiritual and intellectual imagination, needing further theological development.

Womanist theologian Delores Williams has written and spoken powerfully about the surrogate roles that black women have been forced to assume by white men and women as well as black men.[6] That surrogacy extended as well to lynching, as women were sometimes substituted for black men who happened to escape white mob violence. "A significant number of female lynchings were not suspected of any crime," writes historian Patrick

J. Huber. "These 'collateral victims' died in place of an intended male target, such as a father, son, or brother, who had eluded the grasp of a frustrated mob."[7] But as Crystal Nicole Feimster has noted in her important study "Ladies and Lynching," "The evidence . . . reveals that less than 10 black women were lynched solely for their connection or relationship with black men."[8] The great majority of black women became "strange and bitter crop" because they courageously challenged white supremacy, refusing to stay in any place that denied their dignity.

Although women constitute only 2 percent of blacks actually killed by lynching, it would be a mistake to assume that violence against women was not widespread and brutal. Black women were neither incidental objects of white vigilante violence nor marginal participants in the black resistance against it. Like black men, they were tortured, beaten and scarred, mutilated and hanged, burned and shot, tarred and feathered, stabbed and dragged, whipped and raped by angry white mobs. They fought back any way they could—individually and collectively, with black men and by themselves—refusing to submit to white supremacy. Black women suffered when black men suffered and when black men did not. In the physical and spiritual struggle for survival and dignity, some atrocities were "more bitter than death,"[9] and many women, like Addie Hunton of the National Association of Colored Women (NACW), placed rape in that category—especially sexual violation in one's home by white Christian men who regarded black women as whores incapable of being violated.[10]

With many historians and sociologists writing about the lynching of black men, black women have objected to being invisible in lynching discourse, as if they were exempt from mob violence. Furthermore, when black men were lynched, black women not only suffered the loss of their sons, husbands, brothers, uncles, nephews, and cousins but also endured public insults and economic hardship as they tried to carry on, to take care of their fatherless children in a patriarchal and racist society in which whites could lynch them or their children with impunity, at the slightest whim or smallest infraction of the southern racial etiquette.

Such suffering created a deep religious paradox for black women, challenging their faith in the justice and love of God. A free black woman named Nellie, from Savannah, Georgia, expressed the spiritual agony black suffering created for her faith:"It has been a terrible mystery, to know why the good Lord should so long afflict my people, and keep them in bondage— to be abused, and trampled down, without any rights of their own—with no ray of light in the future. Some of my folks said there wasn't any God, for if there was he wouldn't let white folks do as they do for so many years."[11]

The spiritual anguish that lynching created connected blacks with the spiritual wrestling of the prophets, of Job, and the psalmist. In the midst of "destruction and violence," "strife and contention," "justice . . . turned back, and righteousness . . . at a distance" (Hab 1:2-4; Isa 59:14), they too cried out to God, "How long, Lord? . . . How long must I bear pain in my soul, and have sorrow in my heart all day long? How long shall my enemy be exalted over me?" (Ps 13:1, 2). Blacks identified with the way biblical characters wrestled with faith's contradictions and incongruities. "Lord, how come me here? . . . I wish I never was born!" they sang, a despairing declaration similar to that of Job and Jeremiah, who cursed the day on which they were born ("Why did I come forth from the womb to see toil and sorrow, and spend my days in shame?" [Jer 20:15, 18; Job 3:1f.]).

Blacks especially identified with the suffering of Jesus, whom they (like the early Christians) viewed as the Suffering Servant in Isaiah 53—the one who "was despised and rejected by others," "wounded for our transgressions, crushed for our iniquities," and who, unlike Job and Jeremiah, "did not open his mouth" (Isa 53:3, 5, 7; Mt 8:17; Acts 8:32-33; 1 Pet 2:22-25). Blacks identified with

Jesus' rejection in Jerusalem, his agony in the Garden of Gethse-mane, and his suffering on the cross of Calvary. Like Jesus, who prayed to his Father to "let this cup pass from me" (Mt 26:39), blacks also prayed to God to take away the bitter cups of slavery, segregation, and lynching. Just as Jesus cried from the cross, "My God, my God, why hast thou forsaken me?" many lynched victims made similar outbursts of despair to God before they took their last breath, hoping for divine intervention that did not come.

New Testament scholar William Barclay called Jesus' cry of abandonment "the most staggering sentence in the gospel record."[12] Black cultural critic Stanley Crouch called it "per-haps the greatest blues line of all time."[13] Jesus' life and death on a Roman cross spoke to the black condition as defined by the American lynching tree. "Calvary, Calvary, Calvary," blacks sang slowly with a mournful sound, feeling Jesus' suffering as their own. "Surely He died on Calvary." "Don't you hear Him calling His Father?" Jesus was "like a lamb that is led to the slaughter" (Isa 53:7; Rev. 5:6)—the one who suffered as blacks suffered, or as the rap artist Tupac Shakur would put it in his "Black Jesuz," "Somebody that hurt like we hurt. . . . That understands where we coming from."[14]

What is the meaning of this unspeakable black suffering—suf-fering so deep, so painful and enduring that words cannot even begin to describe it? Only the song, dance, and the shout—voices raised to high heavens and bodies swaying from side to side—can express both the wretchedness and the transcendent spirit of empowerment that kept blacks from going under, as they strug-gled, against great odds, to acknowledge humanity denied.

Black faith emerged out of black people's wrestling with suf-fering, the struggle to make sense out of their senseless situa-tion, as they related their own predicament to similar stories in the Bible. On the one hand, faith spoke to their suffering, mak-ing it bearable, while, on the other hand, suffering contradicted their faith, making it unbearable. That is the profound paradox inherent in black faith, the dialectic of doubt and trust in the search for meaning, as blacks "walk[ed] through the valley of the shadow of death" (Ps 23:4).

Some black men could and did run away from mob violence, fleeing to another town, city, county, or state. Sometimes they escaped, like Sydney Johnson, and often they did not, like Sam Hose. Bluesman Charley Patton, born in Mississippi in the 1880s, sounded a familiar refrain in the 1920s that expressed the black man's desire to escape mob violence.

> Every day seem like murder here,
> Every day seem like murder here,
> I'm gonna leave tomorrow,
> I know you don't want me here.[15]

For black women, however, running away was not an easy option. It was difficult for them to leave their children. They had to think about more than trying to secure their own safety. Thus, they often stayed where they were and made the most of a bad situation, trying to survive with dignity, as they wrestled, with limited resources, against the virulent expressions of racial hatred. The faith of black women gave them courage to fight, patience when they could not, and the hope that whatever they did, God would keep them "from sinking down." God was the one reality that whites could not control and whose presence was found in unexpected places, doing surprising things. "God may not come when you want but God is right on time," "making a way out of no way"—these were faith declarations frequently repeated in black churches in troubled times.

Many great crusaders rose up in resistance to lynching. Frederick Douglass was among the earliest. Others joined the struggle: T. Thomas Fortune, publisher of the *New York Age* and founder of the Afro-American League; W. E. B. Du Bois, James Weldon Johnson, and Walter White of the NAACP; sociologist Monroe Work of Tuskegee Institute; and Mary Church Terrell and Anna Julia Cooper of the National Association of Colored Women (NACW). Yet all of their work was built on the work of one woman: Ida B. Wells.[16]

Reflecting back on Wells's life and work, Du Bois correctly called her "the pioneer of the anti-lynching crusade," who "began the awakening of the conscience of the nation."[17] Frederick Douglass, whom Wells called "Old Man Eloquent," acknowledged her leadership in a letter of 1892 about her "paper on the lynch abomination." "There has been no word equal to it in convincing power," he wrote.

> I have spoken, but my word is feeble in comparison. You give what you know and testify from actual knowledge. . . . Brave woman! you have done your people and mine a service which can neither be weighed nor measured. If American conscience were only half alive, if the American church and clergy were only half christianized, if American moral sensibility were not hardened by persistent infliction of outrage and crime against colored people, a scream of horror, shame and indignation would rise to Heaven wherever your pamphlet shall be read.[18]

Born a slave in Mississippi in 1862, Wells achieved a national reputation for militancy when she successfully sued a railroad company after a conductor forcibly evicted her from a train for refusing to give up her first-class seat to a white man. (The company won on appeal with the state Supreme Court.) She took up journalism and became the editor of a black newspaper in Memphis called *The Free Speech*. Her life's work began in 1892 when three black men, including her friend Tommie Moss and two companions (Calvin McDowell and Will Stewart), were lynched in Memphis. Mobilized by this event, she responded with a series of blistering editorials, followed by comprehensive investigations, and a stream of pamphlets and speeches delivered around the country.

No one was more militant than Ida B. Wells. "Our country's national crime is *lynching*," she began her essay "Lynch Law in America." "It is not the creature of the hour, the sudden outburst of uncontrolled fury, or the unspeakable brutality of an insane mob. It represents the cool, calculating deliberation of intelligent people who openly avow that there is an 'unwritten law' that justifies them in putting human beings to death without complaint under oath, without trial by jury, without opportunity to make defense, and without right of appeal."[19] On two occasions, Wells took her anti-lynching crusade to Britain, where she was well received, creating much resentment from southern politicians, clergy, and the press. Her fight against lynching was so radical and uncompromising that many anti-lynching advocates in moderate organizations like the NAACP and NACW shunned her.[20]

In their justification of lynching, southern whites often used the pretext of an alleged "outrage" against white women. Lynching, they claimed, was necessary to protect the virtue of white women from the "unspeakable crime" of the "black male beast," who no longer had slavery in place to keep his bestial behavior in check. Rape "placed him beyond the pale of human sympathy," and "the world accepted the story that the Negro is a monster which the southern white man painted him."[21]

Wells herself regarded rape as an "unspeakable outrage," and this initially inhibited her from speaking out forcefully against lynching. Yet the Memphis lynching had nothing to do with rape. What caused it was envy of black economic success. Whites tolerated no competition from blacks in anything, not even in sports such as baseball and horse racing, but especially in politics and economics. Whites frequently blamed any or all blacks for what one did, accusing them of harboring "nigger criminals," and they would take out their frustrations on the whole black community, as they did in Atlanta in 1906—burning their homes and beating and lynching whoever was unlucky enough to be in the wrong place at the wrong time. Nothing was more detested by whites than the idea that blacks were equal to them. "You don't act in a way to make white persons feel that you don't know they were white," commented an Arkansas interviewee about Jim Crow. Any word or body movement that was perceived to be insufficiently deferential, like standing upright and looking a white person in the eye, could get a black beaten or killed. Lynching was the main weapon of terror to take back the black vote and property and "to keep the race terrorized and to keep the nigger down."[22] The Memphis lynching caused Wells to question the rape claim as the main reason for lynching. In her research, Wells discovered that rape was given as the reason in only about one-third of lynchings. In many of these cases, the claims referred to consensual sexual acts, while in others, the claims were often false.

As reported in the Cleveland, Ohio, *Gazette* (January 16, 1892), a Mrs. J. C. Underwood of Elyria, a minister's wife, falsely raised the accusation of rape against Mr. William Offett, who, she said, "forced his way in the house and insulted her," while her husband was "stumping the state for the Prohibition Party." Though the accused vigorously denied her testimony in court and claimed that the sex was not only consensual but occurred at her invitation, his word was dismissed in court. He served four years in prison until she confessed to her husband that the relationship was indeed consensual. Trying to explain to her husband why she repeatedly had sex with a black man she met at the post office, Mrs. Underwood said, "He had a strange fascination for me, and I invited him to call on me," which he did.

> Then I sat on his lap. He made a proposal to me and I readily consented. Why I did so I do not know, but that I did is true. He visited me several times after that and each time I was indiscreet. I did not care the first time. In fact I could not have resisted, and had no desire to resist.

Since a neighbor "saw the fellow here," and "I feared I might give birth to a Negro baby," she told her husband, "I hoped to save my reputation by telling a deliberate lie." Her confession horrified her husband, who had Offett released from prison and then divorced his wife.[23]

Had the Offett–Underwood sexual encounter occurred in the South, a white mob probably would have castrated him and strung him on a lynching tree or "burned him alive." This is what happened to Ed Coy in Texarkana, Texas (1892), as well as to many blacks in the South and sometimes even in the North and West. Since the rape narrative was most often false, Wells was determined to tell, as she wrote in "The Truth about Lynching" (1892), a truth that few whites wanted to hear. Shortly after the Memphis lynching, she wrote an editorial in *The Free Speech*, which nearly caused her own lynching. "Nobody in this section believes the threadbare lie that Negro men assault white women," she wrote. "If Southern men are not careful, they will over-reach themselves and public sentiment will have a reaction; a conclusion will then be reached which will be very damaging to the moral reputation of their women."[24]

That statement outraged whites, causing the Memphis press to call for white men "to tie the wretch who utters these calumnies to a stake at the intersection of Main and Madison Sts., brand him in the forehead with a hot iron and perform upon him a surgical operation with a pair of tailor's shears."[25] Initially, whites thought the unsigned editorial was written by Ida's co-owner, J. L. Flemings, who was driven out of the city. Whites destroyed *The Free Speech* and, after discovering who wrote the editorial, issued threats against Wells's life, preventing her return to Memphis.

Wells was the first to put her life on the line for the anti-lynching cause. "With me it is not myself nor my reputation, but the life of my people, which is at stake," she wrote, responding to an interview by Frances Willard of the Woman's Christian

Temperance Union (WCTU). Moderation was not a virtue when "men, women, and children were scourged, hanged, shot, and burned." "It may be unwise to express myself so strongly," Wells wrote in her diary, expressing her outrage at the lynching of Eliza Woods of Jackson, Tennessee, "but I cannot help it and I know not if capital may not be made of it against me but I trust God."[26]

What was it that gave Wells the courage to risk her life for others she did not even know? What gave her the audacity to proclaim the truth in an era when women were not even expected to speak in public? The answer is found in her faith, inherited from her ex-slave parents and the African American church community. It was a faith defined by the cross and the black cultural resistance to white supremacy.

Wells's trust in God sustained her when her anti-lynching activity was dangerous and when many blacks shunned her. She did not claim credit for her work but gave it all to God. "No other save Divine Strength," she wrote to Frederick Douglass, "could have helped me so wonderfully and to God I give all the praise and glory." When the ministers of the A.M.E. Church refused to support her work at one of their conferences in Philadelphia, she was not fazed. "Under God I have done work without any assistance from my people," she told them as she exited the meeting.[27]

For Wells, faith in the God of Calvary was not an excuse for passivity. She rebuked those who patiently waited on God to save them from injustice. When she disguised herself and risked her life to visit twelve condemned Arkansas prisoners who had survived the massacre of nearly three hundred blacks in Elaine, Arkansas (1919), they told her: "We think that the Lord will never let us die, for we are innocent. . . . All we can do is to read the scriptures, pray to the Lord and sing, and time passes on." Wells upbraided them: "Why don't you pray to live and ask to be freed? The God you serve is the God of Paul and Silas who opened the prison gates, and if you have all the faith you say you have, you ought to believe that he will open your prison doors too." After that rejoinder and following their acquittal by the U.S. Supreme Court, one of the freed prisoners visited Wells in Chicago and told her family that "we never talked about dying anymore, but did as she told us, and now every last one of us is out and enjoying his freedom."[28]

While faith in God empowered Wells to fight against lynching, the continued mob violence against blacks challenged her faith. "The heart almost loses faith in Christianity," she wrote, "when one thinks of . . . the countless massacres of defenseless Negroes, whose only crime was the attempt to exercise their right to vote." "O God, when will these massacres stop?"[29] Faith and doubt were bound together, with each a check against the other—doubt preventing faith from being too sure of itself and faith keeping doubt from going down into the pit of despair. With faith in one hand and doubt in the other she contended against the evil of lynching.

Like most blacks of her time, Wells dismissed white Christianity as hypocrisy. "Why is mob murder permitted by a Christian nation?" she asked. White Christianity was not genuine because it either openly supported slavery, segregation, and lynching as the will of God or it was silent about these evils. "The nation cannot profess Christianity," Wells said in an essay, "which makes the golden rule its foundation stone, and continue to deny equal opportunity for life, liberty and the pursuit of happiness to the black race."[30] She therefore challenged white liberal Christians to speak out against lynching or be condemned by their silence. "During all the years . . . in which men, women, and children were being scourged, hanged, shot and burned," Wells said of Frances Willard and the Women's Christian Temperance Union, "the WCTU had no word, either pity or protest; its great heart, which concerns itself about humanity the world over, was, toward our cause, pulseless as a stone." She could have said the same thing about Reinhold Niebuhr, his brother H. Richard, Social Gospel theologian Walter Rauschenbusch, and the rest of white theologians and ministers during that time. All of them were silent, as if the meaning of the Christian gospel for America had nothing to do with segregation and lynching.

Wells was especially critical of evangelist Dwight Moody, who segregated his revivals to appease whites in the South. "Our American Christians are too busy saving the souls of white Christians from burning in hellfire to save the lives of black ones from present burning in fires kindled by white Christians." "Christianity is to be the test," Wells claimed, that whites failed miserably in their treatment of blacks. She was "prouder to belong to the dark race that is the most practically Christian known to history, than to the white race that in its dealings with us has for centuries shown every quality that is savage, treacherous, and unchristian."[31]

Black people did not need to go to seminary and study theology to know that white Christianity was fraudulent. As a teenager in the South where whites treated blacks with contempt, I and other blacks knew that the Christian identity of whites was not a true expression of what it meant to follow Jesus. Nothing their theologians and preachers could say would convince us otherwise. We wondered how whites could live with their hypocrisy—such a blatant contradiction of the man from Nazareth. (I am still wondering about that!) White conservative Christianity's blatant endorsement of lynching as a part of its religion, and white liberal Christians' silence about lynching placed both of them outside of Christian identity. I could not find one sermon or theological essay, not to mention a book, opposing lynching by a prominent liberal white preacher.[32] There was no way a community could support or ignore lynching in America, while still representing in word and deed the one who was lynched by Rome. For Ida B. Wells, Christian identity had to be validated by opposing mob violence against a powerless people, and no amount of theological sophistry could convince her otherwise. As far as she was concerned, white Christianity was a counterfeit gospel—"as phony as a two-dollar bill," as blacks often said in Bearden.

It is revealing that in all of Wells's writings against lynching, she did not link the cross and the lynching tree or talk about the lynched victim as the recrucified Christ in America, as did many writers during the Harlem Renaissance. As an investigative journalist and activist, she focused on the facts about specific events involving lynching. Literary and theological imagination were not her main concern. Stopping the lynching of black people by white people was the chief focus of her life. When Frederick Douglass asked Wells whether she was nervous, as he was, before speaking in public, she said no. She told Douglass that he was an orator concerned about his presentation, and that was the source of his anxiety. "With me it is different," she said. "I am only a mouthpiece through which to tell the story of lynching. . . . I do not have to embellish, it makes its own way."[33]

A similar point could be said about other black women activists. Lynching was so blatantly wrong that they did not need theological imagination to show it to be so. All contended that true Christianity focused on the Golden Rule: "Do unto others as you would have them do unto you." White Christianity did not even come close to fulfilling that principle. "Are these people Christians who made these laws which are robbing us of our inheritance and reducing us to slavery?" a character asked in Frances Harper's novel *Iola Leroy*. "If this is Christianity I hate it and despise it. Would the most cruel heathen do worse?"[34]

When reflecting on lynching, black women refused to believe that white Christianity was the true gospel. "The old white preachers talked with their lips without saying nothing, but God told us to talk with our hearts," commented an ex-slave. This radical difference between white and black Christianity began during slavery and has persisted throughout American history. "By some amazing but vastly creative spiritual insight," theologian Howard Thurman said, "the slave undertook the redemption of the religion that the master had profaned in his midst."[35]

There were many ways to resist white supremacy that did not always lead to the lynching tree. Black people, especially women, fought against white domination in a variety of creative ways, in song, word, and dance. Billie Holiday's rendition of "Strange Fruit," which she called "my personal protest," was the most powerful resistance song against lynching. It has been called "a declaration of war" and "one of the songs that changed the world." *Time* magazine called Billie Holiday "history's greatest Jazz singer" and "Strange Fruit" "the best song of the century."

> Southern trees bear strange fruit,
> Blood on the leaves and blood at the root,
> Black body swinging in the Southern breeze,
> Strange fruit hanging from the poplar trees.
>
> Pastoral scene of the gallant South,
> The bulging eyes and the twisted mouth,
> Scent of magnolia sweet and fresh,
> Then the sudden smell of burning flesh!
>
> Here is fruit for the crows to pluck,
> For the rain to gather, for the wind to suck,
> For the sun to rot, for the trees to drop,
> Here is a strange and bitter crop. [36]

The lyrics of "Strange Fruit" were written in the early 1930s by Abel Meeropol (a.k.a. Lewis Allen), a white Jewish school teacher from New York City, who later adopted the two sons of convicted spies Julius and Ethel Rosenberg. Upon seeing the well-known Lawrence Beitler's photograph of the lynching of Thomas Shipp and Abram Smith in Marion, Indiana (1930)[37], Meeropol became so incensed that he wrote a poem to express what he felt. "It . . . haunted me for days," he recalled later. "I wrote 'Strange Fruit' because I hate lynching and I hate injustice and I hate the people who perpetuate it."[38]

Meeropol said in the lyrics of "Strange Fruit" what Reinhold Niebuhr and other white theologians and religious leaders should have said if they had the heart and courage to say what Jesus' cross means for American Christians. The cross bears witness to a brutal atrocity, such as the lynching of Shipp and Smith. Abel Meeropol was a part of a marginalized community who had a long history of suffering at the hands of white Christians. Some Jews, like Leo Frank in Atlanta, were also lynched (1915). When Meeropol saw the images of Shipp and Smith, he identified with them and other victims of injustice, such as the nine Scottsboro boys in Alabama, who were falsely accused of the rape of two white girls on a train, during the same decade. The lyrics of "Strange Fruit" expressed Meeropol's existential solidarity with "the strange fruit hanging from poplar trees."

"Strange Fruit" captures the great contradiction in southern culture and the religion that defined it. "Lynching is part of the religion of our people,"[39] one white man told another. Blacks have always wondered how whites could live comfortably with that absurdity. How could white Christians reconcile the "strange fruit" they hung on southern trees with the "strange fruit" Romans hung on the cross at Golgotha? How could they reconcile the "pastoral scene of the gallant South" with "the bulging eyes and twisted mouth," the contrast between the "scent of magnolia sweet and fresh" and "the sudden smell of burning flesh"? How could the white Christian community reconcile "blood on the leaves and blood at the root" with the blood on their consciences? "Here is a fruit for the crows to pluck" like "the dogs beneath the cross"[40] in Jerusalem when Jesus was crucified. "Here is a strange and bitter crop."

First sung in 1939 at the Café Society, the newly integrated nightclub in New York, Billie Holiday's version of "Strange Fruit," as Farah Jasmine Griffin put it, "helped to establish and maintain a political consciousness among black people about lynching." Griffin contends that Lady Day, as Holiday was called, "built upon the work of anti-lynching activists such as Ida B. Wells by assuring that the issue remained at the forefront of black American consciousness." "In 'Strange Fruit,'" writes Griffin in a deeply moving meditation, "Holiday left us a powerful legacy and enduring song of protest against racial violence—protest that has been cited by each succeeding generation of black singers to follow her from Nina Simone to Abbey Lincoln to Cassandra Wilson and Dee Dee Bridgewater."[41] Each one sang "Strange Fruit" in a style of her own, but in the musical and protest tradition defined by Holiday.

With vivid and horrific imagery, deep and disturbing emotions, Billie Holiday's rendition of "Strange Fruit" forced white listeners to wrestle with the violent truth of white supremacy. No white person could listen to Billie's "Strange Fruit" without feeling indicted and exposed by the sound of truth and contempt in her voice. She made whites look at the brutality they wanted to forget. That was why "Strange Fruit" was often banned from many radio stations and several clubs would not let Billie sing it, especially when whites walked out, claiming that it was not entertainment. Those who stayed to listen were eerily quiet as Billie told the story of lynching in the South. Billie's record company, Columbia, refused to record it, fearing that the South would boycott them.

There is some debate whether Billie understood the lyrics of "Strange Fruit" when they were first given to her—with mostly white and black scholars lining up on opposite sides of the issue. But what is clear is that "Strange Fruit" became Billie's song, and she sang it as if she wrote it for those lost on the lynching trees in the South. How much intelligence does a black person need to understand what "black bodies swinging in the Southern breeze" means? The lynching of African Americans was too widespread in the 1930s and the NAACP's efforts to get federal anti-lynching legislation enacted were too well known (especially in the black community) for any black to be ignorant of "the bulging eyes and the twisted mouth" and "the sudden smell of burning flesh." With Billie Holiday traveling in the South with the Artie Shaw band and experiencing many insults and threats against her life, there was no way she could have failed to understand the lyrics in "Strange Fruit." It became her signature song, the song with which she often closed her set. But in a larger sense, her singing of "Strange Fruit," as Farah Griffin puts it, "has become an indelible part of the African American cultural landscape." Griffin calls Holiday a "musical genius" "whose voice embodies the struggles of black Americans."[42] She is our Lady, our musical icon, whose meaning transcends the suffering this racist society inflicted on her.

Although Billie, unlike most black musical artists, did not develop her craft in a black church, her style draws upon the spirit of the black religious experience—the spirituals, blues, jazz, and gospel, creating a sound uniquely her own. Billie's "Strange Fruit" elicits reverence for the dead from blacks and terrible guilt from whites who still reap privileges from the society that lynching created. When blacks hear Lady Day sing "Strange Fruit," they usually become silent and angry. It is difficult to listen to Lady's haunted and raspy voice without getting mad enough to want to hurt some white people, "to hit them upside their head" for what their ancestors did to black people.

Holiday's singing and recording of "Strange Fruit" in 1939 was a cultural event that raised the political consciousness of musicians and their community—a consciousness that would hit its high-water mark with Nina Simone's "Mississippi Goddam" and Marvin Gaye's "What's Goin' On?" "When Holiday recorded it," the drummer Max Roach said, "it was more than revolutionary." Meeropol said Holiday "gave a startling, most dramatic and effective interpretation . . . which could jolt an audience out of its complacency anywhere. . . . Billie Holiday's styling of the song was incomparable and filled with bitterness and the shocking quality I had hoped the song would have." Lady's pianist Mal

Waldron said, "It's like rubbing people's noses in their own shit," which Billie did with contempt and defiance.

It was best not to say anything as Billie sang "Strange Fruit," because the song often "made her sick to perform it." "I have to sing it," she said, because "Fruit goes a long way in telling how they mistreat Negroes down South." When Maya Angelou's twelve-year-old son, Guy, once interrupted her singing to ask, "What's a pastoral scene, Miss Holiday?" "her face became cruel" and "her voice was scornful." "It means when the crackers are killing the niggers." Holiday said with a "thrust of rage," repelling the boy and stunning her. "It means when they take a little nigger like you and snatch off his nuts and shove them down his god-dam throat. That's what it means." Billie could be mean because, as jazz critic Ralph Gleason put it, she "was a sort of living lyric to the song 'Strange Fruit,' hanging, not on a poplar tree, but on the limbs of life itself."[43]

It was fitting for a Jew to write this great protest song about "burning flesh" because the burning black bodies on the American landscape prefigured the burning bodies of Jews at Auschwitz and Buchenwald. "Strange Fruit" was also "an early cry for civil rights," a prophetic call for blacks to take up the cross of black freedom because nobody was going carry it for them. Without Billie's voice, "Strange Fruit" would hardly be remembered. Abel Meeropol wrote "Strange Fruit," but it really belonged to Billie Holiday, who made the song her own and infused blacks with a militant opposition to white supremacy that found expression in the modern Civil Rights and Black Power movements.

Just as the old slave spiritual "Were You There?" placed black Christians at the foot of Jesus' cross, "Strange Fruit" put them at the foot of the lynching tree. Both songs created a dark and somber mood. One was sung in church and the other in a night-club, but both addressed the deep-down hurt that blacks felt and gave them a way to deal with it. As the great theologian

Howard Thurman said, "[a person] has to handle . . . suffering or be handled by it."[44] Black people did not let trouble handle them, and that was why they made music. In the words of Ralph Ellison, "For the art—the blues, the spirituals, the jazz, the dance—was what we had in place of freedom."[45] Both the blues and the spirituals spoke about the tragic and the comic, sorrow and joy simultaneously.

The struggle to *survive* in a white supremacist society was a full-time occupation for black people. But how to survive with one's *dignity* intact—that was the challenge. Women had the additional challenge of assuring not just their own survival but also the survival of their families. Yet, they too aspired for more, for a certain "quality of life,"[46] as womanist theologian Delores Williams has insisted. Black men seemed less able to navigate the complex relationship between survival and dignity in the violent patriarchal South. Just out of slavery, they wanted to be men, just like white males—providing economic support and physical protection for women and children—but they were not permitted to do so. As a result, black men tended either toward violence, which often placed them on lynching trees, or toward passivity, which led to the loss of dignity: few other options were available.

I remember my father and mother trying to strike the right balance between survival and dignity in rural Arkansas during the 1940s and '50s. My mother was much better at striking the right balance than my father, who refused to be intimidated and who was determined to support his family as well or better than the average white man. With only a sixth-grade education, that was no easy feat. As children, my two brothers and I never worried about our mother's survival or her physical safety, but we often worried about our father—whether whites had waylaid him just for their amusement, or whether he might have been involved in a car accident with a white person. Our mother was vigilant and knew whom to contact about his safety. In a patriarchal white society, defined by lynching and state-sponsored executions, it was not easy for any black to survive with dignity, especially black men. Scholars who criticize blacks for their "otherworldly" religion should look a little deeper into the ways blacks resisted the demonic in their midst.

Yet, although black women's struggles for survival might have been somewhat different from those of men, they were not any easier. Although men, such as W. E. B. Du Bois, James Weldon Johnson, and Walter White, were more prominent in public leadership roles in the anti-lynching movement, women were far more active at the grassroots level in churches, in the NAACP, and other male-led organizations. Black women also created their own organizations in which they gained leadership skills, defending their community against vigilante violence. In all of the churches, women formed organizations where they were the leaders. In 1895, women organized nationally as the National Association of Colored Women (NACW), and made lynching their issue. They linked the lynching of black men with the rape of black women, showing the blatant hypocrisy of those who identified rape as a "crime worse than death" but were not outraged when white men raped black women.

Initially, black women in the NACW, the churches, the NAACP, and other organizations were less militant than Ida B. Wells and even pushed her to the margins of their activities. Many were closer to Booker T. Washington, who advised accommodation instead of protest. Accordingly, black club women focused on the politics of respectability and racial uplift, with the motto "lifting as we climb." They believed that if they presented a respectable image of black womanhood the whole race would benefit. "Only the BLACK WOMAN can say," wrote Anna Julia Cooper, "'when and where I enter . . . then and there the whole Negro race enters with me.'"[47]

Yet black women soon found that such accommodation "failed to protect African Americans from the wave of violence that surged across the nation during the early twentieth century."[48] After World War I they began adopting protest tactics quite similar to Wells. Anna Julia Cooper, Mary Church Terrell, Mary McLeod Bethune, Nannie Helen Burroughs and others participated in the NAACP's campaign for federal anti-lynching legislation, testified before Congress, raised most of the money for the Anti-Lynching Fund, and led speaking campaigns against lynching that would keep the issue constantly before the American public. They appealed to the white public, especially women, to join with the black community in opposition against mob violence. "The negro women of the South," Charlotte Hawkins Brown told white women, "lay everything that happens to the members of her race at the door of the Southern white woman.... We all feel that you can control your men. We feel that so far as lynching is concerned that, if the white woman would take hold of the situation, that lynching would be stopped...."[49]

A few white women and men accepted the challenge of opposing lynching, but they were careful not to violate the separation of the races. The Commission of Interracial Cooperation (CIC) was organized in 1919 and the Association of Southern Women for the Prevention of Lynching (ASWPL) in 1930. Both organizations were comprised of white southern moderates who rejected rape as the justification for lynching and sought to convince whites that lynching had no place in a civilized society. "The real victim in the crime of lynching," the Georgia chapter of the ASWPL stated in their official declaration, "is not the person done to death, but constituted and regularly established government." The CIC's Southern Commission on the Study of Lynching made a similar declaration: "Lynching makes a mockery of courts and citizenship. The state itself has been lynched."[50] Thus, whites focused on the anarchy that lynching created for whites. They hardly said an adequate word about the devastating effect of the lynching atrocity in the black community.

Like Wells and other black Christians, club women viewed

white Christianity as a contradiction of true Christian identity, largely because of its support of segregation and lynching.
"Would to God that it were," complained the National Baptist
leader Nellie Burroughs, when she rejected America's Christian
identity, "but it is the most lawless and desperately wicked nation
on the globe." Lynching, she insisted, was "no superficial thing . . .
it is in the blood of the nation. And the process of eliminating it
will be difficult and long."[51]

Though Nellie Burroughs was a deeply committed Christian, she, like many black women leaders before and after, urged
blacks to resist the temptation of spiritual passivity, as if God
would liberate them without their own participation. Speaking
in 1933 on the theme "What Must the Negro Do to be Saved?"
at Bethel A.M.E. Church in Washington, DC, she said: "Don't
wait for deliverers. . . . There are no deliverers. . . . The Negro
must serve notice to the world that he is ready to die for justice. . . . We are a race on this continent that can work out its own
salvation." Therefore, she urged, "Work as if all depends upon
you. Pray as if all depends upon God."[52]

There was no linking of the cross and the lynching tree among
black club women. Like Wells, they focused their concern on
fighting lynching and achieving full equality for all black people.
While men talked, women walked and got things done. Although
the civil rights movement was headed primarily by male leaders
(such as Martin Luther King Jr., Ralph Abernathy, Andy Young,
and others), there never would have been a black freedom movement without the courageous work of women—such as Fannie
Lou Hamer, Jo Anne Robinson, Ella Baker, Septima Clark, and
many more. "Women were the spine of our movement," Andy
Young said. "It was women going door to door, speaking with
their neighbors, meeting in voter-registration together, organiz-
ing through their churches, that gave the vital momentum and
energy to the movement, that made it a mass movement."[53] That
was why Nellie Burroughs said, "The men ought to get down on

their knees to Negro women," who "made possible all we have around us—church, home, school, business,"[54] and most importantly the civil rights movement.

While it has often been said that the civil rights movement was a religious movement and led by male ministers, that was only partly true. The civil rights movement was also a women's movement. Women started it ("If Rosa Parks had not sat down, Martin Luther King Jr. would not have stood up"), sustained it through difficult times, and made religion its central focus through song—giving hope that "we shall overcome," because, as the great Ella Baker said, "we who believe in freedom shall not rest until it comes." Where there is hope, there is God—that divine presence that prevents despair and empowers poor people to resist. Nowhere were hope and resistance more abundant than among women. Every black male minister knows that he would have no church without the women who make up more than 80 percent of the membership. The same was true of the civil rights movement, whose energy was defined by its religious focus, expressed in prayer and song.

> Walk with me, my Lord, walk with me
> Walk with me, my Lord, walk with me
> While I'm on this tedious journey
> I want Jesus to walk with me.

"Actions speak louder than words" is a well-known saying in the black Christian community. Through their actions, women expressed the conviction that their nonviolent suffering could save not only the black community from white supremacy but even save America from its worst self.

When Fannie Lou Hamer, a Mississippi sharecropper who became a great civil rights heroine, sought to inspire blacks to risk their lives for justice in Mississippi, she turned to the cross and embellished it with her religious imagination. She told blacks who were too afraid to fight for their rights: "When Simon Cyrene was helping Christ to bear his cross up the hill, [Simon] said: 'Must Jesus bear the cross alone and all the world go free? No, there's a cross for everyone and there's a cross for me. This consecrated cross I'll bear, till death shall set me free. And then go home a crown to wear, for there's a crown for me.' "[55] Like other poor blacks, Hamer had no access to sophisticated biblical studies, and thus used a familiar evangelical hymn, popular in the black churches, to make her point about our responsibility to become an agent of change. Her hermeneutics were shaped by the spirituals and the tradition of gospel hymns and her involvement in the black freedom struggle. Yet thousands of poor blacks were inspired by her reflection and followed her throughout Mississippi, many to endure jail, beatings, and even death. Where is a similar example of motivation and courage among religion and theology professors and students in our institutions of higher learning?

Yet Hamer did not embrace the cross uncritically. She was aware of its dangers. "We have always been taught," she said, "that we had to suffer as Christ suffered. He was killed and all of his followers were persecuted. But I think in terms of what David had to do. David was a shepherd boy. He was giving service to his people. But it came a time in his life when he had to slay Goliath."[56] As Bernice Johnson Reagon writes, "Fannie Lou Hamer placed Jesus where his experiences, as [interpreted] through the traditions of the Black Church, could be used in the freedom struggle." She embraced the cross and "brought its full force to bear on the work she had to do."[57] Hamer understood the religious meaning of the cross because she interpreted it in the context of being beaten and shot at and nearly lynched for her civil rights work. But no amount of affliction could stop her resistance work. "They whipped her body but they did not whip her soul."[58] The cross gave her courage to keep on fighting what womanist scholar Angela Sims, reflecting on the "ethical complications of lynching," calls "an ethics of resilience."[59] The truth of what she said about Jesus was defined by its *practical* results.

And if today, like Fannie Lou Hamer, "I cling to the old rugged cross," it is because I have seen with my own eyes how that symbol empowered black people to stand up and become agents of change for their freedom.

After telling the country and the world (at the 1964 Democratic National Convention in Atlantic City) about her attempts to register and vote and the vicious beating that followed in a Mississippi jail, Fannie Lou Hamer asked the poignant question that stirred the conscience of most Americans watching her speak over live television: "Is this America?" Her power and eloquence captivated the nation. She knew that even liberal whites could not deny the truth about white supremacy in America. Yet, they did not want to hear that truth, the fact that America's democracy is hypocrisy in the lives of its black population. President Lyndon Johnson, a Texan, knew all too well the hard truth of Hamer's testimony. Immediately, after seeing and hearing her speak, he called a news conference in order to get that "illiterate woman" off live television.[60]

The black religious experience gave Mrs. Hamer the spiritual power to resist, a power incarnated in many blacks that I've seen throughout the South during my childhood. It was the kind of "Blessed Assurance" that they believed could come only from Jesus' cross, from having been "washed in his blood." "I question America," Mrs. Hamer said to millions of Americans as she ended her address. "Is this America, the land of the free and the home of the brave, where we have to sleep with our telephones off the hooks because our lives be threatened daily because we want to live as decent human beings, in America?"[61] The answer to Fannie Lou Hamer's question was a paradoxical yes and no. Yes, in the sense that this was the America that blacks had experienced, but no, in the sense that we should not accept this America; we would not and could not be satisfied until justice was made a reality in the land. We intended to make America the America it was supposed to be, or die trying.

Langston Hughes expressed the feelings of all blacks when he said back in 1936,

> Let America be America again.
> Let it be the dream it used to be.
> Let it be the pioneer on the plain
> Seeking a home where he himself is free.
>
> (America never was America to me.) . . .
>
> O, yes,
> I say it plain,
> America never was America to me,
> And yet I swear this oath—America will be![62]

"To redeem the soul of America"—to make America a land where "opportunity is real, and life is free"—was the motto of the civil rights movement, as defined by Martin Luther King Jr., the Southern Christian Leadership Conference, the Congress of Racial Equality, and the Student Nonviolent Coordinating Committee, the organization in which Fannie Lou Hamer was an active participant. Women in all the civil rights organizations embodied in their lives the faith that God was in the black freedom movement, redeeming America through nonviolent suffering. "We stood up," a black woman participant said. "Me and God stood up." As the oral historian Charles Payne put it, "Faith in the Lord made it easier to have faith in the possibility of social change. . . . The Civil Rights Movement [was] a sign that God was stirring."[63]

Emile Durkheim's interpretation of religion provides an important insight into its meaning for black women: "The believer who has communicated with his [or her] god is not merely a man [or woman] who sees new truths of which the unbeliever is ignorant; he [or she] is a man [or woman] who is *stronger*. He [or she] feels within him [or her] more force, either to endure the trials of existence, or to conquer them."[64] Black women endured and conquered. They transformed America through their suffering.

To say that black women "transformed America through their suffering" is not intended to valorize their suffering or suggest that God willed it. I intend only to acknowledge the great sacrifice my mother and other black women made to ensure a better future for their children and their community. Like Jesus, black women (as well as men) sacrificed their lives for others, especially their children, as in the case of Laura Nelson, who was lynched for defending her fourteen-year-old son, accused of stealing meat.[65] Dying for others was not unusual for black women, and they taught their sons and daughters to give back to the community, to give even their lives for freedom. Despite the dangers, they believed Jesus, their protector and friend, would walk with them and would see them through hard trials.

Even when black women did not speak explicitly in religious terms, one could feel the spirituality in their words, giving them courage in the face of great danger. Mary Dora Jones, at the risk of her life and threats to burn down her home, took in seven blacks and four whites during the Freedom Summer of 1964 in Marks, Mississippi. "Some of the black folks got the news that they were gonna burn it down," she reflected. "My neighbors was afraid of gettin' killed. People standin' behind buildin's, peepin' out behind the buildin's, to see what's goin' on. So I just told 'em, 'Dyin' is all right. Ain't but one thing 'bout dyin'. That's make sho' you right, cause you gon' die anyway.' . . . If they burnt it down, it was just a house burn down. . . ."[66] Her courage was based on her faith.

When I was young, I heard this faith expressed at home from my mother and at Macedonia A.M.E. Church from the women who sang and prayed and talked about Jesus and how you could take your burdens and leave them at the foot of Jesus' cross. "It ain't enough to talk about God," I often heard the women of Macedonia say, "you've got to feel God moving on the altar of your heart."[67] The black church has always been comprised mostly of male leadership in the pulpit and mostly women in the pew. This means that the faith of the church is defined by women who, through the spirituals, hymns, and gospel songs, placed the crucified Jesus at the center of their faith. The cross sustained them—not *for* suffering but in their resistance to it.

The faith that "God will take care of you" runs deep in the history of the African American community, from the time when Harriet Tubman led slaves to freedom to the activities of Ida B. Wells, Nellie Burroughs, and Fannie Lou Hamer. When young, northern, mostly white students began to debate whether God exists, as they had heard it discussed in their university philosophy classes, Fannie Lou Hamer was quick to respond: "Don't talk to me about atheism. If God wants to start a movement, then hooray for God."[68]

It was black women's faith in the God of Jesus that gave them the courage to face great danger in the black freedom movement. No one was more courageous than Fannie Lou Hamer. She was beaten severely and shot at many times, but she faced it all, confident that God was with her and would bring her through the difficulties she encountered fighting for freedom. "I guess if I'd had a little sense, I'd been a little scared," she said reflecting back. But "the only thing they could do to me was kill me and it seemed like they'd been trying to do that a little bit at a time ever since I could remember."[69]

Black women's faith empowered them to transform America, not just for black people but for all Americans, including white men. They redeemed America through nonviolent suffering, which they, along with Martin Luther King Jr. and others, identified with Jesus' invitation: "If any want to become my followers let them deny themselves and take up their cross and follow me" (Mk 8:34). Like Martin Luther King Jr., black women throughout African American history not only preached the cross but bore it, and sometimes died on it.

Though, for Martin King, nonviolence was a matter of faith, he did accept into the movement young people like Stokely Carmichael and James Forman, for whom it was only a matter of strategy. Most of these young men were in SNCC, which took up the call for Black Power, emphasizing self-defense and the cultural affirmation of blackness. Black Power also challenged young African American ministers to develop an understanding of the Christian gospel that would empower African Americans to affirm their *black* and *Christian* identity. How could one be black and Christian at the same time if the public identity of the Christian faith was identified with white supremacy? Black liberation theology emerged out of black people's struggle with nonviolence (Christianity) and self-defense (Black Power). This was basically a struggle among black men in the movement who were Christian ministers and those who were not. To the young black men nonviolence seemed weak and passive, while they yearned to be strong and active. To speak of nonviolence in a Christian context was to speak of Jesus' cross, which meant suffering without fighting back violently.

Nearly twenty years after the civil rights movement, Delores Williams, a womanist theologian, challenged interpretations of the Christian faith that placed the cross at the center. In her important book, *Sisters in the Wilderness*, and in her widely read essay "Black Women's Surrogacy Experience and the Christian Notion of Redemption," Williams, now the Paul Tillich Emeritus Professor of Theology and Culture at Union Theological Seminary in New York, developed a persuasive critique of the idea of redemptive suffering. She rejected the view common in classic texts of the Western theological tradition as well as in the preaching in African American churches that Jesus accomplished human salvation by dying in our place. According to Williams, Jesus did not come to save us through his death on the cross but rather he "came to show redemption through a perfect *ministerial* vision of righting relationships."[70] She argued that if Jesus were a surrogate, then his gospel encourages black women to accept their surrogacy roles as well—suffering for others as Jesus did on the cross. But if the salvation that Jesus brought could be separated from surrogacy, then black women were free to reject it too.

I accept Delores Williams's rejection of theories of atonement as found in the Western theological tradition and in the uncritical proclamation of the cross in many black churches. I find nothing redemptive about suffering in itself. The gospel of Jesus is not a rational concept to be explained in a theory of salvation, but a story about God's presence in Jesus' solidarity with the oppressed, which led to his death on the cross. What is redemptive is the faith that God snatches victory out of defeat, life out of death, and hope out of despair, as revealed in the biblical and black proclamation of Jesus' resurrection.

> Weep no more, Marta,
> Weep no more, Mary,
> Jesus rise from de dead,
> Happy Morning.

But in the end I am in closer agreement with other womanist theologians like Shawn Copeland, associate professor of theology at Boston College, JoAnne Terrell, associate professor of ethics and theology at Chicago Theological Seminary, and Jacquelyn Grant, professor of theology at the Interdenominational Theological Center (Atlanta, Georgia), who view the cross as central to the Christian faith, especially in African American communities. Interpreting the spirituals in "'Wading through Many Sorrows': Toward a Theology of Suffering in Womanist Perspective," Copeland writes,

> If the makers of the spirituals gloried in singing of the cross of Jesus, it was not because they were masochistic and enjoyed suffering. Rather, the enslaved Africans sang because they saw on the rugged wooden planks One who had endured

what was their daily portion. The cross was treasured because it enthroned the One who went all the way with them and for them. The enslaved African sang because they saw the results of the cross—triumph over the principalities and powers of death, triumph over evil in this world.

In concluding her reflection on the cross and suffering, Copeland states that the slaves liberated the cross from its abuse by whites. "By their very suffering and privation," she writes, "black women under chattel slavery freed the cross of Christ. Their steadfast commitment honored the cross and the One who died for all and redeemed it from Christianity's vulgar misuse."[71]

The roots of my perspective on the cross are found in the lives and teachings of black women (and men) at Macedonia A. M. E. Church, other black churches in Arkansas and the United States, and in the history of black resistance against white supremacy, especially in the civil rights and Black Power movements. In *Black Theology and Black Power* and all the texts that followed, including this one, I begin and end my theological reflections in the social context of black people's struggle for justice. The cross is the burden we must bear in order to attain freedom.

We cannot separate the cross from the Christian gospel as found in the story of Jesus and as lived and understood in the African American Christian community. The resurrected Lord was the crucified Lord. Whatever we think about the meaning of the cross for black women should arise out of their experience of fighting for justice, especially as seen in their collective lives and struggles in the civil rights movement. God's salvation is a liberating event in the lives of all who are struggling for survival and dignity in a world bent on denying their humanity.

Oh Mary, don't you weep, don't you moan,
Oh Mary, don't you weep, don't you moan,

Pharaoh's army got drownded,
Oh Mary, don't you weep.

Legacies of the Cross and the Lynching Tree

They are crucifying again the Son of God and are holding him in contempt.

—Hebrews 6:6

Remember those who are in prison, as though you were there in prison with them, those who are being tortured as though you yourselves were being tortured.

—Hebrews 13:3

The law enforcements 'n' highway patrol was altogether up there—you name 'em, they was there. I wasn't afraid. Because I know I had somebody there who was on my side. And that was Jesus; he was able to take care of me. That's who I can depend on and put my trust in. You can't trust white people; they will fail you. You can't trust black people, they will fail you. Even mother, father, brother or sister may fail you. But Jesus won't fail you. You can trust Jesus. He's my all.

—Bee Jenkins in Holmes County, Mississippi[1]

Perhaps nothing about the history of mob violence in the United States is more surprising than how quickly an understanding of the full horror of lynching has receded from the nation's collective historical memory.

—W. Fitzhugh Brundage[2]

Life is not possible without an opening toward the transcendent; in other words, human beings cannot live in chaos. Once contact with the transcendent is lost, existence in the world ceases to be possible. . . .
                                                                        —Mircea Eliade.[3]

I end this reflection as I began—acknowledging that my interest in the cross and the lynching tree stems from my identity as a black person and a Christian struggling to find justice in America today.

As a child, I remember worrying about my father when he did not come home from work at the usual time in the evening. My brothers and I would watch anxiously out the window, hoping that the lights from every vehicle would be the lights from his pick-up truck. My mother worried too, but she tried to assure us that "God would protect Daddy from any harm that whites could do to him" and that he would arrive home soon. I wanted to believe that, but I had heard too much about white people killing black people to believe what she said without deep questioning. When my father would finally make it home safely, I would run and jump into his arms, happy as I could be. For that moment, at least, my faith was renewed.

My wrestling with faith began in childhood. Belief in a good and just God was no easy matter for any black person living in the so-called Christian South. The first essay I wrote in college was, "Why Do People Suffer?" In graduate school, I deepened that reflection, and I have thought about suffering all my life, especially when my wife, the love of my life, died of breast cancer at thirty-six.

Such personal suffering challenges faith, but social suffering, which comes from human hate, challenges it even more. White supremacy tears faith to pieces and turns the heart away from God. The more I believed in God, the harder it became to sustain any faith. White supremacy was so pervasive that everywhere I went it was there staring me in the face—in the North as well as the South. If God loves black people, why then do we suffer so much? That was my question as a child; that is still my question.

The struggle to make sense of being *black* and *Christian* in white America has motivated all my work as a theologian, starting in June of 1968, two months after Martin King's assassination, when I began to write *Black Theology and Black Power*. While writing that book in my brother's church (Union A.M.E. in Little Rock, Arkansas), a place of worship where blacks regularly "caught the spirit," something happened that I can't explain. It seemed as if a transcendent voice were speaking to me through the scriptures and the medium of African American history and culture, reminding me that God's liberation of the poor is the primary theme of Jesus' gospel.

Consumed by a passion to express myself about the liberating power of the black religious experience, I continued to write and speak about this spiritual revolution erupting in the cultural and political contexts of the African American community. This message of liberation was "something like a burning fire shut up in my bones," to use the language of Jeremiah; "I [was] weary with holding it in, and I [could not]" (Jer 20:9). All of my work since that first book has involved an effort to relate the gospel and the black experience—the experience of oppression as well as the struggle to find liberation and meaning. Inevitably, it has led to these reflections on the cross and the lynching tree: the essential symbol of Christianity and the quintessential emblem of black suffering.

To live meaningfully, we must see light beyond the darkness. As Mircea Eliade put it, "Life is not possible without an opening toward the transcendent." The lynching era was the Heart of Darkness for the African American community. It was a time when fragments of meaning were hard to find. Some found meaning in the blues and others in collective political resistance, but for many people it was religion that helped them to look beyond their tragic situation to a time when they would "cross the river of Jordan," "lay down dat heavy load," and "walk in Jerusalem just like John."

The Christian gospel is God's message of liberation in an unredeemed and tortured world. As such, it is a transcendent reality that lifts our spirits to a world far removed from the suffering of this one. It is an eschatological vision, an experience of transfiguration, such as Jesus experienced at his Baptism (Mk 1:9-11) or on Mt. Tabor (Mk 9:2-8), just before he set out on the road to Jerusalem, the road that led to Calvary. Paul had such a vision—"a light from heaven"—as he traveled the road to Damascus (Acts 9:3). Malcolm X, while in prison, had a vision of God, and so too did Martin King hear God speaking to him in his kitchen at a moment of crisis during the Montgomery bus boycott. For all four, the revelatory moment in their lives helped to prepare them to face their deaths, sustained by the conviction that this was not the end but the beginning of a new life of meaning. To paraphrase Eliade, once contact with the transcendent is found, a new existence in the world becomes possible.

And yet the Christian gospel is more than a transcendent reality, more than "going to heaven when I die, to shout salvation as I fly." It is also an immanent reality—a powerful liberating presence among the poor right *now* in their midst, "building them up where they are torn down and propping them up on every leaning side." The gospel is found wherever poor people struggle for justice, fighting for their right to life, liberty, and the pursuit of happiness. Bee Jenkins's claims that "Jesus won't fail you" was made in the heat of the struggle for civil rights in Mississippi, and such faith gave her strength and courage to fight for justice against overwhelming odds. Without concrete signs of divine presence in the lives of the poor, the gospel becomes simply an opiate; rather than liberating the powerless from humiliation and suffering, the gospel becomes a drug that helps them adjust to this world by looking for "pie in the sky."

And so the transcendent and the immanent, heaven and earth, must be held together in critical, dialectical tension, each one correcting the limits of the other. The gospel is *in* the world, but it is not *of* the world; that is, it can be seen in the black freedom movement, but it is much more than what we see in our struggles for justice. God's word is *paradoxical,* or, as the old untutored black preacher used to say, "inscrutable," a mystery that one can neither control nor fully understand. It is here and not here, revealed and hidden at the same time. "Truly, you are a God who hides himself, O God of Israel, the Savior" (Isa 45:15).

Nowhere is that paradox, that "inscrutability," more evident than in the cross. A symbol of death and defeat, God turned it into a sign of liberation and new life. The cross is the most empowering symbol of God's loving solidarity with the "least of these," the unwanted in society who suffer daily from great injustices. Christians must face the cross as the terrible tragedy it was and discover in it, through faith and repentance, the liberating joy of eternal salvation.

But we cannot find liberating joy in the cross by spiritualizing it, by taking away its message of justice in the midst of powerlessness, suffering, and death. The cross, as a locus of divine revelation, is not good news for the powerful, for those who are comfortable with the way things are, or for anyone whose understanding of religion is aligned with power. The religious authorities of Jesus' time were threatened by his teachings about the reign of God's justice and love, and the state authorities executed him as an insurrectionist—one who "perverts the nation" and "stirs up the people" (Lk 23:2, 5). Even Jesus' disciples misunderstood his teachings "that the Son of Man must undergo great suffering, and be rejected," "mocked and flogged and crucified" (Mk 8:31; Mt 20:19). They slept through his agony in the Garden (Mk 14:32), and deserted him when he was arrested, tortured, and crucified. One disciple betrayed him and another denied him, because a suffering Messiah was not the one they expected. "We had hoped that he was the one to redeem Israel" (Lk 24:21).

This reversal of expectations and conventional values is the unmistakable theme of the gospel. "What is prized by human beings is an abomination in the sight of God" (Lk 16:15). "All who exalt themselves will be humbled, but all who humble themselves will be exalted" (Lk 18:14). This "transvaluation of values," as Niebuhr put it, finds its apotheosis in the cross. "In Jesus' cross God took up the existence of a slave and died the slave's death on the tree of martyrdom" (Phil 2:8). The cross, in Martin Hengel's words, points to God's loving solidarity with the "unspeakable suffering of those who are tortured," and "put to death by human cruelty. . . . In the person and fate of the one man Jesus of Nazareth this saving solidarity of God with [the oppressed] is given its historical and physical form."[4] The cross," writes Dorothy A. Lee-Pollard, "reveals where God's kingdom is to be found—not among the powerful or even the religious, but in the midst of powerlessness, suffering and death."[5] Bonhoeffer was right: "The Bible directs [us] to God's powerlessness and suffering. Only a suffering God can help."[6]

Great preachers preach the cross as the heart of the Christian message. The Apostle Paul preached the cross and transformed a Jewish sect into a faith for the world. Martin Luther preached the cross and started the Protestant Reformation. Karl Barth preached the cross and created a Copernican revolution in European theology. Reinhold Niebuhr preached the cross and developed a creative perspective on Christian social ethics in America. Fannie Lou Hamer sang and preached the cross and ignited a grassroots revolution in Mississippi. Martin Luther King Jr. preached the cross and transformed the social and political life in America, pointing to an American dream of justice, for which he gave his life.

One has to have a powerful religious imagination to see redemption in the cross, to discover life in death and hope in tragedy. What kind of salvation is that? No human language can fully describe what salvation through the cross means. Salvation through the cross is a mystery and can only be apprehended through faith, repentance, and humility. The cross is an "opening to the transcendent" for the poor who have nowhere else to turn—that transcendence of the spirit that no one can take away, no matter what they do. Salvation is broken spirits being healed, voiceless people speaking out, and black people empowered to love their own blackness.

And yet another type of imagination is necessary—the imagination to relate the message of the cross to one's own social reality, to see that "They are crucifying again the Son of God" (Heb 6:6). Both Jesus and blacks were "strange fruit." Theologically speaking, Jesus was the "first lynchee," who foreshadowed all the lynched black bodies on American soil. He was crucified by the same principalities and powers that lynched black people in America. Because God was present with Jesus on the cross and thereby refused to let Satan and death have the last word about his meaning, God was also present at every lynching in the United States. God saw what whites did to innocent and helpless blacks and claimed their suffering as God's own. God transformed lynched black bodies into the recrucified body of Christ. *Every time a white mob lynched a black person, they lynched Jesus.* The lynching tree is the cross in America. When American Christians realize that they can meet Jesus only in the crucified bodies in our midst, they will encounter the real scandal of the cross.

God must therefore know in a special way what poor blacks are suffering in America because God's son was lynched in Jerusalem. Jesus and other subject people suffered punishment under the Roman Empire as blacks suffered in the United States. He was tortured and humiliated like blacks. What are we to make of the striking similarities between the brutality in Rome and cruelty in America? What is most ironic is that the white lynchers of blacks in America were not regarded as criminals; like Jesus, blacks were the criminals and insurrectionists. The lynchers were the "good citizens" who often did not even bother to hide their identities. They claimed to be acting as citizens and Christians as they crucified blacks in the same manner as the Romans lynched Jesus. It is even more ironic that black people embraced the Christian cross that whites used to murder them. That was truly a profound inversion of meaning.

White theologians in the past century have written thousands of books about Jesus' cross without remarking on the analogy between the crucifixion of Jesus and the lynching of black people. One must suppose that in order to feel comfortable in the Christian faith, whites needed theologians to interpret the gospel in a way that would not require them to acknowledge white supremacy as America's great sin. Churches, seminaries, and theological academies separated Christian identity from the horrendous violence committed against black people. Whites could claim a Christian identity without feeling the need to oppose slavery, segregation, and lynching as a contradiction of the gospel for America. Whether we speak of Jonathan Edwards, Walter Rauschenbusch, or Reinhold Niebuhr as America's greatest theologian, none of them made the rejection of white supremacy central to their understanding of the gospel. Reinhold Niebuhr could write and preach about the cross with profound theological imagination and say nothing of how the violence of white supremacy invalidated the faith of white churches. It takes a lot of theological blindness to do that, especially since the vigilantes were white Christians who claimed to worship the Jew lynched in Jerusalem.

What is invisible to white Christians and their theologians is inescapable to black people. The cross is a reminder that the world is fraught with many contradictions—many lynching trees. We cannot forget the terror of the lynching tree no matter how hard we try. It is buried deep in the living memory and psychology of the black experience in America. We can go to churches and celebrate our religious heritage, but the tragic memory of the black holocaust in America's history is still waiting to find theological meaning. When black people sing about Jesus' cross, they often think of black lives lost to the lynching tree. Through their own experience of suffering, African Americans have often found themselves existentially at the foot of Jesus' cross, experiencing his fate, believing that only Jesus understands their lot because he suffered as they have.

> Look-a how dey done my Lord,
> Look-a how they done my Lord,
> Look-a how dey done my Lord,
> Oh, look-a how dey done my Lord,
> Done my Lord, done my Lord,
> Done my Lord, done my Lord.

"Dey carry him to Calvary and dey licked him wid violence." "Wasn't that a pity and a shame."

To understand what the cross means in America, we need to take a look at the lynching tree in this nation's history—that "strange and bitter crop" that Billie Holiday would not let us forget. The lynched black victim experienced the same fate as the crucified Christ and thus became the most potent symbol for understanding the true meaning of the salvation achieved through "God on the Cross." Nietzsche was right: *Christianity is a religion of slaves.* God became a slave in Jesus and thereby liberated slaves from being determined by their social condition.

The real scandal of the gospel is this: humanity's salvation is revealed in the cross of the condemned criminal Jesus, and humanity's salvation is available *only* through our solidarity with the crucified people in our midst. Faith that emerged out of the scandal of the cross is not a faith of intellectuals or elites of any sort. This is the faith of abused and scandalized people—the losers and the down and out. It was this faith that gave blacks the strength and courage to hope, "to keep on keeping on," struggling against the odds, with what Paul Tillich called "the courage to be."[7]

The cross and the lynching tree interpret each other. Both were public spectacles, shameful events, instruments of punishment reserved for the most despised people in society. Any genuine theology and any genuine preaching of the Christian gospel must be measured against the test of the scandal of the cross and the lynching tree. "Jesus did not die a gentle death like Socrates, with his cup of hemlock. . . . Rather, he died like a [lynched black victim] or a common [black] criminal in torment, on the tree of shame."[8] The crowd's shout "Crucify him!" (Mk 15:14) anticipated the white mob's shout "Lynch him!" Jesus' agonizing final cry of abandonment from the cross, "My God, my God, why have you forsaken me?" (Mk 15:34), was similar to the lynched victim Sam Hose's awful scream as he drew his last breath, "Oh, my God! Oh, Jesus."[9] In each case, it was a cruel, agonizing, and contemptible death.

Can the cross redeem the lynching tree? Can the lynching tree liberate the cross and make it real in American history? Those are the questions I have tried to answer.

As I see it, the lynching tree frees the cross from the false pieties of well-meaning Christians. When we see the crucifixion as a first-century lynching, we are confronted by the reenactment of Christ's suffering in the blood-soaked history of African Americans. Thus, the lynching tree reveals the true religious meaning of the cross for American Christians today. The cross needs the lynching tree to remind Americans of the reality of suffering—to keep the cross from becoming a symbol of abstract, sentimental piety. Before the spectacle of this cross we are called to more than contemplation and adoration. We are faced with a clear challenge: as Latin American liberation theologian Jon Sobrino has put it, "to take the crucified down from the cross."[10]

Yet the lynching tree also needs the cross, without which it becomes simply an abomination. It is the cross that points in the direction of hope, the confidence that there is a dimension to life beyond the reach of the oppressor. "Do not fear those who kill the body, and after that can do nothing more" (Lk 12:4).

Though the pain of Jesus' cross was real, there was also joy and beauty in his cross. This is the great theological paradox that makes the cross impossible to embrace unless one is standing in solidarity with those who are powerless. God's loving solidarity can transform ugliness—whether Jesus on the cross or a lynched black victim—into beauty, into God's liberating presence. Through the powerful imagination of faith, we can discover the "terrible beauty" of the cross and the "tragic beauty" of the lynching tree.

Although James Baldwin rejected the Christianity of his youth, he did not reject the spiritual dimension of black existence or the capacity to find beauty in suffering.

> This past, the Negro's past, . . . this endless struggle to achieve and reveal and confirm a human identity, . . . yet contains, for all its horror, something very beautiful. I do not mean to be sentimental about suffering— . . . but people who cannot suffer can never grow up, can never discover who they are. . . . It demands great spiritual resilience not to hate the hater whose foot is on your neck, and an even greater miracle of perception and charity not to teach your children to hate. . . . I am proud of these people not because of their color but because of their intelligence and their spiritual force and beauty. This country should be proud of them, too, but, alas, not many people in this country even know of their existence. And the reason for this ignorance is a knowledge of the role these people played—and play—in American life would reveal more about America to Americans than Americans wish to know.

Out of this wrestling with suffering comes a spiritual beauty and maturity that transcends traditional Christianity. As Baldwin put it:

The man who is forced each day to snatch his manhood, his identity, out of the fire of human cruelty that rages to destroy it knows, if he survives his effort, and even if he does not survive it, something about himself and human life that no school on earth—and, indeed, no church—can teach. He achieves his own authority, and that is unshakable. This is because, in order to save his life, he is forced to look beneath appearances, to take nothing for granted, to hear the meaning behind the words.[11]

The church's most vexing problem today is how to define itself by the gospel of Jesus' cross. Where is the gospel of Jesus' cross revealed today? The lynching of black America is taking place in the criminal justice system where nearly one-third of black men between the ages of eighteen and twenty-eight are in prisons, jails, on parole, or waiting for their day in court. Nearly one-half of the more than two million people in prisons are black. That is one million black people behind bars, more than in colleges. Through private prisons and the "war against drugs," whites have turned the brutality of their racist legal system into a profit-making venture for dying white towns and cities throughout America. Michelle Alexander correctly calls America's criminal justice system "the new Jim Crow."[12] "The criminalization and demonization of black men," writes Alexander, "is one habit that America seems unlikely to break without addressing head-on the racial dynamics that have given rise to our latest caste system."[13] Nothing is more racist in America's criminal justice system than its administration of the death penalty. America is the only industrialized country in the West where the death penalty is still legal. Most countries regard it as both immoral and barbaric. But not in America. The death penalty is primarily reserved, though not exclusively, for people of color, and white supremacy shows no signs of changing it. That is why the term "legal lynching"[14] is still relevant today. One can lynch a person without a rope or tree.

When I heard and read about the physical and mental abuse at the Abu Ghraib prison in Iraq, I thought about lynching. The Roman Empire that killed Jesus at Calvary was similar to the American Empire that lynched blacks in the United States and also created the atrocities in Iraq and Afghanistan. Many white Americans seemed surprised and even shocked that such torture and abuse could come from the U.S. military. But most blacks were neither surprised nor shocked. We have been the object of white America's torture and abuse for nearly four hundred years.

People who have never been lynched by another group usually find it difficult to understand why blacks want whites to remember lynching atrocities. Why bring that up? Is it not best forgotten? Absolutely not! What happened to the hate that created the violence that lynched black people? Did it disappear? What happened to the hate that lynched Henry Smith in Texas (1892), John Carter in Arkansas (1927), and Reverend George W. Lee and Lemar Smith in Mississippi (1955)? Where did the hate go that opposed the black freedom movement and killed Martin Luther King Jr. and a host of white and black civil rights workers?

In 2005 the U.S. Senate formally apologized for its failure ever to have passed an anti-lynching bill. Did the apology get rid of the hate? What happened to the indifference among white liberal religious leaders that fostered silence in the face of the lynching industry? Where is that indifference today? Did the hate and indifference vanish so that we no longer have to be concerned about them? What happened to the denial of whites who claimed that they did not even know about lynching, even though many blacks were lynched during their adult years? Unless we confront these questions today, hate and silence will continue to define our way of life in America. For "if racial healing is ever to come to our society, it will mean remembering and retelling our story of racial injustice and honoring the voices and the actions of those who stood against it."[15]

Just as the Germans should never forget the Holocaust, Americans should never forget slavery, segregation, and the lynching tree. As a nation, we are in danger of forgetting our ugly lynching past. As Fitzhugh Brundage reminds us, "Perhaps nothing about the history of mob violence in the United States is more surprising than how quickly an understanding of the full horror of lynching has receded from the nation's collective memory."[16] Because Emmett Till was remembered, the civil rights movement was born. When we remember, we give voice to the victims. Many white religious leaders, scholars, and churches have done everything they can to forget the vigilante violence unleashed on African Americans. But other white and black scholars, especially historians and writers, are helping us to remember. Whites today cannot separate themselves from the culture that lynched blacks, unless they confront their history and expose the sin of white supremacy.

The cross of Jesus and the lynching tree of black victims are not literally the same—historically or theologically. Yet these two symbols or images are closely linked to Jesus' spiritual meaning for black and white life together in what historian Robert Handy has called "Christian America."[17] Blacks and whites are bound together in Christ by their brutal and beautiful encounter in this land. Neither blacks nor whites can be understood fully without reference to the other because of their common religious heritage as well as their joint relationship to the lynching experience. What happened to blacks also happened to whites. When whites lynched blacks, they were literally and symbolically lynching themselves—their sons, daughters, cousins, mothers and fathers, and a host of other relatives. Whites may be bad brothers and sisters, murderers of their own black kin, but they are *still* our sisters and brothers. We are bound together in America by faith and tragedy. All the hatred we have expressed toward one another cannot destroy the profound mutual love and solidarity that flow deeply between us—a love that empowered blacks to open their arms to receive the many whites who were also empowered by the same love to risk their lives in the black struggle for freedom. No two people in America have had more violent and loving encounters than black and white people. We were made brothers and sisters by the blood of the lynching tree, the blood of sexual union, and the blood of the cross of Jesus. No gulf between blacks and whites is too great to overcome, for our beauty is more enduring than our brutality. What God joined together, no one can tear apart.

The lynching tree is a metaphor for white America's crucifixion of black people. It is the window that best reveals the religious meaning of the cross in our land. In this sense, black people are Christ figures, not because they wanted to suffer but because they had no choice. Just as Jesus had no choice in his journey to Calvary, so black people had no choice about being lynched. The evil forces of the Roman state and of white supremacy in America willed it. Yet, God took the evil of the cross and the lynching tree and transformed them both into the triumphant beauty of the divine. If America has the courage to confront the great sin and ongoing legacy of white supremacy with repentance and reparation there is hope "beyond tragedy."

Notes

Introduction

1.   Richard Wright, *Black Boy* (New York: HarperCollins, Harper Perennial Edition, 1993; orig., 1945), p. 413.

2.   Richard Wright, "Blueprint for Negro Writing," in *The Norton Anthology of African American Literature*, ed. Henry Louis Gates Jr. and Nellie Y. McKay (New York: W. W. Norton, 1997), p. 1386.

3.   See Dietrich Bonhoeffer, *The Cost of Discipleship* (revised and unabridged ed.; New York: Macmillan, 1966), p. 45.

4.   See Richard Wright, "The Ethics of Living Jim Crow, an Autobiographical Sketch," in *The Norton Anthology of African American Literature*, ed. Henry Louis Gates Jr. and Nellie Y. McKay (New York: Norton, 1997), pp. 1388-96.

1. "Nobody Knows de Trouble I See"

1.   Mircea Eliade, *The Sacred and the Profane: The Nature of Religion* (New York: Harper Torchbooks, 1959), p. 64.

2.   See Jacquelyn Dowd Hall, *Revolt against Chivalry: Jessie Daniel Ames and the Women's Campaign against Lynching* (New York: Columbia University Press, 1979; rev. ed., 1993). Since the publication of Hall's excellent text, there has been a great deal of historical research on lynching. For a general history of lynching, see Philip Dray, *At the Hands of Persons Unknown: The Lynching of Black America* (New York: Modern Library, 2002). See also Amy Louise Wood, *Lynching and Spectacle: Witnessing Racial Violence in America, 1890-1940* (Chapel Hill: University of North Carolina Press, 2009); Herbert Shapiro, *White Violence and Black Response: From Reconstruction to Montgomery* (Amherst: University of Massachusetts Press, 1988); W. Fitzhugh Brundage, *Lynching in the New South: Georgia and Virginia, 1880-1930* (Urbana: University of Illinois Press, 1993); idem, *Under Sentence of Death: Lynching in the South* (Chapel Hill: University of North Carolina Press, 1997); Christopher Waldrep, *The Many Faces of Judge Lynch: Extralegal Violence and Punishment in America* (New York: Palgrave Macmillan, 2002); idem, *African Americans Confront Lynching: Strategies of Resistance from the Civil War to the Civil Rights*

Era (Lanham, MD: Rowman & Littlefield, 2009); for an excellent treatment of women and lynching, see Crystal N. Feimster, *Southern Horrors: Women and the Politics of Rape and Lynching* (Cambridge: Harvard University Press, 2009); see also her "'Ladies and Lynching': The Gendered Discourse of Mob Violence in the New South, 1880-1930" (Ph.D. diss., Princeton University, 2000).

3. See Waldrep, *The Many Faces of Judge Lynch*.

4. See Wood, *Lynching and Spectacle*, pp. 163, 164, 166.

5. See David M. Oshinsky, *"Worse than Slavery": Parchman Farm and the Ordeal of Jim Crow Justice* (New York: Free Press, 1996).

6. Rayford Logan, *The Negro in American Life and Thought: The Nadir, 1877-1901* (New York: Macmillan, 1954).

7. See Douglas A. Blackmon, *Slavery by Another Name: The Re-Enslavement of Black Americans from the Civil War to World War II* (New York: Doubleday, 2008).

8. Cited in Leon F. Litwack, "Hellhounds," in James Allen, *Without Sanctuary: Lynching Photography in America* (Santa Fe, NM: Twin Palms, 2003), pp. 12, 13.

9. Atticus G. Haygood, "The Black Shadow in the South," *The Forum* (Oct. 1893): p. 167.

10. Joel Williamson, *The Crucible of Race: Black-White Relations in the American South since Emancipation* (New York: Oxford University Press, 1984), p. 73.

11. See Winthrop Jordan, *White over Black: American Attitudes toward the Negro* (Baltimore: Penguin Books, 1969).

12. Cited in Martin E. Marty, *Righteous Empire: The Protestant Experience in America* (New York: Dial Press, 1970), p. 17. On the role of northern Protestant Christianity in making America a white nation, see the excellent book by Edward J. Blum, *Reforging the White Republic: Race, Religion, and American Nationalism, 1865-1898* (Baton Rouge: Louisiana State University Press, 2005).

13. Cited in Adam Gussow, *Seems Like Murder Here: Southern Violence and the Blues Tradition* (Chicago: University of Chicago Press, 2002), p. 49.

14. See "The Dred Scott Decision," in *The Negro American: A Documentary History*, ed. Leslie H. Fishel Jr. and Benjamin Quarles (Glenview, IL: Scott, Foresman, 1967), p. 204.

15. See Litwack, "Hellhounds," p. 20. For Theodore Roosevelt's quotation, see Shapiro, *White Violence and Black Response*, p. 106. There were a few cases in which black men lynched white men, but that was rare. See W. Fitzhugh Brundage, "Conclusion: Reflections on Lynching Scholarship," in *American Nineteenth Century History* 6, no. 3 (September 2005): p. 406.

See also the important essay by Bruce E. Baker, "Lynch Law Reversed: The Rape of Lula Sherman, the Lynching of Manse Waldrop, and the Debate over Lynching in the 1880s," *American Nineteenth Century History* 6, no. 3 (September 2005): pp. 273-93. He discusses the occasion when black men took it upon themselves to lynch a white man for raping a black girl. Some were put on trial but surprisingly not convicted.

16. Benjamin E. Mays, *Born to Rebel: An Autobiography* (New York: Charles Scribner's Sons, 1971), p. 1.

17. See James Allen, *Without Sanctuary: Lynching Photography in America* (Santa Fe, NM: Twin Palms, 2003), front and back postcard photos 25 and 26, the burnt corpse of William Stanley, August 1915, Temple, Texas.

18. Cited in Jacqueline Goldsby, *A Spectacular Secret: Lynching in American Life and Literature* (Chicago: University of Chicago Press, 2006), p. 19.

19. For an account of the Wilmington riot, see Shapiro, *White Violence and Black Response*, pp. 65-75; Philip Dray, *At The Hands of Persons Unknown: The Lynching of Black America* (New York: Modern Library Paperback Edition, 2003), pp. 122-27.

20. See *Lynching in America: A History in Documents*, ed. Christopher Waldrep (New York: New York University Press, 2006), p. 227.

21. *Respect Black: "The Writings and Speeches of Henry McNeal Turner*, ed. Edwin S. Redkey (New York: Arno Press and New York Times, 1971), p. 153.

22. Cited in Gussow, *Seems Like Murder Here*, p. 3.

23. For an artist's image of this often used phrase, see Dora Apel, *Imagery of Lynching: Black Men, White Women, and the Mob* (New Brunswick, NJ: Rutgers University Press, 2004), p. 120.

24. Robert Johnson, "Hellhound on My Trail" (1937), *Robert Johnson: The Complete Recordings*, Legacy, Columbia Records, Sony Music Entertainment, New York, 1990. For an excellent study of the blues, linking the music with lynching, see Gussow, *Seems Like Murder Here*; Robert Johnson's lyrics, p. 28. See also my *The Spirituals and the Blues* (Maryknoll, NY: Orbis Books, 1991; orig., 1972).

25. Blind Willie McTell, "Mama, 'Tain't long fo' Day" (1927), cited in Gussow, *Seems Like Murder Here*, p. 24.

26. Ralph Ellison, "Richard Wright's Blues," in *Shadow and Act* (New York: Quality Paperback Book Club, 1994; orig., 1964), p. 78.

27. Richard Wright, "Foreword," in Paul Oliver, *The Meaning of the Blues* (New York: Collier Books, 1963), p. 9.

28. See John Dollard, *Caste and Class in a Southern Town* (Garden City, NY: Doubleday, 1957; orig., 1937), p. 359.

29. Cited in Gussow, *Seems Like Murder Here*, p. 53.

30. Abdul R. JanMohamed, *The Death-Bound-Subject: Richard Wright's Archaeology of Death* (Durham, NC: Duke University Press, 2005), p. 2.

31. Richard Wright, *Black Boy (American Hunger): A Record of Childhood and Youth*, with a foreword by Edward P. Jones (New York: Harper Perennial Modern Classics, 2006; orig., 1945), p. 74.

32. Cited in Gussow, *Seems Like Murder Here*, p. 10.

33. William Broonzy, *Big Bill Blues: William Broonzy's Story as Told to Yannick Bruynoghe* (New York: Oak Archives, 1955), p. 70.

34. Albert Murray, *Stomping the Blues* (New York: McGraw-Hill Book Co., 1976), p. 6.

35. Cited in Gussow, *Seems Like Murder Here*, pp. 56-57.

36. Richard Wright, *Twelve Million Voices* (New York: Arno Press, 1969; orig., 1941), p. 131.

37. Gussow, *Seems Like Murder Here*, p. 11.

38. Wright, *Twelve Million Voices*, pp. 130-31.

39. Wright, *Twelve Million Voices*, p. 131.

40. "The Sickness unto Death," in *A Kierkegaard Anthology*, ed. Robert Bretall (New York: Modern Library, 1946), pp. 341-44.

41. *A Kierkegaard Anthology*, p. 353.

42. Lerone Bennett, *The Negro Mood* (Chicago: Johnson, 1964), p. 68.

43. Wright, *Twelve Million Voices*, p. 131.

44. See Thomas Wentworth Higginson, *Army Life in a Black Regiment* (Boston: Beacon, 1962), pp. 209-10. This spiritual is also found in William Francis Allen et al., eds., *Slave Songs of the United States* (Freeport, NY: Books for Libraries Press, 1971; orig., 1867). See also a book on religion in the Old South by Erskine Clarke, *Wrestlin' Jacob: A Portrait of Religion in the Old South* (Atlanta: John Knox Press, 1979). For an excellent interpretation of this wrestling, see William H. Becker, "The Black Tradition of Spiritual Wrestling," *Journal of Religious Thought* 51, no. 2 (Winter 1994-Spring 1995): pp. 29-46.

45. The spirituals about Jacob are also found in Allen et al., eds., *Slave Songs of the United States*.

46. W. E. B. Du Bois, *The Souls of Black Folk: Essays and Sketches* (Chicago: McClurg, 1931), pp. 140, 141.

47. See Ernst Käsemann, "The Pauline Theology of the Cross," *Interpretation* 24, no. 2 (April 1970): p. 177; and his "The Saving Significance of the Death of Jesus in Paul," in *Perspectives on Paul* (Philadelphia: Fortress Press, 1969), p. 56.

48. See Sherrilyn A. Ifill, *On the Court-House Lawn: Confronting the Legacy of Lynching in the Twenty-First Century* (Boston: Beacon, 2007), p. 15.

49. Wood, *Lynching and Spectacle*, p. 39.

50. Wood, *Lynching and Spectacle*, p. 36.

51. Cited in Hortense J. Spillers, *Black, White, and in Color: Essays on American Literature and Culture* (Chicago: University of Chicago Press, 2003), p. 253.

52. Cited in Benjamin E. Mays, *The Negro's God: As Reflected in His Literature*, with a new preface by Vincent Harding (New York: Atheneum, 1969; orig., 1938), pp. 43-44.

53. Cited in Mays, *The Negro's God*, p. 49.

54. Litwack, "Hellhounds," p. 33.

55. James Baldwin, *The Fire Next Time* (New York: Dell, 1964), p. 46.

56. Simone Weil, *Waiting for God*, trans. Emma Craufurd, with an introduction by Leslie A. Fiedler (New York: Harper Perennial Modern Classics Edition, 2009, orig., 1951), p. 27.

2. *"The Terrible Beauty of the Cross"* *and the Tragedy of the Lynching Tree*

1. Ray Stannard Baker, "What Is a Lynching?: A Study of Mob Justice, South and North," *McClure's Magazine* 24, no. 4 (February 1905): p. 422.

2. James E. Cutler, *Lynch-Law: An Interpretation into the History of Lynching in the United States* (New York: Longmans, Green, 1905), p. 1.

3. Paula Frederickson, *Jesus of Nazareth, King of the Jews: A Jewish Life and the Emergence of Christianity* (New York: Vintage, 2000), pp. 233-34.

4. Only a few scholars have made even passing references to the similarity between crucifixion and lynching, and no one has fully explored the connection and its meaning for America's religious imagination. See René Girard, *I See Satan Fall Like Lightning* (Maryknoll, NY: Orbis Books, 2001), esp. pp. 64-70; Jack Miles, *Christ: A Crisis in the Life of God* (New York: Vintage, 2002), p. 3. See also an interview with James Allison, "Violence Undone," in *Christian Century*, September 5, 2006, pp. 30-35. See also Tat-siong Benny Liew, "The Word of Bare Life: Workings of Death and Dream in the Fourth Gospel," in *Anatomies of Narrative Criticism*, ed. Tom Thatcher and Stephen Moore (Leiden: Brill, 2008), pp. 167-93.

5. Ronald Stone, "The Contribution of Reinhold Niebuhr, to the Late Twentieth Century," in Charles W. Kegley, ed., *Reinhold Niebuhr: His Religious, Social, and Political Thought* (2nd ed.; New York: Pilgrim Press, 1984), p. 78.

6. See especially his *Moral Man and Immoral Society* (1932), *Beyond Tragedy* (1937), *The Nature and Destiny of Man* (two vols., 1941, 1943), *Children of Light and the Children of Darkness* (1944), *Faith and History* (1949), and *The Irony of American History* (1952).

7. McGeorge Bundy, "Foreign Policy: From Innocence to Engagement," in Arthur M. Schlesinger Jr. and Morton White, eds., *Paths of American Thought* (Boston: Houghton Mifflin, 1963), p. 306.

8. For a range of commentary on Niebuhr's influence and contributions, see Marion Pauck, "Reinhold Niebuhr, Wilhelm Pauck and Paul Tillich: Legend and Myth," *Dialogue* 4, no. 1 (Winter 1995); A. J. Bacevich, "Introduction," in *The Irony of American History* (Chicago: University of Chicago Press, 2008); the excellent but controversial biography by Richard Fox, *Reinhold Niebuhr: A Biography* (New York: Pantheon Books, 1985); Harvey Cox, "In the Pulpit and on the Barricades," *New York Times Book Review*, January 5, 1986; Robert M. Brown, "Reinhold Niebuhr: His Theology in the 1980s," *Christian Century*, January 22, 1986; Michael Novak, "Reinhold Niebuhr: Model for Neoconservatives," *Christian Century*, January 22, 1986. For the most informed critique of Niebuhr on race, see Herbert O. Edwards, "Racism and Christian Ethics in America," *Katallagete* (Winter 1971): pp. 18-24; idem, "Niebuhr, 'Realism,' and Civil Rights in America," *Christianity and Crisis*, February 3, 1985, pp. 12-15; Langdon Gilkey, "Introduction," in Reinhold Niebuhr, *Moral Man and Immoral Society* (Louisville: Westminster John Knox Press, 2001); idem, *On Niebuhr: A Theological Study* (Chicago: University of Chicago Press, 2001); David Brooks, "Obama, Gospel and Verse," in the *New York Times*, April 26, 2007, section A, p. 25. For an important recent collection, defining his importance for today, with a "Foreword" by Martin E. Marty, see Daniel F. Rice, ed., *Reinhold Niebuhr Revisited: Engagements with an American Original* (Grand Rapids, MI: Eerdmans, 2009). Also Richard Harries and Stephen Platten, eds., *Reinhold Niebuhr and Contemporary Politics: God and Power* (New York: Oxford University Press, 2010); John Patrick Diggins, *Why Niebuhr Now?* (Chicago: University of Chicago Press, 2011). See also Elizabeth Sifton's (Niebuhr's daughter) defense of his authorship of the serenity prayer in *The Serenity Prayer: Faith and Politics in Times of Peace and War* (New York: W. W. Norton, 2003).

9. Reinhold Niebuhr, *The Children of Light and the Children of Darkness* (New York: Charles Scribner's Sons, 1944), p. 118.

10. Reinhold Niebuhr, *Irony of American History* (New York: Charles Scribner's Sons, 1952), p. 63.

11. Reinhold Niebuhr, *Christian Realism and Political Problems* (New York: Charles Scribner's Sons, 1953), p. 119.

12. *Essays in Applied Christianity*, ed. D. B. Robertson (New York: Meridian Books, 1959), pp. 30, 32.

13. See Reinhold Niebuhr, "Transvaluation of Values" and "The Suffering Servant and the Son of Man," in *Beyond Tragedy*, pp. 195-225; 171-193; idem, "The Power and the Weakness of God" in *Discerning the Signs of the Times* (New York: Charles Scribner's Sons, 1946), pp. 132-151; idem, "The Son of Man Must Suffer" in *Justice and Mercy*, ed. by Ursula M. Niebuhr (Louisville: Westminster/John Knox Press, 1974), 85-95. Additional reflections on

God's sacrificial love on the cross are found in Reinhold Niebuhr, *An Inter-pretation of Christian Ethics* (1935) and *Faith and History* (1949). The most comprehensive analysis is found in vol. 2 of his magnum opus, *The Nature and Destiny of Man*, taken from his Gifford Lectures of 1939. On "transvalua-tion of values" in Friedrich Nietzsche, see his "The Antichrist" in *The Portable Nietzsche*, ed. Walter Kaufmann (New York: Viking Press, 1954), pp. 568ff; also in Nietzsche's *Beyond Good and Evil: Prelude to a Philosophy of the Future*, trans. and ed. by Walter Kaufmann (New York: Vintage Books, 1966), p. 60.

14. R. Niebuhr, "The Power and Weakness of God" in *Discerning the Signs of the Times: Sermons for Today and Tomorrow* (New York: Charles Scribner's Sons, 1946), pp. 140, 141, 142; see also R. Niebuhr, *The Nature and Destiny of Man*, vol. 2 (New York: Charles Scribner's Sons, 1943), p. 38, n. 1.

15. See Martin Hengel, *Crucifixion* (Philadelphia: Fortress Press, 1977), p. 4.

16. Reinhold Niebuhr, *Beyond Tragedy: Essays on the Christian Interpreta-tion of History* (New York: Charles Scribner's Sons, 1937), pp. 196, 198, 199, 213.

17. Niebuhr, *Beyond Tragedy*, p. 18.

18. Cited in Richard Fox, *Reinhold Niebuhr*, p, 171.

19. Reinhold Niebuhr, "An American Approach to the Christian Mes-sage," in *A Traffic in Knowledge*, ed. Visser T' Hooft (London: Student Chris-tian Movement Press, 1931), p. 74; see also his "The Truth in Myths," in *The Nature of Religious Experience: Essays in Honor of Douglas Clyde Macintosh* (New York: Harper & Row, 1937).

20. Reinhold Niebuhr, *Essays in Applied Christianity*, ed. D. B. Robertson (New York: Meridian Books, 1959), p. 29.

21. Reinhold Niebuhr, "The Terrible Beauty of the Cross," *The Christian Century*, March 21, 1929, p. 386. The Anglo Irish poet William Butler Yeats used this phrase "terrible beauty" in his poem "Easter, 1916." See Daniel Help-ern, ed., *Holy Fire: Nine Visionary Poets and the Quest for Enlightenment* (New York: HarperPerennial, 1994), pp. 194-96. I want to thank Joan Sullivan Gray, an English and humanities teacher at the Boston Latin School, for the Yeats reference. She wrote to me after hearing me use the phrase in reference to Reinhold Niebuhr on the *Bill Moyer's Journal*, November 23, 2007. Niebuhr may have borrowed the phrase for his understanding of Jesus' cross without reference to Yeats. The phrase "terrible beauty" captures best the profound religious meaning of Jesus' cross and its link with the lynching tree. Countee Cullen used the phrase "tragic beauty" in his poem "The Black Christ," saying in reference to a lynched victim, "Never such tragic beauty shone/As this on any face before." It appeared in January 31, 1929. Niebuhr also used that same phrase in his essay. It is not clear whether Niebuhr borrowed it from Cullen. But he did use Cullen's poetry in a Union Seminary course entitled "Ethical

Viewpoints in Modern Literature" (Countee Cullen, "The Black Christ," in *My High Song: The Collected Writings of Countee Cullen, Voice of the Harlem Renaissance*, ed. Gerald Early [New York: Anchor, 1991], p. 227). Ivone Gebara, a leading Latin American liberation theologian, used the phrase "tragic beauty" in her important text *Out of the Depths: Women's Experience of Evil and Salvation* (Minneapolis: Augsburg Fortress Press, 2002), p. 21. See also Miguel De Unamuno, *Tragic Sense of Life*, trans. J. E. Crawford Flitch (New York: Dover Publications, 1954, originally 1921), which also influenced Niebuhr's understanding of tragedy.

22. Reinhold Niebuhr, *Christianity and Power Politics*, (New York: Charles Scribner's Sons, 1940), p. 213.

23. See Zora Neale Hurston, *Jonah's Gourd Vine* (Philadelphia: J. B. Lippincott, 1971; orig., 1934), pp. 278, 279.

24. Reinhold Niebuhr, *Christianity and Crisis*, Winter, 1943, p. 11; "What Resources Have Christians for Dealing with Racial Problems," *The Lutheran*, April 11, 1956, p. 24; "Christian Faith and the Race Problem," *Christianity and Society*, Spring, 1945, pp. 24, 22, 23; "The Negro Dilemma," *The New Leader*, April 11, 1960, p, 13; "The Struggle for Justice," *New Leader*, July 6, 1964, p. 11; *Reflection on the End of an Era* (New York: Charles Scribner's Sons, 1934), pp. 285-86.

25. Reinhold Niebuhr, "A Question of Priorities," *New Leader*, January 15, 1968, p. 9; idem, "The Supreme Court on Segregation in the Schools," *Christianity and Crisis*, June 14, 1954, p. 76; idem, *Man's Nature and His Communities: Essays on the Dynamics and Enigmas of Man's Personal and Social Existence* (Lanham, MD: University Press of America, 1965), pp. 76-77, 77; idem, "Justice to the American Negro from State, Community and Church," in *Pious and Secular America* (New York: Charles Scribner's Sons, 1958), pp. 78-85; idem, "The Problem of Race Relations," *Reinhold Niebuhr on Politics*, ed. Harry R. Davis and Robert C. Good (New York: Charles Scribner's Sons, 1960), p. 228; idem, "Civil Rights and Democracy," *Christianity and Crisis*, July 8, 1957, p. 89; Malcolm X, "God's Judgment of America," in *The End of White World Supremacy* (New York: Merlin House, 1971), pp. 121-48; Reinhold Niebuhr, "Nullification," *New Leader*, March 5, 1956, pp. 3-4. See Alex Heard, *The Eyes of Willie McGee: A Tragedy of Race, Sex, and Secrets in the Jim Crow South* (New York: HarperCollins, 2010); *The Lynching of Emmett Till: A Documentary Narrative*, ed. Christopher Metress (Charlottesville: University of Virginia, 2002); and Howard Smead, *Blood Justice: The Lynching of Mack Charles Parker* (New York: Oxford University Press, 1986).

26. See Martin Luther King Jr., "Our Struggle," *Liberation*, April 1956, pp. 3-6; also included in *A Testament of Hope: The Essential Writings and Speeches of Martin Luther King, Jr.*, ed. James Washington (New York: Harper Collins, 1991), p. 80; William Faulkner, "A Letter to the North,"

Life, March 5, 1956; Faulkner's letter is reprinted as "Letter to a Northern Editor," in *Essays, Speeches & Public Letters*, ed. James B. Meriwether (New York: Random House, 1965), pp. 86-91: "So I would say to the NAACP and all the organizations who would compel immediate and unconditional integration: Go slow now. Stop now for a time, a moment. . . . You have done a good job, you have jolted your opponent off-balance and he is now vulnerable. But stop there for a moment" (p. 87). See also Faulkner's "A Letter to the Leaders in the Negro Race, 1956," in *Essays, Speeches & Public Letters*, pp. 107-12, first published in *Ebony*, September 1956; here he responds to the controversy generated from the March 5 letter. See also James Baldwin's response to Faulkner, "Faulkner and Desegregation," in *The Price of the Ticket: Collected Nonfiction 1948-1985* (New York: St. Martin's, 1985), pp. 147-52; originally published in *Partisan Review*, Winter 1956. See also Richard Fox, *Reinhold Niebuhr*, p. 282; *Remembering Reinhold Niebuhr: Letters of Reinhold and Ursula Niebuhr*, ed. Ursula Niebuhr (San Francisco: Harper, 1991), p. 311.

27. See Harper Lee, *To Kill a Mockingbird* (New York: Harper Perennial Modern Classic ed., 2006; orig., 1960), p. 321.

28. Reinhold Niebuhr, "The Mounting Racial Crisis," *Christianity and Crisis*, July 8, 1963, p. 121.

29. Cited in Kevin Boyle, *The Arch of Justice: A Saga of Race, Civil Rights and Murder in the Jazz Age* (New York: Henry Holt, 2004), pp. 280-81.

30. See Dietrich Bonhoeffer, "The Negro Church," in *No Rusty Swords* (New York: Harper & Row, 1965), pp. 112-14; Clifford Green, "Bonhoeffer at Union. Critical Turning Points: 1931 and 1939," *Union Seminary Quarterly Review* 62, no. 3-4 (2010): pp. 1-16; Scott Holland, "First We Take Manhattan, Then We Take Berlin: Bonhoeffer in New York," *Cross Currents* 50, no. 3 (Fall 2000): pp. 369-82; Josiah U. Young, *No Difference in the Fare: Dietrich Bonhoeffer and the Problem of Racism* (Grand Rapids, MI: Eerdmans, 1998), pp. 114-20; J. Young, "Theology and the Problem of Racism," in Willis Jenkins and Jennifer M. McBride, eds., *Bonhoeffer and King: Their Legacies and Import for Christian Social Thought* (Philadelphia: Fortress Press, 2010), pp. 69-77; Charles Marsh, "Bonhoeffer on the Road to King: Turning from the Phraseological to the Real," in Jenkins and McBride, eds., *Bonhoeffer and King*, pp. 123-38; on what Bonhoeffer read about lynching, see "Editorial from the Literary Digest: Missouri's Is the Shame," in *100 Years of Lynchings*, ed. Ralph Ginzburg (Baltimore: Black Classic Press, 1988), p. 193; regarding Niebuhr's presence at a meeting with Du Bois, see David L. Lewis, *W. E. B. Du Bois: The Fight for Equality and the American Century, 1919-1963* (New York: Henry Holt, 2000), p. 253; Fox, *Reinhold Niebuhr*, p. 125; Richard Fox, "Reinhold Niebuhr—The Living of Christian Realism," in *Reinhold Niebuhr and the Issues of Our Time*, ed. Richard Harries (Grand Rapids, MI: Eerdmans,

1986), p. 13. I was surprised by Paul Lehmann's concern about Bonhoeffer's deep interest in the black community because he was the most welcoming of all Union faculty when I arrived and engaged racial issues constructively, debating with me before the faculty and Union community. See especially his response to my perspective on black theology: Paul Lehmann, "Black Theology and 'Christian Theology,'" in *Union Seminary Quarterly Review* 31, no. 1 (Fall 1975): pp. 31-37. Also his *The Transfiguration of Politics* (New York: Harper & Row, 1975).

31. Reinhold Niebuhr, *Leaves from the Notebook of a Tamed Cynic* (Cleveland: Meridian Books, 1957; orig., 1929), pp. 168-69; idem, "Race Prejudice in the North," *Christian Century*, March 12, 1927, pp. 583-84; see Niebuhr's "Foreword," in *Mississippi Black Paper* (New York: Random House, 1965); June Bingham, "Reinhold Niebuhr in Detroit," *Christian Century*, March 8, 1961; Niebuhr, *Man's Nature and His Communities*, p. 12.

32. Ronald Stone, *Professor Niebuhr: A Mentor to the Twentieth Century* (Louisville: Westminster/John Knox, 1992), p. 33.

33. See Reinhold Niebuhr's letter "To the Church Council, Bethel Church, Detroit," January 22, 1930; a copy was generously given to me by the Niebuhr scholar Professor Ronald Stone, Niebuhr's last teaching assistant; it is also found in the Library of Congress in Washington, DC; see also *Detroit Times*, August 8, 1931; and Niebuhr, *Leaves*, p. 222.

34. Reinhold Niebuhr, "Meditations from Mississippi," *Christian Century*, February 10, 1937, pp. 183-84, emphasis added; Stone, *Professor Reinhold Niebuhr*, pp. 111-15; Richard Fox, *Reinhold Niebuhr*, p. 176; idem, "Who Can but Prophesy?—The Life of Reinhold Niebuhr," in Kegley, ed., *Reinhold Niebuhr*, pp. 28-42.

35. For Niebuhr's reference to his sermon "The Involuntary Cross," see *Leaves*, p. 19. Also James T. Holly, "The Divine Plan of Human Redemption in Its Ethnological Development" in *AME Church Review* 1, no. 6 (October 1884): 79-85, reprinted in Anthony B. Pinn, *Moral Evil and Redemptive Suffering: A History of Theodicy in African American Religious Thought* (Gainesville: University Press of Florida, 2002), pp. 131-40, quotation on pp. 137-38. James T. Holly's quotation is also cited in Allen D. Callahan, *The Talking Book: African Americans and the Bible* (New Haven: Yale University Press, 2006), p. 161. For a recent interpretation of Simon, see Raymond E. Brown, *The Death of the Messiah*, vol. 2 (New York: Doubleday, 1998), pp. 913-17.

36. Countee Cullen, "Colors," in Gerald Early, ed., *My Soul's High Song* (New York: Anchor Books, Doubleday, 1991), p. 145; see also Cullen's "Simon the Cyrenian Speaks," in Early, ed., *My Soul's High Song*, p. 87. James Weldon Johnson, "The Crucifixion," in his *God's Trombones: Seven Negro Sermons in Verse*, foreword by Maya Angelou (New York: Penguin Classics, 2008, origi-

nally 1927), pp. 42-43. See Ridgely Torrence's 1917 play called *Simon the Cyrenian*, cited in Early, ed., *My Soul's High Song*, p. 87 n. 1; Early also points out that an A.M.E. minister, Reverdy C. Ransom, named his mission the Church of Simon the Cyrenian. See also Scott Holland, "First We Take Manhattan," pp. 369-82.

37. I disagree with Ronald Stone, John Bennett, and other Niebuhr scholars who attribute his lack of involvement in the black struggle for justice to his stroke in 1952. I am sure his illness affected his energy for physical movement and writing. But what about before the stroke? My biggest problem with Niebuhr on race was not merely that he failed to associate himself with black organizations fighting for racial justice but, more importantly, what Niebuhr wrote about America's greatest moral issue was at best *moderate* in a time when he was radical on other issues that were dear to him. Most Niebuhr interpreters either ignore what he said about race, as if it was not important for his ethics and theology, or they tend to overvalue his work in that area. While it is true that "Niebuhr worked in the struggle for the rights of black Americans throughout his ministry" (R. Stone), that work was not radical in any sense. Niebuhr's interpreters on race are not much different from him, which shows how distant they are from the truly radical movements in the black community. Contrary to Bennett's view, Niebuhr did not have a "deep commitment to racial justice," at least not in his writings or his life. See especially R. Stone, "The Contribution of Reinhold Niebuhr to the Late Twentieth Century," and J. Bennett, "Afterword: 1982," in Kegley. ed., *Reinhold Niebuhr*, pp. 60 and 140. For a more recent and insightful assessment of Niebuhr on civil rights, see Robin W. Lovin, "Reinhold Niebuhr in Historical Perspective," in Richard Harries and Steven Platten, eds., *Reinhold Niebuhr and Contemporary Politics* (Oxford: Oxford University Press, 2010), pp. 6-17.

38. Even Martin Luther King Jr. was surprised by the Watts riot in Los Angeles, which happened a few days after the Voting Rights Bill was passed in 1965. Unlike Malcolm X, he had failed to see that the civil rights gains in the South did not change the lives of poor blacks in the northern cities who already had the right to vote but had little to vote for. That was why he chose to take his movement to Chicago.

39. Reinhold Niebuhr, "The Struggle for Justice," *New Leader*, July 6, 1964, p. 10; idem, "Justice to the American Negro from State, Community and Church," in *Pious and Secular America* (New York: Charles Scribner's Sons, 1958), p. 82; *Justice and Mercy*, p. 108.

40. *Amsterdam News*, September 7, 1963, p. 6.

41. Niebuhr, *Leaves*, p. 50.

42. See Jean Wagner, *Black Poets of the United States: From Paul Laurence Dunbar to Langston Hughes* (Urbana: University of Illinois Press, 1973), pp.

229-30; Anne P. Rice, ed., *Witnessing Lynching: American Writers Respond* (New Brunswick, NJ: Rutgers University Press, 2003), pp. 188-90.

43. See Darryl Pinckney, "The Black American Tragedy," *New York Review*, November 1, 2001, p. 68.

44. Cited in Wagner, *Black Poets of the United States*, p. 453.

45. Reinhold Niebuhr, "Green Pastures," *World Tomorrow* 13, no. 6 (June 1930): p. 280.

46. Ursula M. Niebuhr, ed., *Remembering Reinhold Niebuhr*, p. 371.

47. Reinhold Niebuhr (with Alan Heimert), *A Nation So Conceived: Reflections on the History of America from Its Early Visions to Its Present Power* (New York: Charles Scribner's Sons, 1963), p. 7; idem (with Paul E. Sigmund), *The Democratic Experience: Past and Prospects* (New York: Frederick A. Praeger, 1969), p. 20. See also Reinhold Niebuhr, *Faith and Politics: A Commentary on Religious, Social and Political Thought in a Technological Age*, ed. Ronald Stone (New York: George Braziller, 1968), p. 237.

48. R. Niebuhr, "Anglo-Saxon Destiny and Responsibility" in Conrad Cherry, ed., *God's New Israel: Religious Interpretations of American Destiny* (Englewood Cliffs, NJ: Prentice Hall, 1971), p. 304; originally published in *Christianity and Crisis*, October 4, 1943.

49. Niebuhr, "Justice to the American Negro from State, Community and Church," pp. 78-85; compare Niebuhr's essay about Jews, "The Relations of Christians and Jews in Western Civilization," with the one on blacks in the same volume. For his reflections on the nations of Asia, Africa, and Latin America, see *The Structure of Nations and Empires: A Study of the Recurring Patterns and Problems of the Political Order in Relation to the Unique Problems of the Nuclear Age* (New York: Charles Scribner's Sons, 1959). On Arabs and Jews in Palestine, see his "A New View of Palestine," *The Spectator*, August 16, 1946, pp. 162-63; see also Edward Said's response to Niebuhr in *The Question of Palestine* (New York: Vintage Books, 1980).

50. See Abraham Heschel's address "The Religious Basis of Equality of Opportunity—The Segregation of God" at the National Conference on Religion and Race, convened by the National Council of Churches, Synagogue Council of America, and the National Catholic Welfare Conference, commemorating the centennial of the Emancipation Proclamation, attended by more than six hundred delegates in Chicago, January 14-17, 1963. Heschel defined a prophet as "a person who suffers harm done to others" "as if the prophet were the victim and the prey." It is revealing that Niebuhr was not even present, which meant that race was a low priority for him. Perhaps this also partly explains why Heschel marched with King, creating a deep and lasting relationship with him, and Niebuhr did not. The civil rights movement could have used Niebuhr's powerful theological voice. For the addresses of this major conference, which initiated the white church's involvement in

the civil rights movement, see Mathew Ahmann, ed., *Race: Challenge to Religion* (Chicago: Henry Regnery, 1963). Martin Luther King Jr. was present and presented "A Challenge to the Churches and Synagogues."

51. See the *New York Times*, Thursday, August 29, 1963, p. 21; see also: Jewish Women's Archive ("Rabbi Joachim Prinz Speech at the March on Washington" http://jwa.org/node/11438 [February 24, 2011]).

52. See Reinhold. Niebuhr, *Moral Man and Immoral Society*, pp. 277, 81, 221.

53. Reinhold Niebuhr, "The Twilight of Liberalism," *The New Republic*, June 14, 1919; idem, "Let Liberal Churches Stop Fooling Themselves!" *Christian Century*, 1931; idem, "The Confession of a Tired Radical," *Christian Century*, August 30, 1928; idem, "Why Is Communism So Evil," in *Christian Realism and Political Problems* (New York: Charles Scribner's Sons, 1953), pp. 33-42. *Moral Man* is Niebuhr at his best; however, what he says about African Americans, though useful, lacks that passion one expects from one with an empathic feeling for their suffering.

54. James Baldwin and Reinhold Niebuhr, "The Meaning of the Birmingham Tragedy," audio tape, no date, in author's possession. On the Birmingham bombing and President Kennedy sending a former football coach and a former Army Secretary to calm things down, see David Garrow, *Bearing the Cross: Martin Luther King, Jr., and the Southern Christian Leadership Conference* (New York: Morrow, 1985), p. 295.

55. Reinhold Niebuhr, "The Negro Minority and Its Fate in a Self-Righteous Nation," *Social Action* 35, no. 2 (October 1968): p. 61. It is important to note that Niebuhr's "foreword" in the pamphlet of the "Clergy and Laymen Concerned about Vietnam" expressed support for King at a time when the latter was under severe criticism from many quarters for his opposition to the Vietnam War, calling him "one of the great religious leaders of our time and he has a right to speak out on any issue which concerns mankind": "Dr. Martin Luther King, Jr., Dr. John C. Bennett, Dr. Henry Steele Commager, Rabbi Abraham Heschel Speak on the War in Vietnam," a "foreword by Dr. Reinhold Niebuhr," Clergy and Laymen Concerned about Vietnam, p. 3.

56. Niebuhr, *Moral Man and Immoral Society*, p. 253.

57. See John C. Bennett to Reinhold Niebuhr, June, 16, 1969; and Reinhold Niebuhr to John Bennett, June 18 and 24, 1969, Reinhold Niebuhr Papers, Library of Congress, Washington, DC. See also John Bennett's comment on Niebuhr's reaction to *Black Theology and Black Power* in his "Afterword: 1982," in Kegley, ed., *Reinhold Niebuhr*, pp. 140-41.

58. Cited in Charles C. Brown, *Niebuhr and His Age: Reinhold Niebuhr's Prophetic Role and Legacy* (Harrisburg, PA: Trinity Press International, 2002), p. 15. Also, Niebuhr, *Beyond Tragedy*, p. 85; *Leaves*, p. 131. Niebuhr seemed to encourage the label and was embarrassed by it. "I should have been

allowed to end my days without anyone trying to make a 'prophet' out of me," Niebuhr wrote to a friend in response to June Bingham's book about him (cited in Richard Fox, *Reinhold Niebuhr*, p. 273). See June Bingham, *The Courage to Change: An Introduction to the Life and Thought of Reinhold Niebuhr* (New York: Charles Scribner's Sons, 1961).

59. John C. Bennett, *Social Salvation: A Religious Approach to the Problem of Social Change* (New York: C. Scribner's Sons, 1935); and *The Radical Imperative: From Theology to Social Ethics* (Philadelphia: Westminster Press, 1975).

60. Walter Rauschenbusch, "The Problem of the Black Man," *The American Missionary* 68, no. 3 (March 1914): p. 732.

61. Cited in Ralph Luker, *The Social Gospel in Black and White: American Racial Reform, 1885-1912* (Chapel Hill: University of North Carolina Press, 1991), p. 25. Luker's text is an account of both black and white religious figures involved in the Social Gospel movement.

62. On Quincy Ewing, see especially Quincy Ewing, "The Heart of the Race Problem," *Atlantic Monthly*, March 1909, pp. 389-97. See also his sermon, "The Beginning of the End," which was published in an African American magazine, *The Colored American Magazine*, October 1901, pp. 471- 78; Charles E. Wynes, "The Reverend Quincy Ewing: Southern Racial Heretic in the 'Cajun' Country," *Louisiana History: The Journal of the Louisiana Historical Association* 7, no. 3 (Summer 1966). On Andrew Sledd, see Andrew Sledd, "The Negro: Another View," *Atlantic Monthly* (June 1902); Terry L. Matthews, "The Voice of a Prophet: Andrew Sledd Revisited," *Journal of Southern Religion* 6 (December 2003); "Professing Justice: A Symposium on the Civil Rights Legacy of Professor Andrew Sledd," held in his memory at Emory University, April 22, 2002. On E. T. Wellford, see E. T. Wellford, *The Lynching of Jesus: A Review of the Legal Aspects of the Trial of Christ* (Newport News, VA: Franklin Printing Co., 1905), p. 17; and *Atlanta Constitution*, September 14, 1903. In his essay "The Protestant Churches and Lynching, 1919-1939," Robert M. Miller, using denominational minutes, claims that major denominations, especially those in the Federal Council of Churches, opposed lynching. It is not a persuasive argument because churches are good at passing resolutions against racism but doing nothing about it. The small number of southern preachers who opposed lynching did not oppose white supremacy. The only minister I found who came close to opposing both lynching and white supremacy was Quincy Ewing. In his book *Christ*, Jack Miles makes a revealing comment: "The crucifix is a violently obscene icon. To recover its visceral power, children of the twenty-first century must imagine a lynching, the body of the victim swollen and distorted, his head hanging askew above a broken neck, while the bystanders smile their twisted smiles" (pp. 3-4). This

is an excellent statement, as far as it goes. Like most white scholars, Miles failed to mention that lynched victims in America were mostly *black*, especially the ones who were tortured. To leave out the racial aspect of lynching misses the point completely.

63. Cited in David Margolick, *Strange Fruit: Billie Holiday, Café Society, and an Early Cry for Civil Rights* (Philadelphia: Running Press, 2000), pp. 103, 101.

3. Bearing the Cross and
Staring Down the Lynching Tree

1. See King's sermon "Pride versus Humility: The Parable of the Pharisee and the Publican," on September 25, 1955, in *The Papers of Martin Luther King, Jr.*, 6 vols.; senior editor, Clayborne Carson (Berkeley: University of California Press, 1992-2007), 6:232. In contrast, my research has not discovered one white theologian of the time who made a reference to the lynching of Emmett Till. They were much more likely to reference European theology—Barth, Bultmann, Tillich, and the New Quest of the Historical Jesus—than to comment on the violence against blacks in the 1950s and 60s.

2. *Memphis Commercial Appeal*, September 1, 1955, cited in *The Lynching of Emmett Till: A Documentary Narrative*, ed. Christopher Metress (Charlottesville: University of Virginia Press, 2002), p. 16.

3. Martin Luther King Jr. and A. Philip Randolph in *The Papers of Martin Luther King, Jr.*, 5. "Threshold of the New Decade," January 1959—December 1960; Clayborne Carson, senior editor, and Susan Carson et al., eds. (Berkeley: University of California Press, 2005), quotation at the front of text.

4. Cited in Howell Raines, *My Soul Is Rested: The Story of the Civil Rights Movement in the Deep South* (New York: Penguin Books, 1983), p. 235; *The Lynching of Emmett Till*, p. 3. See also John Lewis's discussion of the impact of the Till lynching on him and others in the civil rights movement in his *Walking with the Wind* (New York: Simon & Schuster, 1998), p. 57.

5. Cleveland Sellers, with Robert Terrell, *The River of No Return: The Autobiography of a Black Militant and the Life and Death of SNCC* (New York: Morrow, 1973); also cited in *The Lynching of Emmett Till*, p. 263.

6. Cited in *The Lynching of Emmett Till*, p. 21.

7. *Jet*, September 1955.

8. *The Lynching of Emmett Till*, pp. 29, 30, 227, 32.

9. Lewis, *Walking with the Wind*, 57.

10. *The Lynching of Emmett Till*, pp. 29, 232.

11. *The Lynching of Emmett Till*, p. 232.

12. See Clenora Hudson-Weems, *Emmett Till: The Sacrificial Lamb of the Civil Rights Movement* (Troy, MI: Bedford, 1994).

13. Albert Camus, *The Rebel*, trans. Anthony Bower (New York: Random House, 1956), p. 15.

14. Dietrich Bonhoeffer, *The Cost of Discipleship* (revised and unabridged ed.; New York: Macmillan, 1959), p. 99.

15. As one of King's professors at Boston University, L. Harold De Wolf, later observed, "regardless of the subject matter, King never tired of moving from a one-sided thesis to a corrective, but also one-sided antithesis and finally to a more coherent synthesis beyond both" (cited in David J. Garrow, *Bearing the Cross: Martin Luther King, Jr., and the Southern Christian Leadership Conference* [New York: Morrow, 1986], p. 46). King also spoke of Palm Sunday as the thesis and Good Friday as the antithesis and Easter as the synthesis. See his sermon "Questions that Easter Answers" at Dexter Avenue Baptist Church (April 21, 1956) in *The Papers of Martin Luther King, Jr.*, 6. "The Advocate of the Social Gospel," September 1948-March 1963; Clayborne Carson, senior editor; Susan Carson et al., eds. (Berkeley: University of California Press, 2007), p. 287.

16. See King's sermon "It's Hard to Be a Christian," Dexter Avenue Baptist Church, February 5, 1956, in *Papers*, 6:252; also "An Experiment in Love" in his *A Testament of Hope: The Essential Writings and Speeches of Martin Luther King, Jr.*, ed. James M. Washington (New York: HarperCollins, 1991), p. 16.

17. See Reinhold Niebuhr, *Moral Man and Immoral Society* (New York: Charles Scribner's Sons), p. 254.

18. See James Weldon Johnson, "The Crucifixion," in *God's Trombones: Seven Negro Sermons in Verse* (New York: Penguin Classics, 2008; orig., 1927), p. 43; James Cone, *The Spirituals and the Blues* (Maryknoll, NY: Orbis Books, 1991; orig., 1972), pp. 48, 49.

19. For an important interpretation of the meaning of Jesus' death in the black religious experience, see JoAnne Marie Terrell, *Power in the Blood? The Cross in the African American Experience* (Maryknoll, NY: Orbis Books, 1998). See also the important collection *The Passion of the Lord: African American Reflections*, ed. James A. Noel and Matthew V. Johnson (Minneapolis: Fortress, 2005). Included in this volume are the following essays: Matthew Johnson, "Lord of the Crucified," pp. 1-32; James Noel, "Were You There?" pp. 33-50; JoAnne Terrell, "What Manner of Love?" pp. 51-76; Demetrius Williams, "Identifying with the Cross of Christ," pp. 77-110; Karen Baker-Fletcher, "Womanist Passion," pp. 111-44; Rosetta Ross, "Passionate Living," pp. 145-59; Robert Franklin, "The Passion and African American Pilgrimage," pp. 160-74. These essays are responses to the Mel Gibson movie *The Passion of the Christ*.

20. See "Meet the Press" Television News Interview in Martin Luther King Jr., *A Testament of Hope*, p. 385.

21. Martin Luther King Jr., *Strength to Love* (Philadelphia: Fortress Press, 1963), pp. 83, 51.

22. See his "Application for Admission to Crozer Theological Seminary," in *The Papers of Martin Luther King, Jr.*, 1. "Call to Serve," January 1929-June 1951; Clayborne Carson, senior editor; Ralph Luker and Penny Russle, eds. (Berkeley: University of California Press, 1992), pp. 142, 144; Coretta Scott King, *My Life with Martin Luther King, Jr.* (New York: Holt, Rinehart, & Winston, 1969), p. 85.

23. The Reverend Martin Luther King, Sr., with Clayton Riley, *Daddy King: An Autobiography* (New York: Morrow, 1980), p. 29-31.

24. *Daddy King*, p. 30. Many blacks have tragic stories of lynching to tell. When I was about six, I saw a black man nearly lynched in Bearden, in the presence of his wife and son, after a white woman ran a stop light and crashed into him. In any altercation with whites, no matter the circumstances, blacks were always wrong, especially when a white woman was involved. While in college during the 1950s, I nearly started a riot when I sat down near a white woman on a newly integrated Little Rock city bus. I was only seventeen, about 130 pounds at the time. A burly looking white man bolted from his seat, grabbed me from behind and lifted me up as if he was going to kill me. Fortunately, a black man of similar size came to my defense and said, "Put him down! Pick on somebody your own size." The white man was caught off guard and obeyed. When I got off the bus and told a policeman what happened he replied, "I agree with the white man who attacked you. Complain to the Attorney General." It was much later while researching the white male mind on lynching that I realized how close I came to starting a riot.

25. See Martin Luther King Jr., "Thou Fool," August 27, 1967, a sermon preached at Mt. Pisgah Baptist Church, Chicago, Illinois, Martin Luther King Jr. Papers, Martin Luther King Jr. Center for Nonviolent Social Change, Atlanta, Georgia. See also his recall of the same crisis experience in *Stride toward Freedom: The Montgomery Story* (New York: Harper, 1958), p. 134-35; and in *Strength to Love*, pp. 112-14. See also his sermon "A Knock at Midnight," in *Strength to Love* pp. 56-66.

26. See King's sermon "Antidotes for Fear," in *Strength to Love*, pp. 125-26 (emphasis added).

27. The song "Never Alone" is found in *Gospel Pearls* (Nashville: Sunday School Publishing Board, National Baptist Convention, U.S.A., 1921), p. 33. This songbook is widely used in black Baptist churches. King senior and junior were members of this group until the latter inspired the founding of the Progressive National Baptist Convention in 1961.

28. King Jr., *Stride toward Freedom*, pp. 135, 136, 137, 138.

29. Cited in Garrow, *Bearing the Cross*, p. 75.

30. Cited in Garrow, *Bearing the Cross*, p. 89; see also King, *Stride toward Freedom*, p. 179; *New York Times*, January 28, 1957.

31. See "Thou Fool"; and "The Death of Evil upon the Seashore," in *Strength to Love*, p. 85; Martin Luther King Jr., "Paul's Letter to American Christians," in *A Knock at Midnight*, ed. Clayborne Carson and Peter Holloran (New York: Warner Books, 1998), p. 34.

32. *The Papers of Martin Luther King, Jr.*, 5:531-32. Through the intervention of Senator and then-presidential candidate John Kennedy, who called Mrs. King to express his concern, and Robert Kennedy, who called the Atlanta judge to express his outrage for imprisoning King for a minor traffic violation, Martin King was released a few days later—causing Daddy King to publicly switch his support to Kennedy from Richard Nixon (who said and did nothing) with many blacks following suit, tipping a close election to Kennedy. Martin King, however, kept SCLC nonpartisan. He was more worried about the crosses of white supremacy ahead of him and others in the civil rights movement.

33. See Martin King's reference to a "martyr's complex" in "Suffering and Faith," in *A Testament of Hope*, p. 41.

34. Martin Luther King Jr., "A Walk through the Holy Land," in *The Papers of Martin Luther King, Jr.* 5. "Threshold of a New Decade," January 1959-December 1960; ed. Tenisha Armstrong et al. (Berkeley: University of California Press, 2005), p. 169; see James T. Holly in Chapter 2, pp. 46-47.

35. Cited in Garrow, *Bearing the Cross*, pp. 229, 602.

36. Garrow, *Bearing the Cross*, p. 229.

37. Martin Luther King Jr., "A Challenge to the Churches and Synagogues," in *Challenge to Religion: Original Essays and an Appeal to the Conscience from the National Conference on Religion and Race*, ed. Matthew Ahmann (Chicago: Henry Regnery, 1963), pp. 168-69.

38. "Speech at Staff Retreat, Penn Center, Frogmore, South Carolina, May 22, 1967," Martin Luther King Jr. Center for Nonviolent Social Change, Atlanta, Georgia.

39. For a classical interpretation of the theories of atonement in Western theology, see Gustaf Aulen, *Christus Victor: An Historical Study of the Three Main Types of the Idea of the Atonement* (London: S.P.C.K, 1953).

40. Martin Luther King Jr., "O That I Knew Where I Might Find Him!" in *The Papers of Martin Luther King, Jr.*, 6:598.

41. Coretta Scott King, *My Life with Martin Luther King, Jr.*, 244; see also Garrow, *Bearing the Cross*, p. 307.

42. Martin King, "Shattered Dreams," in *Strength to Love*, p. 95.

43. Martin Luther King Jr., "Suffering and Faith," in *A Testament of Hope*, pp. 41-42.

44. Martin Luther King Jr., "Eulogy for the Martyred Children," in *A Testament of Hope*, pp. 221-22.

45. Martin Luther King Jr., "A Knock at Midnight," in *A Knock at Midnight*, p. 75.

46. John Macquarrie, *Jesus Christ in Modern Thought* (London: SCM Press, 1990), p. 357.

47. See H. Raines, "Interlude: Benjamin Mays and Martin Luther King, Sr.," in *My Soul Is Rested*, p. 460.

48. See Martin Luther King Jr., "I See the Promised Land," in *A Testament of Hope*, p. 286.

49. Martin Luther King Jr., "A Christmas Sermon on Peace," in *The Trumpet of Conscience* (New York: Harper & Row, 1967), pp. 75, 76.

50. For critiques of King's view of redemptive suffering, see especially Delores Williams, *Sisters in the Wilderness: The Challenge of Womanist God-Talk* (Maryknoll, NY: Orbis Books, 1993), pp. 199-203; Joanne Carlson Brown and Rebecca Parker, "For God So Loved the World?" in Joanne Carlson Brown and Carole R. Bohn, eds., *Christianity, Patriarchy and Abuse* (New York: Pilgrim, 1989), pp. 1-30; Anthony B. Pinn, *Why, Lord? Suffering and Evil in Black Theology* (New York: Continuum, 1995), pp. 71-89.

4. The Recrucified Christ in Black Literary Imagination

1.   Rubin Stacey was lynched in Fort Lauderdale, Florida, July 19, 1935; Laura Nelson and her son in Okemah, Oklahoma, in 1911; and Cleo Wright in Sikeston, Missouri, January 27, 1942. For their images, see James Allen, *Without Sanctuary: Lynching Photography in America* (Santa Fe, NM: Twin Palms, 2003). Images of Stacey and Wright are also found in Doral Apel, *Imagery of Lynching: Black Men, White Women, and the Mob* (New Brunswick, NJ: Rutgers University Press, 2004), pp. 41, 38.

2.   Trudier Harris, *Exorcising Blackness: Historical and Literary Lynching and Burning Rituals* (Bloomington: Indiana University Press, 1984), p. 187.

3.   Cited in Richard Fox, *Reinhold Niebuhr: A Biography* (Ithaca, NY: Cornell University Press, 1996; orig., 1985), p. 171.

4.   Countee Cullen, "Yet Do I Marvel," in James Weldon Johnson, ed., *The Book of American Negro Poetry* (rev. ed.; New York: Harcourt, Brace & World, 1959), p. 231.

5.   See Mark Twain, "The United States of Lyncherdom" (1901), in his *Collected Tales, Sketches, Speeches, & Essays 1891-1910*, ed. Louis J. Budd (New York: Library of America, 1992), pp. 479-86.

6. Countee Cullen, *The Black Christ & Other Poems*, with Decorations by Charles Cullen (New York: Harper & Brothers, 1929), p. 69.

7. Cullen, *The Black Christ*, p. 72; "Christ Recrucified" in *Kelley's Magazine*, October 1922, p. 13; also included in Anne P. Rice, ed., *Witnessing Lynching: American Writers Respond* (New Brunswick, NJ: Rutgers University Press, 2003), pp. 221-22.

8. Walter Everette Hawkins, "A Festival in Christendom," in Arthur P. Davis and Michael W. Peplow, eds., *The New Negro Renaissance* (New York: Holt, Rinehart & Winston, 1975), pp. 41-42.

9. See Claude McKay, "The Lynching," in *Harlem Shadows: The Poems of Claude McKay* (New York: Harcourt, Brace, 1922), p. 51; also in Rice, *Witnessing Lynching*, p. 190.

10. Gwendolyn Brooks, *Blacks* (Chicago: Third World Press, 1991), p. 348.

11. My question is similar to Hilton Als's question in his important essay in Allen, *Without Sanctuary:* "What is the relationship of the white people in these pictures to the white people who ask me, and sometimes pay me, to be Negro on the page?" See his "*GWTW*," p. 39.

12. Cullen, *The Black Christ*, p. 96.

13. Cullen, *The Black Christ*, pp. 77, 98, 72.

14. Catherine Fox, "Lynching Apology Just a Start, Collector Says," *Atlanta Journal-Constitution*, June 23, 2005, p. B1. See also Roberta Smith, "An Ugly Legacy Lives On, Its Glare Unsoftened by Age," *New York Times*, January 13, 2000, p. E1; Richard Lacayo, "Blood at the Root," *Time*, April 10, 2000, pp. 122-23; Jim Auchmutey, "Mississippi College to Show Exhibit of Lynching Photos," *Atlanta Journal-Constitution*, January 30, 2004, p. E3; J. R. Moehringer, "The Lynching Collector," *Toronto Star*, October 29, 2000 Sunday, Edition 1.

15. This work was interpreted by some critics as a "sentimental glorification of the martyred Negro." See especially Dora Apel, "The Antilynching Exhibitions of 1935: Strategies and Constraints," in her *Imagery of Lynching*, for Campbell's and other drawings, paintings, prints, and sculptures and also an excellent discussion of these issues on pp. 83-131. See also "An Art Exhibit against Lynching," *The Crisis* 42 (1935): p. 106, which reproduced the Campbell drawing for its cover. Other important discussions include Helen Langa, "Two Anti-Lynching Art Exhibitions: Politicized Viewpoints, Racial Perspectives, Gendered Constraints," *American Art* 13, no. 1 (1999): pp. 11-39; Marlene Park, "Lynching and Antilynching: Art and Politics in the 1930s," *Prospects* 18 (1993): pp. 311-65; and Margaret Rose Vendryes, "Hanging on Their Walls: An Art Commentary on Lynching, The Forgotten 1935 Art Exhibition," in *Race Consciousness: African-American Studies for the New Century*, ed. Judith Jackson Fossett and Jeffrey A. Tucker (New York: New University Press, 1997), pp. 153-76.

16. See Apel, *Imagery of Lynching*, pp. 111-12.

17. See especially Herbert Aptheker, "W. E. B. Du Bois and Religion: A Brief Reassessment," *The Journal of Religious Thought* 39 (Spring-Summer 1982): pp. 5-11.

18. W. E. B. Du Bois, "The Riddle of the Sphinx" (originally published in *Crisis* [1914] as "The Burden of Black Women") in his *Darkwater: Voices from Within the Veil* (New York: Schocken, 1920), p. 54. I am especially grateful to Edward Blum for his excellent text, *W. E. B. Du Bois: American Prophet* (Philadelphia: University of Pennsylvania Press, 2007). He has persuasively shown not only the importance of religion in Du Bois' perspective but also how his idea of the Black God and the Black Christ anticipates black liberation theology in the 1960s and womanist theology in the 1980s. See especially pp. 17, 129, 139.

19. See Du Bois, "Jesus Christ in Texas" (published in *Crisis*, 1911, as "Jesus Christ in Georgia") in *Darkwater*, pp. 125, 126, 129, 133.

20. W. E. B. Du Bois, "The Second Coming," in *Darkwater*, p. 106.

21. W. E. B. Du Bois, "Religion in the South," in Booker T. Washington and W. E. B. Du Bois, *The Negro in the South*, with an introduction by Herbert Aptheker (New York: Citadel, 1970; orig., 1907), p. 171.

22. W. E. B. Du Bois, "The Church and the Negro," *Crisis* 6, no. 6 (October 1913): p. 290. This essay has been reprinted in many places. See especially the excellent collection in Phil Zuckerman, ed., *Du Bois on Religion* (Walnut Creek, CA: Altamira, 2000).

23. W. E. B. Du Bois, "The Gospel According to Mary Brown," *Crisis* 19, no. 2 (December 1919): pp. 41-42, 48.

24. W. E. B. Du Bois, *The Souls of Black Folk*, ed. Henry Louis Gates Jr. and Terri Hume Oliver (New York: Norton, 1999), p. 10.

25. W. E. B. Du Bois, "Pontius Pilate," *Crisis* 21, no. 2 (December 1920): pp. 53-54; also in Zuckerman, *Du Bois on Religion*, pp. 157-59.

26. W. E. B. Du Bois, "The Son of God," *Crisis* 40, no. 12 (December 1933): pp. 276-77; also in Zuckerman, *Du Bois on Religion*, pp. 181-85.

27. W. E. B. Du Bois, "Easter," *Crisis* 3 no. 6 (1912): p. 244; also in Zuckerman, *Du Bois on Religion*, pp. 107, 108.

28. W. E. B. Du Bois, *Darkwater*, pp. 25-28.

29. Robert Hayden, "Night, Death, Mississippi" (1962), in his *Angle of Accent: New and Selected Poems* (New York: Liveright, 1975), pp. 87-88.

30. James E. Andrews, "Burnt Offering," in *Opportunity: Journal of Negro Life* 17, no. 3 (March 1939): p. 84.

31. Claude McKay, *Harlem Shadows: The Poems of Claude McKay* (New York: Harcourt, Brace, 1922), p. 51.

32. Lorraine Hansberry, "Lynchsong," *Masses and Mainstream* 4, no. 7

(July 1951): pp. 19-20. Angela Y. Davis compared Hansberry's poem to Billie Holiday's "Strange Fruit." See her "Billie Holiday's 'Strange Fruit': Music and Social Consciousness," in *Speech and Power: The African-American Essay and Its Cultural Content, from Polemics to Pulpit*, vol. 2, ed. Gerald Early (Hopewell, NJ: Ecco Press, 1993), pp. 33-43. "Rosalee" in the poem refers to Willie McGee's wife. The first trial of Willie McGee took only two-and-one-half minutes. However, it took four years to execute him in a portable electric chair with a crowd of one thousand screaming whites. His alleged crime was "rape"—the "old threadbare lie" that Ida B. Wells exposed as consensual sex. For a recent study of the Willie McGee tragedy, see Alex Herd, *The Eyes of Willie McGee: A Tragedy of Race, Sex, and Secrets in the Jim Crow South* (New York: HarperCollins, 2010). See Ida B. Wells, *Southern Horrors and Other Writings: The Anti-Lynching Campaign of Ida B. Wells, 1892-1900*, ed. Jacqueline Jones Royster (Boston: Bedford/St. Martin's, 1997), p. 1; Wells is discussed in the next chapter.

33. Walter White, *Rope and Faggot: A Biography of Judge Lynch* (Notre Dame, IN: University of Notre Dame Press, 2001; orig., 1929), p. 40.

34. Cullen, *The Black Christ*, p. 78.

35. Cited in Arnold Rampersad, *The Life of Langston Hughes*. 2 vols. (New York: Oxford University Press, 1986, 1988), vol. 1, p. 223.

36. Sterling Brown, *Negro Poetry and Drama and the Negro in American Fiction* (New York: Atheneum, 1969; orig., 1937), p. 65.

37. W. E. B. Du Bois, "Criteria of Negro Art" (1926), in Henry Louis Gates Jr. and Nellie Y. McKay, eds., *The Norton Anthology of African American Literature* (New York: W. W. Norton, 1997), pp. 752-59, here p. 757. Alaine Locke, Harvard Ph.D., Rhodes scholar, and author of the classic text on the Harlem Renaissance, *The New Negro* (New York: Atheneum, 1969, originally 1925), disagreed with Du Bois about art and politics. See his "Art or Propaganda?" in *Voices from the Harlem Renaissance*, ed. Nathan Irvin Huggins (New York: Oxford University Press, 1975), pp. 312-13; originally published in *Harlem*, vol. 2 (November 1928). On the same theme, see especially Langston Hughes, "The Negro Artist and the Racial Mountain," *The Nation* 122 (June 1926); and Richard Wright, "Blueprint for Negro Writing" (1937), in *Richard Wright Reader*, ed. Ellen Wright and Michel Fabre (New York: Harper & Row, 1978).

38. Cited in Arnold Rampersad, *The Life of Langston Hughes*, vol. 1. *1902-1941. I, Too, Sing America* (New York: Oxford University Press, 1986), pp. 224, 225.

39. Cited in Arnold Rampersad, *The Life of Langston Hughes*, vol. 2. *1941-1967. I Dream A World* (New York: Oxford University Press, 1988), pp. 50-51.

40. Cited in Arnold Rampersad, *The Life of Langston Hughes*, vol. 1, p. 226.

41. Langston Hughes, "Good Morning Revolution," *New Masses*, September 1932, p. 5; also cited in Rampersad, *Life of Langston Hughes*, vol. 1, p. 252.

42. Cited in Rampersad, *Life of Langston Hughes*, vol. 1, pp. 252-53.

43. Cited in Blum, *W. E. B. Du Bois, American Prophet*, p. 198.

5. "O Mary, Don't You Weep"

1. Wells is writing about the lynching of Eliza Woods of Jackson, Tennessee, August 19, 1886. See Jacqueline Goldsby, *A Spectacular Secret: Lynching in American Life and Literature* (Chicago: University of Chicago Press, 2006), p. 62; see also Paula J. Giddings, *Ida: A Sword among Lions, Ida B. Wells and the Campaign against Lynching* (New York: Amistad, 2008), pp. 117, 152, 173; Christopher Waldrep, *The Many Faces of Judge Lynch: Extralegal Violence and Punishment in America* (New York: Palgrave Macmillan, 2002), p. 107.

2. See Philip Dray, *At the Hands of Persons Unknown: The Lynching of Black America* (New York: Modern Library, 2003), p. 246; also Christopher Waldrep, *Lynching in America: A History in Documents* (New York: New York University Press, 2006), p. 197.

3. Cited in Dora Apel, *Imagery of Lynching: Black Men, White Women, and the Mob* (New Brunswick, NJ: Rutgers University Press, 2004), p. 13.

4. Cited in Jacqueline Goldsby, *A Spectacular Secret*, p. 62.

5. See Jacquelyn Grant, *White Women's Christ and Black Women's Jesus: Feminist Christology and Womanist Response* (Atlanta: Scholars Press, 1989), pp. 220, 216.

6. See Delores Williams, "Black Women's Surrogacy Experience and the Christian Notion of Redemption," in Paula M. Cooey et al., eds., *After Patriarchy: Feminist Transformations of the World Religions* (Maryknoll, NY: Orbis Books, 1991); and Delores Williams, *Sisters in the Wilderness: The Challenge of Womanist God-Talk* (Maryknoll, NY: Orbis Books, 1993).

7. Patrick J. Huber, "'Caught Up in the Violent Whirlwind of Lynching': The 1885 Quadruple Lynching in Chatham County, North Carolina," *The North Carolina Historical Review* 65, no. 2 (April 1998): p. 137.

8. Crystal Nicole Feimster, "'Ladies and Lynching': The Gendered Discourse of Mob Violence in the New South, 1880-1930" (Ph.D. diss., Princeton University, 2000), p. 237.

9. Addie Hunton, "Negro Womanhood Defended," cited in Crystal Feimster, "Ladies and Lynching," p. 206.

10. For a historical account of the rape of black women and how their resistance led to the rise of the civil rights and black power movements, see the excellent text by Danielle L. McGuire, *At the Dark End of the Street: Black*

Women, Rape and Resistance—A New History of the Civil Rights Movement from Rosa Parks to the Rise of Black Power (New York: Alfred A. Knopf, 2010).

11. Cited in Albert J. Raboteau, "'The Blood of the Martyrs Is the Seed of Faith': Suffering in the Christianity of American Slaves," in *The Courage to Hope: From Black Suffering to Human Redemption*, ed. Quinton H. Dixie and Cornel West (Boston: Beacon, 1999), p. 31.

12. William Barclay, *The Gospel of Matthew, chs. 11-28: The New Daily Study Bible*, vol. 2; introduction by John Drane (Louisville, KY: Westminster John Knox Press, 2001; orig., 1957), p. 430.

13. Stanley Crouch, "Do the Afrocentric Hustle," in *The All-American Skin Game, or, The Decoy of Race: The Long and the Short of It, 1990-1994* (New York: Pantheon Books, 1995), p. 44.

14. Tupac Shakur, "Black Jesuz," 2PAC+OUTLAWZ, *Still I Rise*, 1999, Interscope Records, 4904132.

15. See Adam Gussow, *Seems Like Murder Here: Southern Violence and the Blues Tradition* (Chicago: University of Chicago Press, 2002), pp. 16, 196.

16. There has been a great deal of historical work on the life and times of Ida B. Wells. The place to begin is her *Crusade for Justice: The Autobiography of Ida B. Wells*, ed. Alfreda M. Duster (Chicago: University of Chicago Press, 1970); and *Southern Horrors and Other Writings: The Anti-lynching Campaign of Ida B. Wells, 1892-1900*, ed. Jacqueline Jones Royster (Boston: Bedford/St. Martin's, 1997). The best biography is Giddings, *Ida*. See also Mia Bay, *To Tell the Truth Freely: The Life of Ida B. Wells* (New York: Hill & Wang, 2009); Patricia A. Schechter, *Ida B. Wells-Barnett and American Reform, 1880-1930* (Chapel Hill: University of North Carolina Press, 2001); Emilie M. Towns, *Womanist Justice, Womanist Hope* (Atlanta: Scholars Press, 1993); and Mildred I. Thompson, *Ida B. Wells-Barnett: An Exploratory Study of an American Black Woman, 1893-1930* (Brooklyn: Carlson, 1990).

17. Cited in Giddings, *Ida*, p. 658. See also W. E. B. Du Bois, "Ida B. Wells-Barnett: Postscript," *The Crisis* (June 1931): p. 207.

18. Douglass's letter in Ida B. Wells, *Southern Horrors*, p. 51; see also Giddings, *Ida*, pp. 284, 318.

19. See Ida B. Wells, "Lynch Law in America," in Thompson, *Ida B. Wells-Barnett*, pp. 235-43, quotation, p. 235.

20. See Giddings, *Ida*, p. 423; for the reactions of the press, politicians, and clergy to Wells's speeches in Britain, see "A New English Craze," *The Atlanta Constitution*, May 30, 1894, p. 4; "'Tis Miss Ida: Whose Words are now Charming the English Ear," *The Atlanta Constitution*, July 28, 1894, p. 2. See also Wells, *Southern Horrors*, pp. 136f.

21. Wells, *Southern Horrors*, p. 78.

22. Cited in Paul Harvey, *Freedom's Coming: Religious Culture and the*

Shaping of the South from the Civil War through the Civil Rights Era (Chapel Hill: University of North Carolina Press, 2005), p. 112; for an account of the Memphis lynching, see Giddings, *Ida*, 177f.; and Wells in Patricia A. Schechter, *Ida B. Wells-Barnett and American Reform* (Chapel Hill: University of North Carolina Press, 2001), pp. 75-79.

23. Wells, *Southern Horrors*, pp. 120-21.

24. Wells, *Southern Horrors*, pp. 50, 79, 122f.; see also Giddings, *Ida*, pp. 221, 222ff.

25. Cited in Wells, *Southern Horrors*, p. 52, from "Evening Scimitar."

26. Wells, *Southern Horrors*, pp. 143, 144; see Goldsby, *Spectacular Secret*, 62; also Giddings, *Ida*, 117.

27. Wells, *Crusade for Justice*, p. 221; cited in Giddings, *Ida*, pp. 319, 310.

28. Wells, *Crusade for Justice*, pp. 402-4; Robert Whitaker, *On the Laps of Gods: The Red Summer of 1919 and the Struggle for Justice that Remade a Nation* (New York: Crown, 2008), pp. 229, 210; Giddings, *Ida*, p. 642.

29. Wells, *Southern Horrors*, p. 77; Giddings, *Ida*, p. 91.

30. Wells, "Our Country's Lynching Record," in Thompson, *Ida B. Wells-Barnett*, p. 280.

31. Giddings, *Ida*, p. 153; Wells, *Crusade for Justice*, pp. 154-55; see Edward J. Blum, "'O God of a Godless Land': North African American Challenges to White Christian Nationhood, 1865-1906," in *Vale of Tears: New Essays on Religion and Reconstruction*, ed. Edward J. Blum and W. Scott Poole (Macon, GA: Mercer University Press, 2005), pp. 101, 102; Wells, *Southern Horrors*, p. 144.

32. One possible exception was perhaps Quincy Ewing. See chapter 2, p. 62. I found no prominent liberal theologian in the North who made a vigorous stand against lynching. Unlike Ewing, they were free to express their outrage but they had none. It is revealing that Harry Emerson Fosdick, the well-known liberal pastor of Riverside Church in New York, spoke out vigorously against fundamentalism during the 1920s but was nearly silent on lynching.

33. Cited in Giddings, *Ida*, p. 319.

34. Cited in Blum, "'O God of a Godless Land,'" p. 104.

35. Howard Thurman, *Deep River: Reflections on the Religious Insight of Certain of the Negro Spirituals* (Port Washington, NY: Kennikat, 1969; orig., 1945), p. 36.

36. See David Margolick, *Strange Fruit: Billie Holiday, Café Society, and an Early Cry for Civil Rights* (Philadelphia: Running Press, 2000); *Time*, December 31, 1999; Billie Holiday, with William Dufty, *Lady Sings the Blues* (reprt., New York: Penguin, 1984), p. 84; also cited in Angela Y. Davis, *Blues Legacies and Black Feminism: Gertude 'Ma' Rainey, Bessie Smith, and Billie Holiday* (New York: Pantheon Books, 1998), p. 186.

37. For account of the lynching and its photo by Beitler, see James H. Madison, *A Lynching in the Heartland: Race and Memory in America* (New York: Palgrave, 2001); a third person, James Cameron, was also taken from the jail to be lynched but was not because someone in the mob said, "Take this boy back. He had nothing to do with the raping and killing!"; see also James Cameron, *A Time of Terror: A Survivor's Story* (Baltimore: Black Classic Press, 1982), p. 74. An account of his return to jail is also found in Madison's *Lynching in the Heartland*.

38. Cited in Margolick, *Strange Fruit*, p. 31.

39. See Donald G. Mathews, "Lynching Is Part of the Religion of Our People," in *Religion in the American South: Protestant and Others in History and Culture*, ed. Beth B. Schweiger and Donald G. Mathews (Chapel Hill: University of North Carolina Press, 2004), pp. 153-94.

40. See John Dominic Crossan, *Jesus: A Revolutionary Biography* (New York: HarperCollins, 1994), p. 123.

41. Farah Jasmine Griffin, *In Search of Billie Holiday: If You Can't Be Free, Be a Mystery* (New York: Ballantine Books, 2001), pp. 132, 131. Also, Robert O'Meally, *Lady Day: The Many Faces of Billie Holiday* (New York: Da Capo Press, 1991); and Donald Clarke, *Wishing on the Moon: The Life and Times of Billie Holiday* (New York: Viking, 1994).

42. Griffin, *In Search of Billie Holiday*, p. 132; see also Donald Clarke, *Wishing on the Moon*, pp. 163-70.

43. See Maya Angelou, *The Heart of a Woman* (New York: Random House, 1981), pp. 6-18; David Margolick, "Strange Fruit," http://www.lady-day.net/stuf/vfsept98.html, pp. 1, 2, 4. Margolick's essay was first published in *Vanity Fair*, September 1998, and later developed into a book. The literary influence of Holiday's "Strange Fruit" can be seen in Lillian Smith's novel about an interracial relationship, also called *Strange Fruit* (New York: Harcourt Brace, 1944). See Billie Holiday's reference to Lillian Smith's novel in Holiday's *Lady Sings the Blues*, pp. 85-86.

44. Howard Thurman, *A Strange Freedom*, ed. Walter E. Fluker and Catherine Tumber (Boston: Beacon Press, 1998), p. 44.

45. See Ralph Ellison's review of LeRoi Jones's (Amiri Baraka) *Blues People*, in *Imamu Amiri Baraka (LeRoi Jones): A Collection of Critical Essays*, ed. Kimberly W. Benston (Englewood Cliffs, NJ: Prentice-Hall, 1978), p. 60.

46. The emphasis on "survival" and "quality of life" was first introduced in theological discourse by Delores Williams as a way of defining womanist theology, separating it from black and feminist theologies. See her *Sisters in the Wilderness*.

47. Cited in Paula J. Giddings, *When and Where I Enter . . . The Impact of Black Women on Race and Sex in America* (New York: William Morrow,

1984), p. 82; see also *Black Women in Nineteenth-Century American Life*, ed. Bert James Loewenberg and Ruth Bogin (University Park: Pennsylvania State University Press, 1976).

48. Cited in Feimster, "Ladies and Lynching," p. 234.

49. Charlotte Hawkins Brown, "Speaking up for the Race at Memphis, Tennessee, October 8, 1920," in Gerda Lerner, ed., *Black Women in White America* (New York: Random House, 1972), p. 470; Anna Julia Cooper (1858-1964) received her Ph.D. from the Sorbonne in Paris and was the author of *A Voice of the South by a Black Woman of the South* (1892). Mary Church Terrell (1863-1954), who earned her Masters degree from Oberlin College, was one of the founders and the first president of the National Association of Colored Women, and author of the important essay "Lynching from A Negro Point of View," *North American Review* 178 (June 1904). Charlotte Hawkins Brown (1883-1961) was the founder of the Palmer Memorial Institute and a founding member of the National Council of Negro Women. Mary McLeod Bethune (1875-1955) was founder and president of Bethune-Cookman College, advisor to President Franklin Roosevelt, and creator and head of the National Council of Negro Women. Nannie Helen Burroughs (1879-1961) was the founder and president of the National Training School for Women and Girls in Washington, DC, and deeply involved in the formation of the Woman's Convention Auxiliary of the National Baptist Convention. For more information on these and other black women, see especially Feimster, "Ladies and Lynching." See also Barbara Dianne Savage, *Your Spirits Walk beside Us: The Politics of Black Religion* (Cambridge: Harvard University Press, 2008); Darlene Clarke Hine, ed., *Black Women in America: An Historical Encyclopedia* (New York: Carson, 1993); Evelyn Higginbotham, *Righteous Discontent: The Women's Movement in the Black Baptist Church, 1880-1920* (Cambridge: Harvard University Press, 1993); Hazel V. Carby, "On the Threshold of Women's Era: Lynching, Empire, and Sexuality in Black Feminist Theory," *Critical Theory* 12, no. 1 (Autumn 1985).

50. Cited in Amy L. Wood, *Lynching and Spectacle: Witnessing Racial Violence in America, 1890-1940* (Chapel Hill: University of North Carolina Press, 2009), p. 217.

51. Cited in Savage, *Your Spirits Walk beside Us*, 47; and Jacquelyn D. Hall, *Revolt against Chivalry: Jessie Daniel Ames and the Women's Campaign against Lynching* (New York: Columbia University Press, 1979), p. 244.

52. Cited in Allen D. Callahan, *The Talking Book: African Americans and the Bible* (New Haven: Yale University Press, 2006), p. 133; also in Stewart Burns, *To the Mountaintop: Martin Luther King Jr.'s Sacred Mission to Save America 1955-1968* (San Francisco: Harper, 2004), p. 176.

53. Cited in Mary King, *Freedom Song: A Personal Story of the 1960s Civil Rights Movement* (New York: Quill/Morrow, 1987), pp. 469-70.

54. Cited in Savage, *Your Spirits Walk beside Us*, p. 42.

55. Cited in Bernice Johnson Reagon, "Women as Culture Carriers in the Civil Rights Movement: Fannie Lou Hamer," in *Women in the Civil Rights Movement: Trailblazers and Torchbearers, 1941-1965*, ed. Vickie Crawford et al. (Brooklyn: Carlson, 1990), p. 211.

56. See "'Never Turn Back': The Life of Fannie Lou Hamer," videotape narrated by Debbie Allen, Rediscovery Productions, Inc., Westport, CT; also "Eyes on the Prize," videotape narrated by Julian Bond, a Blackside, Inc., production.

57. Reagon, "Women as Culture Carriers," p. 211.

58. Cited in Reagon, "Women as Culture Carriers," p. 208.

59. See Angela D. Sims, *Ethical Complications of Lynching: Ida B. Wells' Interrogation of American Terror* (New York: Palgrave Macmillan, 2010). See also Samuel G. Freedman, "Seeking Lynching Stories as Accounts of Faith," *New York Times*, February 26, 2011, p. A17. Sims is currently working on an important book based on "the recollections of African American elders about lynching."

60. See Nick Kotz, *Judgment Days: Lyndon Baines Johnson, Martin Luther King, Jr., and the Laws that Changed America* (New York: Houghton Mifflin, 2005), p. 216.

61. For Fannie Lou Hamer's speech to the Democratic National Convention in Atlantic City (1964), see "Fannie Lou Hamer: Testimony before the Credentials Committee, Democratic National Convention, 1964," in *Say It Plain: A Century of Great American Speeches*, ed. Catherine Ellis and Stephen D. Smith (New York: New Press, 2005), pp. 49-53. See also the video "Never Turn Back," and the award-winning documentary "Eyes on the Prize," produced by Blackside, Henry Hampton; also Reagon, "Women as Culture Carriers," pp. 203-17, 208, 209.

62. Langston Hughes, "Let America Be America Again" (1936), in *The Poetry of the Negro 1746-1970*, ed. Langston Hughes and Arna Bontemps (New York: Doubleday Anchor Book, 1970), pp. 193, 195; also in Jean Wagner, *Black Poets of the United States: From Paul Laurence Dumbar to Langston Hughes*, trans. Kenneth Douglass (Urbana: University of Illinois Press, 1973), p. 451.

63. Charles Payne, "Men Led, but Women Organized: Movement Participation of Women in the Mississippi Delta," in Crawford et al., eds., *Women in the Civil Rights Movement*, pp. 7, 5.

64. Emile Durkheim, *The Elementary Forms of the Religious Life*, trans. Joseph Wardswain, with a new introduction by Robert Nisbet (London: George Allen & Unwin, 1976, originally 1915), p. 416; also cited in Payne, "Men Led, but Women Organized," p. 6.

65. See James Allen, *Without Sanctuary: Lynching Photography in America* (Santa Fe, NM: Twin Palms, 2003), pp. 178-80.

66. Cited in Howard Raines, *My Soul Is Rested: The Story of the Civil Rights Movement in the Deep South* (New York: Penguin, 1983), p. 280.

67. The quotation I heard at Macedonia was handed down from slavery; it is also cited in Albert Raboteau, *Canaan Land: A Religious History of African Americans* (New York: Oxford University Press, 1999), p. 45.

68. Cited in David Chappell, *A Stone of Hope: Prophetic Religion and the Death of Jim Crow* (Chapel Hill: University of North Carolina Press, 2004), pp. 71, 72.

69. Chana Kai Lee, *For Freedom's Sake: The Life of Fannie Lou Hamer* (Urbana: University of Illinois Press, 2000), p. 26.

70. Delores S. Williams, "Black Women's Surrogacy Experience and the Christian Notion of Redemption," in Cooey et al., *After Patriarchy*, pp. 1-14. Additional reflections on the cross by womanist theologians include Jacquelyn Grant's *White Women's Christ and Black Women's Jesus: Feminist Christology and Womanist Response* (Atlanta: Scholars Press, 1989); Grant, "'Come to My Help, Lord, for I'm in Trouble': Womanist Jesus and the Mutual Struggle for Liberation," in *Reconstructing the Christ Symbol: Essays in Feminist Christology*, ed. Maryanne Stevens (Mahwah, NJ: Paulist Press, 1994); Kelly Brown Douglas, *The Black Christ* (Maryknoll, NY: Orbis, 1994); and Kelly Brown Douglas, *What's Faith Got to Do with It: Black Bodies/Christian Souls* (Maryknoll, NY: Orbis Books, 2005); JoAnne M. Terrell, *Power in the Blood? The Cross in the African American Experience* (Maryknoll, NY: Orbis Books, 1998); "Our Mothers' Gardens: Rethinking Sacrifice," in *Cross Examinations: Readings on the Meaning of the Cross Today*, ed. Marit Trelstad (Minneapolis: Fortress Press, 2006); and M. Shawn Copeland, *Enfleshing Freedom: Body, Race, and Being* (Minneapolis: Fortress Press, 2010); M. Shawn Copeland, "Wading through Many Sorrows: Toward a Theology of Suffering in Womanist Perspective," in *A Troubling in My Soul: Womanist Perspectives on Evil and Suffering*, ed. Emilie Townes (Maryknoll, NY: Orbis, 1993); M. Shawn Copeland, "To Live at the Disposal of the Cross: Mystical-Political Discipleship as Christological Locus," in *Christology: Memory, Inquiry, Practice*, ed. Anne M. Clifford and Anthony Godzieba (Maryknoll, NY: Orbis Books, 2003).

71. Copeland, "'Wading through Many Sorrows,'" pp. 120, 124.

Conclusion: Legacies of the Cross and the Lynching Tree

1. Cited in Gary S. Shelby, *Martin Luther King and the Rhetoric of Freedom: The Exodus Narrative in America's Struggle for Civil Rights* (Waco, TX: Baylor University Press, 2008), p. 42.

2. W. Fitzhugh Brundage, *Lynching in the New South: Georgia and Virginia, 1880-1930* (Urbana: University of Illinois Press, 1993), p. 258.

3. Mircea Eliade, *The Sacred and the Profane: The Nature of Religion* (New York: Harper Torchbooks, 1959), p. 34.

4. Martin Hengel, *Crucifixion* (Philadelphia: Fortress Press, 1977), p. 88.

5. Dorothy A. Lee-Pollard, "Powerlessness as Power: A Key Emphasis in the Gospel of Mark," *Scottish Journal of Theology* 40 (1987): p. 188.

6. Dietrich Bonhoeffer, *Letters and Papers from Prison*, ed. Eberhard Bethge (enlarged ed.; New York: Macmillan, 1974), p. 361.

7. Paul Tillich, *The Courage to Be* (New Haven: Yale University Press, 1952).

8. Hengel, *Crucifixion*, p. 90.

9. Cited in Leon F. Litwack, *Trouble in Mind: Black Southerners in the Age of Jim Crow* (New York: Alfred Knopf, 1998), p. 281.

10. Jon Sobrino, *No Salvation outside the Poor: Prophetic-Utopian Essays* (Maryknoll, NY: Orbis Books, 2008), pp. 1-17.

11. James Baldwin, *The Fire Next Time* (New York: Vintage International, 1993; orig., 1963), pp. 98, 99, 100, 101.

12. See Michelle Alexander, *The New Jim Crow: Mass Incarceration in the Age of Colorblindness* (New York: New Press, 2010).

13. Michelle Alexander, "Obama's Drug War," *The Nation*, December 27, 2010, p. 27.

14. One of the best interpretations of the connection between the lynching legacy and the death penalty is the important text, *From Lynch Mobs to the Killing State: Race and the Death Penalty in America*, ed. Charles J. Ogletree and Austin Sarat (New York: New York University Press, 2006); see also Rev. Jesse L. Jackson, Rep. Jesse L. Jackson Jr. and Bruce Shapiro, *Legal Lynching: The Death Penalty and America's Future* (New York: Anchor Books, 2001); Gene Miller, *An Invitation to a Lynching* (New York: Random House, 1975). On race and the death penalty, see The Death Penalty Resource Center: www.deathpenalty info.org.

15. Gary Selby, *Martin Luther King and the Rhetoric of Freedom*, p. xi.

16. Brundage, *Lynching in the New South*, p. 258.

16. Robert Handy, *Christian America: Protestant Hopes and Historical Realities* (New York: Oxford University Press, 1971).

Index